*The Other Side
of the Mirror*

TURKEY

Tigris R.
Cizre
Ain Divar
Nusaybin
Qamishli

Tell Halaf ▲
Jaghjagh R.
Ras-al-Ain
▲ *Tell Brak*

Cyrrhus (Hagiopolis) ▲
Jerabulus
Qalaat Najm
Khabur R.
Haseke

Azaz
Afrin R.
Ain Dara
Manbij
Balikh R.
Tell Mashnaqa ●

MEDITERRANEAN SEA

Harim
Deir Semaan (Telanissos)
▲ St. Simeon
Lake Asad

JEBEL ANSARIYYA
Qalb Lozeh
Ruweiha
Idlib
Aleppo
Qinnesrin
Raqqa ●

Orontes R.
▲ Ebla
Ma'arat al-Numan
Euphrates R.
Halebiye (Zenobia) ●
ZALEBIYE

Ugarit
Bara
Serjilla
Latakia
Apamea
● Anderin
Resafa (Sergiopolis) ●
Qaedaha
Isriya ●

Jeble
Baniyas
▲ Shaizar
Qalaat Burzey
Hama
Deir ez-Zor ●
Circesium ▲

Qalaat Marqab ▲
Masyaf
Qasr Ibn Wardan
Qalaat Saladin
(Château de Saône) ▲
Qalaat Rahba ▲

Tartous
ARWAD
Hosn Suleiman
▲ Krak des Chevaliers
Qasr al-Hayr (East) ▲
Dura Europus ●
Mari ▲

Amrit
Homs (Emesa)
Palmyra (Tadmor) ●
S Y R I A
Abu Kemal ● Baghuz

Safita
(Chastel Blanc)
Qadesh
Tell Nebi Mend
Qasr al-Hayr (West) ▲

LEBANON
▲ Deir Mar Musa

Maaloula
Seidnaya
ANTI LEBANON MTS.
● Dumeir
JEBEL SEIS

Maysalun ⊛
Damascus

Wadi Barada

ISRAEL
Quneitra
Ezraa
Shahba
Suweida
Qanawat
Deraa

Yarmuk R.
Bosra

WEST BANK
Jordan R.
J O R D A N
I R A Q

N

| 0 | | 50 | | 100 Miles |
| 0 | 50 | | 100 kilometers | |

▲ Antiquities (ruins)

BROOKE ALLEN

The Other Side of the Mirror

❖❖❖❖❖❖❖❖❖❖❖❖❖❖❖❖❖❖❖

AN AMERICAN TRAVELS
THROUGH SYRIA

PAUL DRY BOOKS

Philadelphia   2011

First Paul Dry Books Edition, 2011

Paul Dry Books, Inc.
Philadelphia, Pennsylvania
www.pauldrybooks.com

Typefaces: Janson and Gill Sans families
Designed and composed by P. M. Gordon Associates

1 3 5 7 9 8 6 4 2
Printed in the United States of America

Library of Congress Cataloging-in-Publication Data
Allen, Brooke
  The other side of the mirror : an American travels through Syria /
Brooke Allen. — 1st Paul Dry Books ed.
      p. cm.
  Includes bibliographical references.
  ISBN 978-1-58988-068-9 (alk. paper)
  1. Allen, Brooke—Travel—Syria. 2. Syria—Description and travel.
3. Syria—Social life and customs. I. Title.
  DS94.A55 2011
  915.69104'42—dc22
                                                    2010044837

Contents

Illustrations

Figures

Color plates

The Other Side
of the Mirror

1 ❖ *The Destination*

This is not a book about militant Islam, or women and the veil, or terrorism, or the Arab-Israeli crisis, or any of the other subjects Americans have come to expect every time they pick up a volume on the Middle East. Instead, it will be an old-fashioned series of traveler's impressions: observations and thoughts about a country whose reality confounded all my preconceived notions and inspired me to seek out many historical and literary sources for enlightenment. It is simply my attempt to convey a bit of what makes Syria one of the most captivating countries I have ever visited, and certainly the most welcoming.

I took my first trip to Syria in the spring of 2009 with my husband and two teenaged daughters. I returned there the following autumn with an old school friend, Catherine. Each visit was a revelation.

For while Syria was not actually named by George W. Bush as part of the axis of evil, it might as well have been. Official American policy had ensured that it was linked in the popular imagination with our much-hyped enemies in the Middle East; the Bush administration had imposed a series of crippling economic sanctions against the country; and Syria was routinely portrayed in the American media as a scary police state with an old-style strong-arm leader (first the long-time president Hafiz al-Asad, who ruled the country from 1970 until his death in 2000, and thereafter his son Bashar). Not that there were very many mentions of it at all; if the distant and mysterious nation did pop up in the pages of the *New York Times*, my hometown paper, it was usually in the sinister context of its existential opposition to Israel, its roles in the 1967 and 1973 Arab-Israeli wars, or its government's alleged support of international terrorism. No other aspect of Syrian life was presented, and from what I could glean from television and newspapers of every political stripe—and how else is one to judge?—the country was principally populated with militant, bomb-hurling Islamists who hated America and aspired to develop a nuclear arsenal in order to pulverize Israel as quickly as possible.

So when our friends Alex and Katya suggested that we all visit the country together during the Easter holiday, I was naturally intrigued. Alex, an artist with a special interest in religious matters, had been reading a book about the early Christian monks of Syria—in particular the fanatical St. Simeon Stylites, who stood on a pillar for forty years—and conceived a desperate wish to see the country where these religious excesses had occurred. Peter and I needed no further prompting; we bought tickets for ourselves and our sixteen-year old twin daughters and sent off to Washington for the visas. Alex and Katya, as it turned out, were never able to go, but my husband, Peter, and I were launched.

I was not really quite as ignorant about the country as I might have been, for I had long been interested in the Crusades. Syria was the epicenter of crusading activity, and I knew that many of the famous castles tussled over by European Crusaders and Arab defenders still existed and could be visited: Marqab and Tartous on the coast; Masyaf, the lair of the terrifying Assassins; the great and impregnable citadel of Aleppo; the Château de Saône, considered by T. E. Lawrence ("of Arabia") "the most sensational thing in castle-building I have seen"; and the massive stronghold of the Hospitallers, Krak des Chevaliers, one of the largest and best preserved medieval castles in the world. I knew, too, that Syria contained some spectacular classical remains, like the Greco-Roman ruins at Palmyra and Apamea, not to mention early Christian churches and famous Bronze Age sites like Mari and Ebla.

Still, I didn't expect the country to be an easy spot for a family vacation. At the very least, I assumed there would be hassles about border-crossings and visas, secret police keeping an eye on our doings, and a pervasive sense of being watched, as in the old Soviet Union, Syria's long-time patron. This image was reinforced by the U.S. State Department's Travel Warning for those of us who might be reckless enough to venture into this heart of darkness. "American citizens," it said forbiddingly, "are urged to consider the risks of travel to Syria and to take adequate precautions to ensure their safety." Well, we were game, and so we prepared ourselves to brave official trouble from the country's administration and unofficial hostility from its people. After all, we had encountered knee-jerk anti-Americanism before; Europe is rife with it.

My husband, Peter, who is Jewish, wanted to take the trip but seemed to approach it with an uneasy feeling that he was in some way betraying his heritage. His eighty-five-year-old mother couldn't imagine why we would go, and expressed her distaste for our proposed journey in no uncertain terms. That this automatic opposition came from a tolerant, cosmopolitan, and politically liberal woman says everything you need to know about Jewish-American views. An atheist, my mother-in-law is culturally rather than religiously Jewish; in fact a couple of years previously she had startled the assembled company at her annual Rosh Hashanah dinner by ranting against the text of the Haggadah, to which she had never before, apparently, given full consideration. "My religion isn't about plagues and burning bushes!" she shouted. "It's about family and friends and celebration!" Still, she had no problem lumping the Arab world together as a united, malignant force. It seemed not to occur to her that Arab countries contain plenty of people who share her definition of religion—or that the Holocaust took place not in the Middle East but in Europe, her favorite travel destination.

I didn't take the direst of the warnings all that seriously. Even so, our first brush with Syrian officialdom was something of a surprise, for after a cursory examination of our passports, the immigration officer at the Damascus Airport said simply, "Welcome." This phrase—*ahlan wa sahlan* in Arabic—was to be the most common utterance we heard on this visit. "Is this your first trip to Syria? You are welcome. How do you like our town? You are very welcome."

It was literally impossible for us to walk down a street without passersby trying to strike up a conversation. On my very first evening in Damascus, wandering half-stunned and jet-lagged through the ancient spice market in the gathering darkness, I was ushered by one young vendor into the little room at the rear of his stall. Here he poured me some tea and summoned his brother to translate. The two of them showed me their photograph album, a great treasure. There was a picture of my host with President Bashar al-Asad, which he pointed out with some pride, but he was even more eager to point out a shot of himself with John Kerry, to whom he had had the privilege of serving coffee during a diplomatic visit the senator had made to Damascus.

When told about the warmness of our welcome, friends have often made knowing remarks about Potemkin villages, or red carpets rolled out by the wily Syrian Ministry of Tourism. But there is nothing like that here, nothing remotely like the old Soviet Intourist that micromanaged tourists' experiences of the country. Visitors are not required to register with any agency (indeed there doesn't appear to be such an agency) or to employ a guide or to join a group. You can travel and stay wherever you like without ever encountering officialdom in any form. And the fact that everyone we met wanted to talk to us would seem to indicate that, unlike in the Soviet Union, citizens' encounters with foreigners are not monitored. Far from shying away from being seen with Americans, the locals sought out our company.

Everyone, it seemed, wanted to know who and what we were. "Are you English? German?" At first we were a little nervous about admitting to being Americans—after all, if their political rhetoric is anything like ours they must hate us, right? But we needn't have worried: once we admitted our nationality there was a bit of surprise, but then the interest became even more intense: "We have so few Americans coming to our country. How are you enjoying your trip? You are very welcome." Almost without exception, they spoke of their admiration for Jimmy Carter and his peacekeeping efforts. Barack Obama had recently been sworn into office; hopes were very high.

Occasionally we voiced a regret that our countries were not better friends, and when we did so the reply was invariably the same: "Everyone knows that's just politics, not people." Well—*do they*? Not on our side of the pond, I reflected, and tried to envision the kind of reception a family of Syrian tourists might find in New York. First, an endless grilling at immigration and security, where they would be approached as potential criminals and enemies rather than as guests, which is how Syrian officialdom treated us. Then, assuming they were lucky enough to get into the country at all, they would encounter reactions ranging from indifference to outright hostility. It would be most unlikely for anyone to bid them welcome, much less invite them into their homes for tea, coffee, or a meal, as so many strangers invited us into their homes in Syria. So far from sensing danger in the air, we felt far safer in Damascus than we usually do in New York, and even gave up locking our hotel rooms after the first couple of days. The many European tourists we encountered (Syria is a popular destination among Europeans) seemed to have no particular fears.

As for the dreaded red tape—difficulties changing money and reserving hotels, passport and visa hassles—there simply wasn't any. I was able to renew my visa in less than five minutes, literally, at Aleppo's passport office. Hotel managers reserve your room the old-fashioned way, not through a credit card deposit but simply by writing your name in a book, then erasing it again if you cancel. Changing money can be done at any bank or *Bureau de Change* without even filling out forms or keeping receipts, though because there is no reciprocity between American and Syrian banks you can't use an ATM machine or travelers' checks—you simply have to bring a wad of American cash and change it bit by bit. This might seem to be a problem, for everyone is nervous about carrying large sums of currency. But there is practically no petty crime in Syria, and you are most unlikely to have your pocket picked.

Syria is classified by human rights organizations as a police state, and its citizens have to watch what they say and write. In 1968—even before the first Asad's time—a special court, the Supreme State Security Court, was set up to try those accused of dissent or offences against state security. Under the control of the executive branch of the government, the SSSC still exists, and Amnesty International has deemed its proceedings "grossly unfair."[1] Syria's prisons contain quite a few people found guilty of vague crimes like "spreading false news," "weakening national morale," and "inciting sectarian sentiments."

The cult of the Asad family is immediately noticeable, with posters and statues of the current president and his father littering the urban landscape. It is very unusual to hear any criticism of the president or his regime: the general belief seems to be that the walls have ears, and people we chatted with would frequently throw in some positive comment about Bashar al-Asad, apparently as a sort of propitiatory magic. We came across a couple of openly disaffected people, but such encounters were rare. What we were most surprised by was the fact that there is obviously a significant measure of genuine enthusiasm for the president mixed with all the *pro forma* compliments. The attitude of Syrian citizens toward the Asad regime turns out to be exceedingly complex (more of all this in chapter six) and there is a real appreciation of the benefits Asad and his father have brought on the country—mixed, of course, with resentment over one-party rule and a government-controlled press.

The general principle seems to be that if you want to be left alone, don't get involved in politics. With the exception of traffic cops, there is no visible police presence, and no armed guards in front of hotels and public buildings as there are in countries like Egypt. Big Brother might be lurking, but his presence is not immediately obvious. And so far from being dangerous for foreigners, as the State Department would have had us believe, Syria (as I discovered later) has been deemed the third safest country in the world, after Malaysia and Singapore.

Why should this be so? The police presence in Syria is nothing at all like ultra-repressive Singapore, where theft is punished with lashes of a cane and narcotics offenses will get you the death penalty. On the contrary, Syria possesses a certain Mediterranean casualness, and its citizens openly flout laws pertaining to minor offenses like littering or smoking. Perhaps, as some Syrians suggested to us, it's because the country has a "shame culture": someone caught stealing brings great shame on their family.

I struggled to make sense of all these seeming contradictions, ultimately deciding that a fortnight was not nearly long enough. I started to plan a second, more leisurely trip, with the idea of writing a book or article. My friend Catherine, a Washington lawyer with a lifelong interest in classical history and culture, agreed to come along with me; another friend, Arthur, agreed to join us for a week as we swung through Crusader country. And so I arrived back in Syria at the beginning of November.

Only seven months had passed, but I sensed a subtle change in the way we were approached. For one thing, the bloom was already off Obama's rose. A full year had now passed since the election, and the Arabs, even the most hopeful and well disposed among them, couldn't see that much progress had been made in international relations. In fact President Obama was at that very moment trying to decide whether to commit yet more troops to the war in Afghanistan that was widely unpopular in the Middle East and Europe. He had also made the decision, a bitter disappointment to Syrians, to renew Bush's 2003 sanctions against the country, the Syria Accountability and Lebanese Sovereignty Restoration Act. Notwithstanding his fine words in Cairo a couple of months previously, nothing much had improved and the Syrians, who had initially looked upon the new president with such goodwill and optimism, were already allowing themselves to become cynical. We heard no more cries, as we had back in April, of "Obama!" accompanied by fist pumping or thumbs-up signs.

I also found that I received a rather less ecstatic reception in the absence of my pretty teenaged daughters. Lizzy in particular, a six-foot redhead who had refused to modify her *outré* fashion choices for the benefit of Muslim sensibilities, had cut quite a swath through the streets of Damascus. "You could get a lot of camels for Lizzy," a Bedouin acquaintance of ours remarked dryly. One of the things I found attractive about the country was that while both the girls attracted plenty of open admiration, we never heard a single offensive comment—unusual for a Mediterranean society, which it is, after all. It was mostly just a wildly enthusiastic "Good *morning*!" or "How are *you*?"

Two middle-aged women, however well preserved, simply could not garner this level of rapture. But when all is said and done, everyone Catherine and I encountered was unfailingly polite, and often very friendly indeed. Catherine, who is half English and travels under her husband's Irish passport, and Arthur, who is originally Dutch, both feared anti-Americanism and did not like to admit to being from the United States. On the other hand, I figured if I said up front that I was from New York, whether the reaction was positive or negative, at least it was unlikely to be a yawn. This turned out to be true, and though occasionally someone would express distress at the actions of the late Bush regime, I encountered none of the knee-jerk, virulent anti-Americanism that is so common in Western Europe.

Criticism of America took a less personal and vindictive form than the kind you encounter in France or England. America—its government, not its people—is perceived to be a clumsy, destructive giant, running roughshod over the rest of the world, imposing its will with no thought for the human pain caused by its actions. Syria, which has absorbed some million and a half Iraqi refugees since the 2003 American invasion, is in a position to observe a great deal of that human pain, and while I was made aware

of the general anger over it, I never felt that I was being personally blamed for the actions of my leaders. Instead I was implored
to recognize everyone's common humanity and to tell the people
back home that Syrians wished them well. "Please ask them not
to like us, but simply to tolerate us," begged one old man.

And everyone I met fell over backwards to present themselves as peacekeepers. Aware of the widespread Western horror
of militant Islam, they spoke passionately about their commitment to peace. Even the Tishreen Panorama, a propagandistic
museum dedicated to the country's military glory and "victory"
in the 1973 war against Israel, was full of little coded indications
of Syria's identity as a peaceful nation: a painting of the signing
of the first peace treaty in recorded history, for instance, at Ebla
in the third millennium B.C., or of the victorious Saladin liberating Jerusalem from the Christian Crusaders in 1188, with both
mosque and church in the background—equal beneficiaries, it is
implied, of his just new order.

Back in the twelfth century the Spanish traveler Ibn Jubayr
observed while voyaging through Syria that "If in all these eastern lands there were nothing but the readiness of its people to
show bounty to strangers and generosity to the poor, especially
in the case of the inhabitants of the countryside [it would be
enough]. For you will find admirable their eagerness and kind-
ness to guests, which is enough to bring them honor."[2] Not
much seems to have changed. Walking through Damascus's Old
City at night, I was struck by the sensation that also prevails in
some small Italian cities: the feeling that you are in a community of neighbors rather than a metropolis of strangers. To lift
a phrase from Dickens, the Syrians seemed to treat us, and one
another, as fellow passengers to the grave rather than as anonymous Others.

One day Catherine and I found ourselves in the so-called
"Museum Caffé" near Aleppo's National Museum. It was one

of those cavernous hostelries patronized almost exclusively by men in traditional dress, who sat about drinking tea and playing backgammon and dominoes while the television set showed some silly Arab farce. We never felt entirely comfortable in such places as two women on our own, but we braved them anyway, and to be truthful, no one ever looked at us askance. Here, indeed, we were approached by an elderly man who clearly hoped to be invited to join us.

His name was Wadjih, and he made his living as an English interpreter and teacher. When he heard Catherine's mellifluous English accent—and discovered that she had a doctorate in English literature from Oxford with an emphasis in seventeenth-century poetry—he was almost beside himself with pleasure. "Oh, this is truly a parcel of joy for me!" he cried. "I wonder if you could recite any part of Thomas Gray's 'Elegy'?"

Catherine was equal to the challenge. "'The Curfew tolls the knell of parting day,'" she began boldly;

"The lowing herd wind slowly o'er the lea,
The plowman homeward plods his weary way,
  And leaves the world to darkness and to me.

Now fades the glimmering landscape on the sight,
  And all the air a solemn stillness holds,
Save where the beetle wheels his droning flight,
  And drowsy tinklings lull the distant folds . . ."

But here she ran out of steam. Wadjih tried to mask his disappointment. "Perhaps more of it will come back to you in a moment. It gives me so much pleasure to hear it as it should be spoken. Tell me—Is Eliot still fashionable?"

We said that we doubted whether Eliot had ever fallen out of fashion.

"Yes," he said with satisfaction. "*The Waste Land.* A very great poem." He considered it in silence for a moment. "I like specially the bit about the secretary going home and lying on her *diwan.*"

"Ah," said Catherine:

"The typist home at teatime, clears her breakfast, lights
Her stove, and lays out food in tins.
Out of the window perilously spread
Her drying combinations touched by the sun's last rays
On the divan one piled (at night her bed)
Stockings, slippers, camisoles and stays."

"And the young man with skin eruptions?" Wadjih asked
eagerly.
Catherine went on:

"He, the young man carbuncular, arrives,
A small house-agent's clerk, with one bold stare
One of the low on whom assurance sits
As a silk hat on a Bradford millionaire."

"It is beautiful to hear you say it," Wadjih sighed.
The next day we met again, and this time Wadjih was clutch-ing a well-thumbed volume of English verse. His object, of course, was to hear more poetry read in Catherine's lovely accent, and his first choice for her to read was a sly, courtly gesture to us: "The Autumnal," John Donne's elegy in praise of an older wom-an's beauty.

. . . Call not these wrinkles, graves; if graves they were,
    They were Love's graves, for else he is no where.
Yet lies not Love dead here, but here doth sit
    Vow'd to this trench, like an anachorit . . .

Wadjih's deep and passionate engagement with poetry, as we discovered, was not unusual in this part of the world. Through-out our Syrian travels we came upon people who were eager to establish a personal relationship, and to discuss serious and meaningful ideas rather than go through the usual social niceties and chit-chat. Poetry, with Wadjih and with others, was a subject that seemed irresistible to educated Syrians and helped establish a link between their culture and ours. By Western standards there are very few novels written in the Arab world, but this does not mean that theirs is not a literary culture; it is one, but it is a culture in which the national consciousness has traditionally been expressed through poetry rather than prose. Over and over, people wishing to establish a link with us sought to do so through a shared feeling for the Anglo-American poetic tradition, with which they were surprisingly familiar.

There was Abed for instance, a twenty-year-old student at Aleppo University who had directed and acted in three plays there—in English—by the Jacobean dramatist Christopher Marlowe. He showed us photographs of himself in the role of Dr. Faustus. We were astounded, for even in an American university all this would have been a little recondite. How much of an audience did he find for it in Aleppo? Abed admitted that it was hard to fill the theater for every performance, but he did the plays anyway, "for love." Shades of *A Chorus Line*!

And then there was Muthanna, who served as my personal guide through the Tishreen Panorama. A freckled redhead in his mid-twenties, Muthanna was earnest, thoughtful, and very eager not only to pass a pleasant morning with me, but to establish some sort of meaningful communication. He wished me to know he was a serious person and a studious one. "I don't watch football," he told me. "I don't go out. Every night I read, I read." Before I knew it, he was quoting Poe's "Annabel Lee," which he knew perfectly, along with many other Poe works.

It was all very well to keep discussing the English and American classics, but I was actually becoming more interested in Arabic poetry, of which there are few readily available English translations. The name I kept hearing was that of al-Mutanabbi, the tenth-century poet who, of all Arab writers, seems to be the most beloved. I asked Wadjih for a good English translation of the great Mutanabbi, but he pooh-poohed this, taking the line (something I have heard often enough from American poetry critics) that poetry is precisely that which cannot be translated. Still, I couldn't let it go. Right here in Aleppo, not a stone's throw from the Museum Caffé, had flourished the brilliant court of al-Mutanabbi's patron Sayf ad-Dawla, the most famous member of Aleppo's medieval Hamdanid dynasty. Sayf ad-Dawla patronized a dazzling literary circle whose brightest lights included not only al-Mutanabbi but the almost equally famous Abu Firas, most notable for his *Rumiyyat*, a series of verses the poet wrote while in captivity among Sayf ad-Dawla's Byzantine enemies. Another ornament of the Hamdanid court was Kushajim al-Sindi, author of "Etiquette of the Cup Companions and Refined Jests of the Elegant," a sort of precursor to Castiglione's *Book of the Courtier*. Kushajim was especially well known for his charming poems about food, including a few written for a symposium on food in the year 947, in which various poetic courtiers offered verses in praise of delicious eatables—a sort of medieval poetry slam.

There is still a Sayf ad-Dawla Street in Aleppo, but the monarch's palace has disappeared. Yet there is more than enough left of the medieval city, and enough of the local taste for poetry, to keep the connection alive. It is one of the countless examples of physical, intellectual, and spiritual continuity that tie modern Syria to its distant past. So is the interest in food, which in Aleppo does not seem to have changed much from Sayf ad-Dawla's day to our own—for the town is still the gastronomic capital of the region and a destination for foodies from as far away as France. Granted, its restaurant menus advertised some of the weirdest items I have ever seen. Just one of them had listed all of the following dishes, some comprehensible and some utterly mysterious:

Goat milky
Chit lings
Filet tricky (Dower with caramel and Soya sauce and cream)
Raw Leon
Watercress with pastrami
Varied of kinora from cheese French fiction

Sweat cakes
Cear Off Let Tuch with Rakford
Shanghlesh
Fries bird
Coll Slow
Filet of Humor

And our favorite,

Crap Salad.

Given a bit more time I might have worked my way through this entire menu and would probably have found even the nastiest-sounding dishes (watercress with pastrami?!) to be delicious, for there is almost no such thing as a bad meal to be had here: the country is agriculturally self-supporting and everything is fresh and local. The markets are colorful with oranges, pomegranates, radishes, and every possible variety of pickle and olive and cheese. Aleppo, which as one of the major stops on the Silk Road was always a meeting spot for a myriad of nationalities and ethnicities, developed a particularly sophisticated cuisine, with specialties such as lamb in cherry sauce, lamb with mint, eggplant with pomegranate sauce, and multiple varieties of *kibbe*, crispy cracked wheat around various fillings. Pistachios, figs, and pine nuts, all grown around Aleppo, are frequent garnishes. At the upscale Sissi House we had the thinnest little lamb chops I have ever tasted, and the sweetest eggplant, and one of the best desserts I have ever had, a simple dish of fresh persimmons with a local sweet, creamy cheese. The working-class neighborhoods have their own delicacies, and Aleppo even boasts a Seinfeldian Soup Nazi: Abu Abdo, where people line up first thing in the morning with their own plastic containers to take away portions of the restaurant's wildly popular *ful*, fava bean soup.

Two hundred twenty miles south of Aleppo, Damascus was known for centuries as the Pearl of the East, in large part because of its situation at the center of a heavenly oasis called the Ghouta. Pistachios, apricots, olives, pomegranates, persimmons, almonds, dates: the groves and orchards were famous around the world, and survived right up into modern times. The Ghouta was admired, and wondered at, by every visitor to the city. In the 1180s, Ibn Jubayr was in ecstasies: Damascus, he said, "is garnished with the flowers of sweet-scented herbs, and bedecked in the brocaded vestments of gardens. In the place of beauty she holds a sure position, and on her nuptial chair she is most richly adorned . . . Its rivulets twist like serpents through every way, and the perfumed zephyrs of its flower gardens breathe life to the soul. To those who contemplate her she displays herself in her bridal dress calling to them: 'Come to the halting place of beauty, and take the midday repose.'"[3] As recently as the early twentieth century, travelers were describing it in much the same way—it was a paradise, they said, of jasmine-scented fertility bathing one's senses after a long voyage in the desert. The Barada River ran swiftly through it, giving life to the orchards and the surrounding city.

Nowadays all this is hard to credit, for urban sprawl has swallowed up nearly all of the Ghouta and choked the lovely Barada until it is almost extinct. Nizar Qabbani's poem conveys a sense of the river's importance in the national imagination, the almost human character it took on:

Barada, oh father of all rivers
Oh, horse that races the days
Be, in our sad history, a prophet
Who receives inspiration from his lord
Millions acknowledge you as an Arab
Prince . . . so pray as an imam

Oh eyes of the gazelle in the desert of Sham
Look down. This is the age of lavender
They have detained you in the pavilions for a long time
We have woven tents from tears

God has witnessed that we have broken no promise
Or secured protection for those we love.[4]

I decided to make my own journey on foot through the
Ghouta to see if anything remained of it. Heading off from Bab
Sharqi—the east gate—I left the beautiful Old City behind and
walked immediately into the sort of urban wasteland that has
grown up in so many places since World War II, thanks to the
population explosion and, simultaneously, the advent of the auto-
mobile. Damascus remained within virtually the same footprint
from Roman times until the twentieth century; after World War
II, it burst through its boundaries. It now encompasses a population of more than four million.

The walk to the Ghouta passes through a squalid post-
industrial landscape full of car repair joints, rundown factories,
stinking refuse—the same muck that can be found all over the
so-called developing world and even in the developed. After I
had walked for about thirty minutes, fields and groves of trees
began to appear behind the crumbled cement and other rubbish
that lined the road, and there were glimpses of what must once
have been a rural Eden. A family harvesting their olives; yellow
squashes ripening on the ground; cows taking their ease in the
shade—a pastoral scene right out of a Hobbema or a Ruisdael
landscape. The contrast of these vignettes with the grim vistas
of modernity, the shoddy highways and uniformly hideous twentieth-century cement apartment blocks, broke my heart.

What are the consequences of all this unplanned growth?
The Old City of Damascus, like all cities built before the auto-
mobile, is on a *human* scale. Shops are small and manageable,
people know each other, and you can carry your bags from one
place to the next. Sprawling suburbs are on an inhuman scale,
as we are also learning to our cost in America. The car and the
shopping mall have caused everything to balloon to a greater-
than-human scale; shopping at the giant new Walmarts and
Costcos is a positively oppressive experience. All this ugliness is

happening in Syria, now, and in an even more makeshift fashion because of the speed with which the cities are growing.

The government is trying to reverse some of the damage, though the numbers that continue to pour into the city—recent refugees from Iraq account for a million and a half new inhabitants of Damascus—make it hard to keep illegal houses from springing up. Bashar al-Asad recently spearheaded a successful communal project, involving all parts of Damascus society, to plant a million jasmine trees in the city; a million olive trees are planned for the near future. But it will be very hard to keep pace with the unplanned sprawl and the endless stretches of drab concrete.

One doesn't travel to Syria for the landscapes, though in fact there are some beautiful ones. And one doesn't travel there for the food, good as it is. One goes there for the history, which is of a richness and complexity scarcely conceivable to someone accustomed to Western countries, even those with as many-layered a history as France's or Italy's. On my travels I was often reminded of Agatha Christie's amusing description of her husband, the archaeologist Max Mallowan, as he excavated an Iron Age tell near the Euphrates: picking up from the ground some interesting artifact, he would toss it aside as he muttered with infinite contempt, "Roman!" In Syria, the Roman Empire indeed qualifies as recent history. Remains of palace complexes at Ebla and Mari along the Euphrates reveal that sophisticated cities flourished in this region as early as the third millennium B.C. The country was settled by the Phoenicians, invaded by Sargon of Akkad in the third millennium B.C., by Hammurabi the lawgiver in the second, the Hittites a few centuries later, then Egypt's all-conquering Ramses II, the Assyrian monarch Tiglath-Pileser, the Achaemenid Persians under Cyrus, and by Alexander the Great when he scooped up the Persians' empire after the Battle of Issus in 333 B.C. After Alexander's death Syria was grabbed by his general Seleucus I Nikator, founder of the

Seleucid empire, who made it a central part of the Hellenistic world. In 64 A.D. it was taken by the Roman general Pompey the Great, subsequently conquered by Marc Antony (who presented it to Cleopatra as a wedding gift), then reincorporated into the Roman Empire by Augustus. It was on the road to Damascus that St. Paul was struck blind; he later took refuge in the city itself at the home of a Christian, Ananias—a structure that can still be visited. Syria became a center of early Christian culture under the Byzantine empire. In all, the country formed part of the Greco-Roman world for a thousand years. Conquered by the Arabs from the Byzantine Greeks in the seventh century, it became the capital of the Umayyad caliphate until 750, when the caliphate changed hands and moved to Baghdad under the new Abbasid dynasty. In the Middle Ages the Seljuk Turks overran the country and set up independent principalities within it. Much of the region fell to the Crusaders in the Middle Ages and was subsequently reconquered by the Muslims under the new Ayyubid dynasty, which was followed by the upstart Mamluk dynasty from Egypt. Syria eventually succumbed to the Ottoman armies in 1516, continuing as part of that empire for the next four centuries and winning its liberation from the Turks after World War I, only to fall almost immediately to the French, who took advantage of a Mandate they wangled from the League of Nations to invade the country, kick out its newly chosen king, dismantle it, and stay on for more than twenty years until Syria finally gained permanent independence after the Second World War. Principally Muslim since the seventh century, Syria has always, officially at least, tolerated its non-Muslim minorities, particularly the Christians, who still make up ten percent of its population. And far from rejecting its long pre-Muslim past (a time referred to in Islam as the *Jahiliyya*, "days of ignorance"), Syria is exceedingly proud of its major role in the continuing evolution of monotheism.

Yet the average American knows almost nothing about the country, not even its geographic outlines. "Why don't Americans know where Syria is?" a high-school student asked me. "We know where America is. We know where England and France are." And of course he is right: while most Americans can place Syria somewhere in the Middle East, few would be able to tell you that it has a coastline along the Mediterranean, and the popular assumption at home seems to be that this officially secular country is under the iron rule of *sharia* law. "They think we are all like the Saudis!" scoffed our hotel manager, a Christian, as he and his *zaftig* receptionist shared a hookah and a cup of tea with Peter and me on our first evening in the country.

So what are the geographical boundaries of the nation, and how was it formed? Modern Syria, the Syrian Arab Republic, consists of a rump, what was left of the country after the victors of the twentieth-century wars carved off large bits of it. For up until the First World War, "Syria," then a part of the Ottoman Empire, was a region that included not only modern Syria but also modern Lebanon, Israel, Jordan, the Golan Heights, and what is now the Turkish province of Hatay, which includes the Mediterranean port of Alexandretta and the ancient city of Antioch (Turkish Antakya), once the capital of Christian Syria. To judge by official maps of the country, Syria's current government is in a state of denial about its reduced status. These make no mention of Israel, which is invariably labeled "Palestine," and Syria's borders with "Palestine" and Lebanon are depicted not as international borders but as "regional" ones, whatever that means. They also show the Golan Heights to be under Syrian control, which has not been the case since the 1967 Six-Day War with Israel (though a small part of the Heights was taken back in 1973). The fantasy seems to be that Greater Syria—*Bilad al-Sham*—is still inviolate, still a historical reality. Hence the sort of attitude embodied in this speech delivered by Hafiz al-Asad in 1991 upon the signing of the Treaty of Brotherhood, Cooperation, and Coordination between Syria and Lebanon on May 22, 1991:

> We [the Syrians] did not create [that which binds] us to Lebanon—this is God's handiwork. We all share a common his-

tory, a common geography, and bloodties. Therefore, the ties we establish today between the two countries are a reflection of our common heritage. This heritage cannot be erased, nor will it disappear with the passing of time, for brothers are brothers, whether or not they live in the same house. We are one people, even if we live in two separate states. This is the truth, and no one can ignore it. Turning away from this truth does not serve the interests of either of the two independent states, or of the people who live in them.[5]

The destruction of Bilad al-Sham resulted from the dismemberment of the Ottoman Empire by the victorious powers (primarily England and France) after the First World War. The British, who needed the Arabs' help to defeat the Ottoman Turks, had supported—indeed helped to foment—the successful 1916–18 Arab Revolt against them and promised that after the war the Arabs would be rewarded with an independent Arab state in Syria and the Levant. Sharif al Hussein—the Emir of Mecca, keeper of the Holy Places of Mecca and Medina—had been picked to act as the spiritual leader of the revolt, and his charismatic son Faisal, a firm friend to British interests, was put forward as leader of the new state.

But the British had made other promises to other allies. The secret 1916 Sykes-Picot Agreement between Britain and France had established spheres of influence in the Middle East for each country, with France being awarded what are now Syria and Lebanon while Britain got Palestine and what are now the countries of Iraq and Jordan. And in November of 1917, British Foreign Secretary (and former Prime Minister) Arthur Balfour had informed Zionist leaders that his government favored the establishment of a national home for the Jewish people in Palestine and would do what they could to facilitate its founding.

All this came to a head during the Paris Peace Conference where the British and French got to work dividing the spoils; it became evident even to the hopeful Faisal that any Arab state created would be independent in name only. The future historian

Arnold Toynbee, then acting as adviser to the British delegation, remembered one of Prime Minister David Lloyd George's unguarded moments. "Lloyd George, to my delight," he wrote, "had forgotten my presence and had begun to think aloud. 'Mesopotamia . . . yes . . . oil . . . irrigation . . . we must have Mesopotamia; Palestine . . . yes . . . the Holy Land . . . Zionism . . . we must have Palestine; Syria . . . h'm . . . what is there in Syria? Let the French have that.'"[6]

Not that the colonial powers admitted any of this to the world. Presenting (for once) a united front, the British and French issued a declaration, in Arabic, that their principal wartime goal in the East had been "the complete and definite emancipation of the peoples so long oppressed by the Turks and the establishment of national governments and administrations deriving their authority from the initiative and free choice of the indigenous populations."[7] Still, the only people actually to consult the Arabs about their fate were the Americans, though even this was done in a half-hearted manner: President Wilson had no wish to become embroiled in the Middle East. One of his Fourteen Points had specified that "other nationalities which are now under Turkish rule should be assured of an undoubted security of life and an absolutely unmolested opportunity of autonomous development," and he did send a commission of inquiry to the region in 1919. The King-Crane Commission would determine that a great majority of the inhabitants wanted an independent nation encompassing Syria, Palestine, and Lebanon, but no one paid any attention to this; the Commission report was not even published until 1922, after the fateful decisions had already been made. As the future Field Marshal Earl Wavell remarked in 1919, "After 'the war to end war' they seem to have been pretty successful in Paris at making a 'Peace to end Peace.'"

At the San Remo Conference of 1920, the League of Nations Mandates were set up: Britain took control of Palestine, and France of Syria. The unabashedly paternalistic language of the Creation of Mandates document, Article 22 of the Covenant of the League of Nations, formalized the status of Syria and other Middle Eastern countries as "developing" nations (though not quite as "developing" as countries in Africa and the South Pacific) and legitimized the "civilizing mission" of the European powers:

> To those colonies and territories which as a consequence of the late war have ceased to be under the sovereignty of the states which formerly governed them and which are inhabited by peoples not yet able to stand by themselves under the strenuous conditions of the modern world, there should be applied the principle that the well-being and development of such peoples form a sacred trust of civilization and that securities for the formance of this trust should be embodied in this Covenant.
>
> The best method of giving practical effect to this principle is that the tutelage of such peoples should be entrusted to advanced nations who by reason of their resources, their experience or their geographical position can best undertake this responsibility, and who are willing to accept it, and that this tutelage should be exercised by them as Mandatories on behalf of the League . . .
>
> Certain communities formerly belonging to the Turkish empire have reached a stage of development where their existence as independent nations can be provisionally recognized subject to the rendering of administrative advice and assistance by a Mandatory until such time as they are able to stand alone. The wishes of these communities must be a principal consideration in the selection of the Mandatory.[8]

That final clause was strictly *pro forma*; certainly no one paid any attention to the wishes of the Syrians in the selection of the Mandatory, for the French were the very last nation they would have chosen. If the Syrians had to endure a Mandatory power, Faisal informed the Peace Conference, they would prefer it to be the United States, but at that time the Americans had no wish to take up the White Man's Burden. The French duly assumed the

Mandate, momentarily maintaining the fiction that Syria was independent "subject to the rendering of administrative advice and assistance." The Syrian Congress had proclaimed Faisal king, and in 1920 persuaded him to declare unconditional independence—though the Lebanese Christians, backed by France, declared their own independence. The French finally sickened of the game and crushed Syrian nationalism by force of arms, defeating Faisal's brave but inadequate army in the summer of 1920 and sending the king into exile. A year later, the British paid him off for services rendered by making him king of their newly created Iraq.

This is how the Bilad al-Sham was reduced to a new and slimmer Syria, shorn of Lebanon (now an independent Christian-dominated state), Palestine (under the British League of Nations Mandate), and the territories incorporated into the new Hashemite Kingdom of Jordan, which were placed by the British under the rule of Faisal's brother Abdullah, great-grandfather of the current King Abdullah of Jordan. In 1939, the French would reduce Syria still further by handing over the Hatay Province to Turkey.

This new and reduced Syria is slightly larger than the state of New York. It's easy enough to cover most of its area in a month's time. My traveling companions and I did a certain amount of traveling by bus, minibus, and service taxi, but in order to cover as much turf as possible in a limited time we mostly depended on drivers—all of whom, curiously enough, were named Muhammed. There was Muhammed One, who took Peter, Evie, Lizzy, and me around the country on our first trip: a sweet-natured teddy bear. Then Muhammed Two, who worked for our Damascus hotel and drove Catherine and me round the Hauran in southern Syria. Then Muhammed Three, out of Aleppo, who showed us the Dead Cities and early Christian sites in the north. And finally, Muhammed Four—dear Muhammed Four, an intelligent, discreet man in his forties, who accompanied Catherine and me on our rather aimless peregrinations up and down the country. Muhammed Four eventually seemed to twig to the fact that I was writing something, for his proposed itineraries became ever more imaginative.

It was during the course of all these drives that I was struck, again and again, by the essential continuity of history in Syria, how the same trends and themes and cultural traits would crop up again and again, in different guises, throughout the centuries. Religion or warfare or art might change from one historic period to the next, but there are always strong regional connections that allow many customs to stay the same at heart, however different they might appear on the surface.

And what about the courteous national character? For despite Syria's melting-pot history, there does seem to be such a thing, and the observations of medieval travelers like Benjamin of Tudela do not differ substantially from more recent ones like Freya Stark—or from my own, for that matter. Why would we, standard-issue American tourists, receive such an effusive welcome? I speculated that it might be due to more than just cultural norms. Yes, hospitality is a sacred duty among the Arabs, enjoined by the Prophet and enforced by the necessity of mutual aid for survival in a harsh desert environment. But the attitude goes deeper than that, and might on some level even be attributable to the country's one-party political situation. For in Syria, the man in the street appears able to differentiate between government propaganda and actual news; after decades—no, centuries—of authoritarian government, well aware that their press is not free, the people approach its dicta with a certain skepticism. In America we find it very hard to make that distinction: with our naive faith in our supposedly free press, we tend to accept the spin put on the news by our politicians and our media. We may laugh at primitive appeals to our natural xenophobia through slogans like "Evil Empire," "bad guys," or "axis of evil," but when these are repeated often enough they tend to get through to us, whether we like it or not.

Then, too, there is the fact that Syria has always been overrun by people of so many creeds and races that xenophobic fears are hard to maintain. This is something that Gertrude Bell noticed on her voyages there prior to World War I. "You will find in the East," she commented, ". . . a wider tolerance born of greater diversity . . . [T]he European may pass up and down the wildest places, encountering little curiosity and of criticism even less. The news he brings will be heard with interest, his opinions will be listened to with attention, but he will not be thought odd or mad, nor even mistaken, because his practices and the ways of his thought are at variance with those of the people among whom he finds himself."[9]

The foreigner here is an object of interest rather than mistrust, and offers of hospitality appear to be genuine rather than just casual politeness. Take Mylène, for instance, the friend of a friend of a friend, who when we called her to introduce ourselves instantly put her life on hold and devoted the next two days to entertaining us and showing us every beauty spot of her native Aleppo. An Armenian Christian, Mylène is one of those enviably elegant women one rarely encounters in the Anglo-American world: beautiful and cultivated, she is fluent in eleven languages—including Turkish and Farsi as well as Arabic, French, English, Italian, etc. Not content with dragging us all over town she also invited us home for "a light lunch—nothing really," with her husband Iskander, an adorable, roly-poly dental surgeon. We probably shouldn't have been surprised when the light lunch turned out to be composed of nine dishes and lasted for three hours.

And then Saeed. How to describe Saeed? I met him one afternoon when an eccentric cab driver had shanghaied me off to see a sight he said "couldn't be missed," far on the outskirts of Damascus, almost at the airport. Where *could* he be taking me? At the end of a long and lonely road, we finally found ourselves at something called the Sham Village Resort ("Sham" is an Arabic name used to designate both the city of Damascus and the country of Syria). This turned out to be a high-kitsch tourist center, aimed not at Western tourists but at the Gulf Arabs who repair to Syria during the hot months. In the spirit of Walt Disney, the proprietors of the Sham Village had created a phony

Damascus as it might have looked a hundred years ago, with room upon room of wax figures re-enacting traditional scenes: the spice market, the bakery, the barber shop, the coffee shop, etc. I wondered why anyone would look at all this when the real thing can still be seen, relatively unchanged, only a few miles away; but of course there is no accounting for the psychology of mass tourism. More interesting than the museum was the set, also housed at the Sham Village, of *Bab al-Hara*, Syria's most popular soap opera. Set in the Mandate era, *Bab al-Hara* reproduces pre-modern Damascus faithfully, and I was enjoying looking at the pasteboard mock-up of a 1925 neighborhood.

The security guard, a tall, plump boy of nineteen or twenty, looked prudishly disapproving when my middle-aged driver addressed me as *habibi*, "darling."

"Do you know what he is calling you?" he demanded.

"Oh, I call everyone *habibi*," the driver said carelessly.

The guard, who had introduced himself as Saeed, rolled his eyes. "Here is my telephone number," he said, pressing a piece of paper into my hand. "My mother and I would be happy to take you to dinner before you leave and show you around Damascus at night."

When the evening came the mother couldn't join us, but Saeed took me to his favorite restaurant and all around the Bab Touma district, chattering away with puppy-like friendliness. He was only a senior in high school, as it turned out, and was working at the Sham Village as a part-time job. His father had left the family when he was a small child, his mother suffered from back trouble, and he and his brother had to contribute to the family budget. Saeed longed to be a fashion designer—he had every episode of *Project Runway* practically memorized— but he figured that with all his responsibilities, training for a career in fashion was nothing but a pipe dream. He was planning instead to study Japanese at the university and go into business.

"I wish I could have got dressed before meeting you so I could show you my style," he said, "but I had to come straight from work." Saeed is an avid consumer of international pop culture, a passionate devotee of Britney Spears, Beyoncé, and 50 Cent. His fifteen-year-old brother helps support the family by doing web design and Photoshop after school, and also performs and records techno-rap with his girlfriend: he aspires to be the Arab Eminem. Their mother, Saeed said, is completely addicted to Oprah and quotes Dr. Phil whenever an occasion arises.

As we walked, Saeed reached up and plucked branches of jasmine for me, crushing the blossoms in his fingers so I could get a richer waft of their fragrance. He spoke without bitterness about his dreams for a career and how unlikely it was that they would come true. "We are all the family we have, so we must take care of each other," he said. "My mother has done everything for us. We must care for her."

These encounters led me to some profound rethinking, both about the country I was visiting and my own. "What went wrong?" historian Bernard Lewis asked about the Islamic world, in his recent book by that title, and the phrase has caught on. Some things have gone wrong there, unquestionably; but others seem, at least to my foreign eyes, to have gone right. Whether because of the Prophet's enjoinder on the faithful to practice charity and hospitality or because of some other cultural conditioning in that direction, Syrians seem to have developed a far more civil and polite public arena than our own.

One might profitably transpose Lewis's question and ask what went wrong with *us*—with America. For my trips East have made it clearer to me than ever before that something has gone very wrong: a cultural hardening that set in, I have come to believe, in the Reagan 80s, when greed suddenly became good. In the intervening quarter-century our country succumbed to a grim Social Darwinist philosophy according to which our neighbor is defined not as a fellow-creature but, if not exactly an enemy, then at least a potential competitor. One might have expected the resurgence of American Christianity over the same period to have mitigated this dog-eat-dog attitude, but too many of our Christian churches seem to have incorporated the philosophy of competition directly into their creeds.

What do Christianity and Islam teach us about our duties to others? Christ urged us to sell all we have and give to the poor. An admirable goal, but not very realistic—how many people in history have actually followed these instructions? Muhammed, on the other hand, proposed an entire social system, a series of laws that anyone can realistically follow and still remain part of the larger social structure. The Muslim *zaka*, an obligatory charity amounting to 2.5 percent of one's income (as distinct from private charity, also important), is eminently do-able. That system seems to have instilled some respect for the humanity of the dispossessed, while our own Social Darwinism seems only to have engendered contempt for them as pathetic losers. I was struck by the Syrians' shocked reaction to the health care debate going on back at home at the time of my visit: they simply could not conceive of a system that let poor people fall through the cracks, that allowed someone to die unnecessarily if they couldn't pay for care. The whole thing made me think it quite probable that Islam is philosophically incompatible with the doctrinaire capitalism we have been trying to spread around the world. But then again, so is Christianity—*real* Christianity, that is—as I see it.

American media coverage of the Middle East for the last forty years or so—probably since the 1967 war—has engendered a knee-jerk prejudice that will be almost impossible to cure. To visit Syria is to confront the unhappy truth about our media, which is that much of the international news we read or see, from whatever portion of the political spectrum, serves not as a window looking out at the world but as a mirror: a mirror that reflects our own fears and obsessions and shines them right back at us.

2 ✤ *Time*

> The Arab Islamic civilization was at bottom the
> Hellenized Aramaic and the Iranian civiliza-
> tions as developed under the aegis of the caliphate
> and expressed through the medium of the Arabic
> tongue. In another sense it was the logical con-
> tinuation of the early Semitic civilizations of the
> Fertile Crescent originated and developed by the
> Assyro-Babylonians, Phoenicians, Aramaeans
> and Hebrews. In it the unity of the Mediterra-
> nean civilization of Western Asia found its final
> culmination.
>
> —Philip K. Hitti, *History of the Arabs*

Seated at one of the cluster of cafés beneath the
looming medieval Citadel of Aleppo, a spot that still
functions as the heart of this ancient city, you are
treated to the best people-watching you're likely to
find anywhere (fig. 1). There are fully veiled ladies
on pilgrimage from Iran; there are Bedouin wives in
black relieved by bright spots of color, gypsy-like ex-
otics who stand out even in this ultra-exotic crowd.
Gulf Arabs stride along in their telltale white garb.
Old men on donkeys scuttle past; others, in long
robes and *keffiye*, stroll along, dignified and unhurried. Added to the mix are more modern types, for as

29

well as being a crossroad of cultures, Aleppo is a living amalgam of historic periods. Trophy girlfriends strut alongside their men in what might here be considered the height of fashion: clinging little scarlet miniskirts worn with tights, along with perilously teetering high heels. On cobblestones these shoes become treacherous, making the girls cling tightly to their companions' arms to keep from falling—and maybe that is the whole point of the exercise, after all. One young woman wore a hijab that modestly covered her body but happened to be gleaming gold and coated with glitter. Fashion in footwear is particularly striking. Aleppo's young spivs tend to sport leather shoes, unremarkable except for weirdly long and pointy toes, the distant descendants, perhaps, of curly-toed Ottoman slippers. Women, even those completely concealed by burqas, favor highly-polished boots of a rather S & M aspect, sharply high-heeled with glittering silver panels at the side—boots *not* made for walking.

The scene is not so very different from what it was in the 1920s when the archaeologist Leonard Woolley, excavator of Carchemish and Ur, visited the place. "And then the people!" he exclaimed:

> Syrians in European clothes and fez, town Arabs with cloaks of thin light-tinted silks embroidered with silver, swaggering Circassians with their long black coats, high boots, and crossed bandoliers stuffed with silver-plated cartridge-cases, Dervishes with tall sugar-loaf hats of brown felt, red-slippered villagers in gaudy prints with brown *abas* and heavy black ropes over their head-cloths, driving donkeys laden with garden produce, Bagdadis with their slender 'brims' or head-ropes bound and tasseled with silver, Anatolian Turks with baggy trousers and voluminous waist-bands, Kurds from Lake Van, drovers from Samarkand or Teheran heralded by the fivefold bells which dangle from the necks of their camels whose swaying bales block the narrow streets, black-cloaked Bedouin, Jews and Persians, Afghans and Turkmans, kavasses with their gold-embroidered

Zouave jackets and silver scimitars, all these and many more crowd on the cobbled ways, all with their distinctive dress and their own manner of speech; it is a kaleidoscope of color and a mixing-pot of races.[1]

The Western view of the "Arab world" as a homogenous, purely Muslim place full of anonymous black-clad crowds is blown to pieces as soon as you arrive in this complex civilization. On the level of sheer human spectacle, Syria's cities are astounding. It is an easy cliché to call the country a crossroad of civilization, but here, in the streets of Aleppo or Damascus, the cliché comes true. Where the Mediterranean meets the Arab world, the desert meets the metropolis. Syria was for many centuries a key stop on the Silk Road, its markets a depot for the goods of all the world. The result is that the country has been a melting pot and a multi-cultural society for a very, very long time.

Damascus and Aleppo both lay claim to being the oldest continually inhabited city on earth, with life-spans somewhere in the neighborhood of eight millennia. No scholar has been able to determine which is older, for dense habitation on both sites has kept archaeologists from being able to dig down to the earliest signs of civilized life, but there can be no doubt that both cities are very ancient. One of the most extraordinary aspects of the country, and the most compelling reason to make the trip there, is the spectacle it offers of life being lived, *totally unselfconsciously*, just as it has been for thousands of years. In America we often turn what is left of our old architecture into Disneyfied theme parks: think of what has happened to Colonial Williamsburg—or even old Santa Fe or Nantucket, now populated not by ranchers and whalers but by CEOs. The well-preserved centers of European cities like Paris or Amsterdam have essentially become open-air museums. This is not at all the case in Damascus or Aleppo, whose souqs, khans (caravansarais), and houses of prayer are still being used for their original purposes. Here, history is not over; it lives on. In the 1860s Mark Twain, stunned by his first sight of Damascus, marveled that the city "measures time not by days and months and years, but by the empires she has seen rise and prosper and crumble to ruin . . . Damascus has seen all that has ever occurred on earth, and still she lives. She has looked upon the dry bones of a thousand empires, and will see the tombs of a thousand more before she dies."[2]

This is a feeling that must be shared by anyone who walks for the first time into the square outside Damascus's Umayyad Mosque. The site, like so many of the major holy places in this part of the world, is very ancient, with origins dating to long before the advent of Islam. A thousand years before Christ the Semitic god Hadad was worshiped on this spot; many centuries later, the Romans converted the building into a temple to Jupiter, assimilating the cult of Hadad into that of the Roman deity. After the adoption of Christianity by the Roman Empire, the temple was converted again, this time into a church— possibly by the emperor Theodosius—and dedicated to St. John the Baptist, whose head is supposed to lie within the mosque and is now venerated equally by Christians and Muslims, both of whom worship John, or Yahya as he is known in Arabic, as a prophet. When the Muslim armies took the city in 636, they allowed the church to remain in operation; as the decades went on, more and more Muslims came to pray there alongside Christians, with members of both faiths entering through the original entrance to the Jupiter Temple. It is hardly surprising that the Umayyad Caliph al-Walid chose this spot, rendered holy by countless generations of worshipers, when he set out to build his great mosque.

Al-Walid filled in the Jupiter Temple doorway in the process of reorienting the building, but it is still clearly visible in the mosque wall, and so is the Greek inscription over it, dating to Byzantine times: "Thy Kingdom, O Christ, is an enduring Kingdom, and Thy dominion endureth throughout all generations." The fact that the new Muslim dispensation left this relic of Christian rule undisturbed says a great deal about the clemency *and* the confidence of the new faith. Islam had triumphantly superseded the old religions; it could afford to be generous. And the Great Mosque is above all a triumphalist statement. The Umayyads were asserting their ascendancy not only over the Islamic Empire but also over the Byzantine Christians who had ruled the region during the previous centuries. They were the new heirs of the Roman Empire, and they intended to show it. The Mosque cost al-Walid seven years of the total income of the Damascus treasury. It was huge; it was a *statement*: Islam was here to stay.

We are accustomed to thinking of the monotheistic religions as being mutually intolerant, and equally hostile to paganism. We are accustomed, also, to a certain amount of city planning, often of a rather ruthless variety. The architectural synchronism of this great Levantine city, in which each age and faith has left visible relics of the previous ones to make up part of the ensemble, is unlike anything to be seen even in that most synchronistic city of Western Europe, Rome. The sight in Damascus of the enormous propylaeum of the Roman Temple, with its Corinthian capitals and its entablature half smashed away, rearing forty feet into the air over the great walls of the mosque, the old souq spread beyond it covered with its gracious nineteenth-century arched roof, is an unforgettable image, especially considering the casual street life going on all around it (fig. 2): stalls selling books, a wagon piled high with pomegranates and black-berries, peanut-sellers, *shwarma* stands, the bustling crowds, the gawping tourists, whether Japanese with cameras or burqa-clad Iranians in town to visit the spot where the martyr Husayn's head is said to have touched ground (on the site of the mosque, of course, the timeless holy site) after the Battle of Karbala.

The Mosque was completed in 715, the year of al-Walid's death. It has inevitably metamorphosed over the centuries, with fires, earthquakes, and unsatisfactory reconstruction efforts wreaking their damage. One fire in 1893 was particularly disastrous, and a 1964 restoration project has generally been judged a mistake. But the effect is still one of great splendor. Ibn Jubayr called the large, stately courtyard "one of the most beautiful and splendid of sights. Here the population congregate, for it is the place of care-dispelling and recreation, and here every evening you will see them, coming and going from east to west, from Bab Jairun to Bab al-Barid, and others you will see talking to their friends, and some reading. In this manner they will go on, coming and going, until the end of the last evening prayers, and then depart."[3]

This is still absolutely the case, and as long as you take off your shoes and don the robes provided for visiting tourists (they are handed out in a chamber signposted "Putting On Special Clothes Room"), you are welcome to join the congregants strolling through the courtyard, sitting on the ground and schmoozing, or performing their ritual ablutions at the pretty Ottoman-era fountain. For like many such expanses in mosques, the courtyard functions as a social space: it is in fact the direct descendant of the Greek *agora* and began its life as an assembly hall. It is also a place for relaxation and refreshment, both physical and spiritual. Muslims' attitude toward their place of worship might seem strange to Protestants—less so perhaps to Catholics. Within the mosque's great courtyard some folks lie down and take a nap; congregations of old men, swathed in keffiyes, sit in contemplation; a mother pours out tea and distributes cakes to her family (plate 1). Tourists are obvious from the uniform robes meted out to visitors, but we seemed to attract no special attention, and certainly no onus. Quite a few people even smiled in a welcoming manner. Maybe this is because tourists are relatively thin on the ground. In Europe I have seen churchgoers driven practically to distraction by hordes of noisy rubberneckers and once, at the Church of the Carmine in Florence, I even witnessed an enraged old woman shouting for the infidels to get out of the church. Here infidels like ourselves are few enough to be unobtrusive, and no one seems to resent us.

What makes this courtyard a masterpiece rather than simply a handsome and imposing structure are the mosaics that cover the lower arcade, a glimmering dream of green and gold, with the façades of walls and transept covered in panel after fantastic panel depicting the Islamic vision of paradise (plate 2, fig. 3).

Against a background of gold we see an intense interweaving of trees, plants, fruits, orchards, fields, rivers, houses, and palaces, all in chromatic tones of green. In accordance with Islamic rules, there are no humans or animals here; like the Sleeping Beauty's overgrown landscape the scene is frozen in one otherworldly, enchanted moment, richly alive but absolutely still. The Barada panel along the western wall intensifies the surrealistic effect by presenting, in stylized and dreamlike form, a landscape well known to the old Damascenes, that of the Ghouta oasis.

Travelers who have seen the great mosaics created in Ravenna two hundred years before these, or in Sicily under the Norman kings, will immediately be reminded of these places, for they all share the bold uses of color and the large-scale, all-encompassing decorative vision. As in Ravenna, the mosaics of the Umayyad Mosque were fashioned by Greek as well as local craftsmen, and they certainly have a strong Byzantine flavor: it is an Arab ideal—the Islamic paradise—but seen through Byzantine tradition and Byzantine aesthetics, another unforgettable example of eccentric Syrian syncretism. Robert Byron, who visited Damascus in 1933 on the road to Oxiana, called these mosaics "the first landscapes of the European tradition," and while this is typical of the kind of high-handed generalizations he was in the habit of tossing out, I found myself unable to come up with any real counter examples. "For all their Pompeiian picturesqueness," Byron wrote, ". . . they are real landscapes, more than mere decoration, concerned inside formal limits with the identity of a tree or the energy of a stream. They must have been done by Greeks, and they foreshadow, properly enough, El Greco's landscapes of Toledo. Even now, as the sun catches a fragment on the outside wall, one can imagine the first splendor of green and gold, when the whole court shone with those magic scenes conceived by Arab fiction to recompense the parched eternities of the desert."[4]

The effect is heart-stopping even now; but the mosaics were originally still more extensive, covering all the surfaces of the arcaded walls. This remains the largest-scale use of mosaic ever attempted. It was meant to overwhelm, and even in its reduced form it succeeds in doing this. So does the great prayer hall, though it is merely a rebuilding of the original Umayyad adaptation and synthesis of various Muslim, Byzantine, Eastern, and Mediterranean elements, much of which was lost in the 1893 fire. So different from the tiny, intimate, almost domestic mosques that proliferate through the ancient alleys and souqs of the cities, the Umayyad Mosque, like the Great Mosque in Aleppo, was designed to dominate the cityscape and express the worldly as well as the spiritual power of its rulers.

In the shadow of the Mosque is the Bab Touma district, named for the Gate of St. Thomas, an ancient city gate rebuilt in the thirteenth century using classical masonry. An outpost of international student/bohemian culture, the neighborhood is oddly reminiscent of Paris's Latin Quarter, with a polyglot young crowd patronizing its little boutiques, internet cafés, and restaurants. There is even, wonder of wonders, a tiny English bookstore—though of course the books on sale are far too pricey to buy. The nighttime scene is festive and noisy and most of the goings-on would not seem out of place on the Boul' Mich.

In the lee of the mosque looking in the direction of Bab Touma, the Café Nawfara looks absurdly romantic (fig. 4). Fairy lights are festooned around the outdoor part of the café, nestled under the mosque's eastern wall, while patrons smoke their nargilehs and gaze into the dusk. Inside, the last *hakawati*, or public storyteller, still plies his trade, playing to a mixed crowd of locals and foreigners. Here on most evenings—the actual time of the performance varies, so listeners must take their chances—Abu Shadi, a slight, intelligent-looking man in his sixties, sits on a raised dais in the back of the café, book and sword in hand and cup of tea at his side. For about an hour he will read from whatever classic tale he happens to be perusing at the moment. Typical choices include the chivalric *Romance of Prince Antar*, or the tale of the twelfth-century Mamluk Sultan Baybars, or the *Sirat Banu Hilal*, a medieval epic, or the *Thousand and One Nights*. Abu Shadi reads with great verve, giving special emphasis to accents and eccentric voices, and when a particularly dramatic moment presents itself he whacks on his little metal table with the sword, causing the audience to jump and roar their approval. He indulges in a good deal of repartee with his listeners, who shout good-natured responses to his sallies (plate 3).

The tea-boy moves silently through the room, topping people's glasses and using tongs to pluck burning coals from a brazier to keep the nargilehs alight (fig. 5). The décor is a characteristically Syrian mixture of venerable decay and modern trash: the furniture is battered, and the ancient walls are hung with plastic ferns and a cheap 1950s American autumn scene. The hakawati in his fez and ordinary suit jacket, waving his sword, personifies the slightly confused nature of this corner of the Middle East, poised uneasily but not ungracefully between the old world and the new.

Abu Shadi is well aware that he is an anachronism. For the hakawati tradition has of course been killed by television and other forms of canned entertainment. If it weren't for the Café Nawfara and the government, which sponsors hakawati performances at various arts festivals and Ramadan celebrations, the art form would be entirely dead. Purists, especially those who are old enough to remember a half-century back, bemoan great hakawatis of the past, men like Abu Ahmad Monis who held court at the Nawfara for many years. But for those of us without such long memories, listening to Abu Shadi is still a thrill, whether you can understand his words or not.

Why don't I feel this way about American "storytellers," who irk me to distraction? Maybe because the storytelling we now hear at fairs and festivals seems like such an artificial, self-conscious genre, and because it is so often aimed at children. Abu Shadi is nothing like that: he is an adult, speaking to adults, making adult jokes. And in any case, he is not reviving a dead medium but still working in a living one, ancient and moribund though it might be.

Characteristically Damascene is the al-Hamadiye souq, the great covered market that follows the path of the Roman processional way leading down to the Jupiter Temple (now the mosque). Rebuilt and covered with an arched metal roof in the nineteenth century during the reign of the Sultan Abdul Hamid II, for whom it was named, the souq was the brainchild of his governor Rashid Nasha Pasha, who hoped it would rival the grand new shopping galleries that were going up in Istanbul and Europe at that time. In the event, he outdid even the splendid Constantinopolitan emporia: for sheer scale, the al-Hamadiye souq surpasses anything in Turkey or anywhere else in the Arab world, and to enter its dark maw, like a great cave or a cathedral, is like being sucked into a vortex. A long line of shops curves off into the unknown. High overhead, little stars of light twinkle through the arched metal roof: these are bullet holes left by the French guns when they struck back against a major uprising in 1925.

Unlike most Syrian souqs with their essentially medieval aspect, the Hamadiye looks like a gigantic, shabby, Eastern take on nineteenth-century European models like the Burlington Arcade in London or Paris's Passage des Panoramas. Shops loom behind tall plate-glass vitrines, with offices and countinghouses in the upper stories. We see wandering vendors selling toys and, weirdly, stuffed eagles with raised wings, apparently a popular item; we see a tea-vendor (fig. 6) in tarboosh, swelling pantaloons, and tight waistcoat, a gigantic samovar hung over his shoulder, pouring tea for a couple of passing policemen. We stop for a break at Bakdash, a magnificent Ottoman-era tea-room where big, burly men in the front window slap dollops of what looks like vanilla ice cream or taffy into shape (fig. 7). Inside, every table is occupied by shoppers eating one of the only two items on the menu: the white stuff, which is indeed ice cream, or a bland milk pudding, both offerings sprinkled with fresh pistachios. Paneled oak walls lined with mirrors and photographs of Ottoman Damascus give off a whiff of faded grandeur.

I did a lot of Christmas shopping at the Hamadiye souq, for nothing there seemed to cost much more than a dollar. The mild local soap stamped "Gren Vegetal." Loofahs—the real thing, dried ridged plant gourds, not industrially made copies. Depilatory kits that included little pans, something like Jiffy Pop popcorn poppers, filled with gaily colored wax. Rosewater for the complexion. Perfume in little glass bottles: not only Damascus standards like jasmine and rose, but concoctions proudly advertised as Dolce Cabannis, Mor Amor, Jacomo, and Issey Myake. And the piled up spices in the spice souq: the cardamom, the saffron, the sumac; fragrant piles of Damascene roses; ginger and cinnamon tea; grape seed oil. And hanging above these shops, dried lizards, wolf skins, and tortoise shells (fig. 8).

And the lingerie! All the souqs here have special lingerie sections full of outrageously over-the-top ensembles that are not sexy so much as just plain funny and playful, adorned with sequins, feathers, plastic foliage, fur, even rubber cockroaches and cell phones. One thong is covered by a big squishy pair of lips; a bra is made up of two gigantic eyeballs. All of this is sold quite openly, and the vendors took it in good part when I photographed their displays (fig. 9).

Then there is the gold souq, with rows of gold jewelry displayed in nearly identical little shops along a narrow covered walk. As a New Yorker, I found something startling about this, for it is so clearly the ancestor of the noisy, garish Diamond District along Forty-seventh Street in Manhattan. No doubt the New York vendors' grandfathers presided in just such souqs as these.

Some of the fashion displays hardly harmonize with our anorexic Western ideal of female beauty—one window we passed every day contained so many chunky mannequins that we took to calling it the Hefty Ladies Shop. For some reason a couple of them were even turned around to display ample posteriors. One display that we admired featured five female dummies wildly gyrating in what looked like the frug.

There is still a strong Levantine flavor to these souqs. Do any of the other cities of the Levant retain this same atmosphere? Jerusalem, Beirut, Amman? Unlike the Hamadiye souq in Damascus which has a nineteenth-century feel, the Aleppo souqs are purely medieval, with people living and working much as they must have done seven or eight hundred years ago (fig. 10). They are a warren comprising eight miles of narrow alleys all interconnected and covered with vaulted ceilings of rough stone; there are no motor vehicles other than mopeds (fig. 11), and you can still see merchants riding along on heavily-laden donkeys (fig. 12). Each alley leads into the next by way of secret passageways and doors, tiny mosques are set into walls, and khans open out from hidden alleys. The Roman policy of providing public drinking fountains was continued under Arab rule: the fountains are there still (fig. 13). Specific ethnic "neighborhoods" exist within the souq, with Armenian businesses, for example, clustered together. Having no sense of direction, I got lost almost as soon as I entered the souq and wandered about quite blindly.

Despite the big ambitions of tourism boosters in Aleppo and the plethora of wonderful sights there, the city is still not easy for foreign visitors to negotiate without a guide. The al-Jdeideh district is full of tantalizing old houses that have been converted into upscale hotels and restaurants, but it is a maze of alleys with no signage in English or any other Western language; even the city maps made specifically for tourists are useless, since they show only major thoroughfares. All you can really do is point yourself in what you imagine to be the right direction and hope for the best.

The parts of the souq directed toward the tourist trade are attractive, but I found myself much preferring the areas devoted to ordinary housewares and food. For one thing, no one tries to sell you anything; your presence as a mere gawker is accepted, and you are ignored. There is a perfume souq, the Souq al-Attareen. There is also a wool souq, where Mylène showed us the shop her grandfather had founded a century earlier. I bought quite a few pairs of socks on my wanderings and also a pair of the plastic bath sandals furnished by hotels, so comfortable that I inadvertently wore them down to breakfast a few times. But I was not tempted by the myriad Bridget-Jones-sized panties. The food shops were the most fun of all: every part of the sheep hanging on hooks together, testicles, lungs, liver, heart; delicious green frittata-type sandwiches with red pepper sauce; outsized potatoes looking almost human in shape. In fish shops, water lies ankle-deep on the floor and quantities of catfish (or some Levantine equivalent of them) swim around in the murky liquid while the vendors walk about in high rubber boots. Leaving the fish market, you exit the souq at the Bab Antakya, one of the gates of the medieval city, where hawkers, in from the country with their fresh produce, cry out to advertise their wares: almonds, grapes, pomegranates, peaches. A century ago, T. E. Lawrence described a scene not all that different today:

> Sweetmeat sellers, the icedrink man who sells syrups, crying out 'Take care of thy teeth' or 'Refresh thy heart', 'This for a metalik' (1/2 d.), or the man with plain water in a goatskin with brass spout, then the fruit sellers, 'if an old woman eats my cress she is young tomorrow'; and funniest of all men with women's ornaments crying 'appease your mother-in-law', and then as you are looking on at this comes a coarse cry of 'dahrak' (your back) and a porter crashes into you with a fresh-killed sheep on his back, or a load of charcoal, or perhaps a camel loafs through the crowd with its bell round its neck giving notice.[5]

These souqs have lasted for a couple of thousand years, evolving somewhat but still recognizably what they must have been in early Arab and even perhaps in Roman times. How will they fare in the age of the shopping mall? Will they go the way of America's mom-and-pop stores? This is a question that is very sensitive, as malls are now popping up in Syria at a rapid rate. They have been late in coming, mostly because for years the government kept strict control over the sales of international brands in hopes of encouraging local manufacturers. In the last few years, though, these controls have been relaxed. There is now a gigantic mall on the road between Aleppo and Turkey and several new ones going up in Damascus, though compared with other Middle Eastern cities Damascus is still traditional, with less than a fifth of the mall space of neighboring Beirut. Will the new malls siphon off shoppers from the souqs and fundamentally change the country's shopping habits? No one is sure, but the fact that the malls cater to wealthier customers than the average souq-shopper means that there has been little thinning of the crowds in the old souqs so far. One mall owner points out, "The shoppers we target used to go to Lebanon to shop. We target the middle-to-upper-middle-class shoppers in the 14-to-40 age range who don't usually go to the souqs."[6]

Hafiz al-Asad decreed a centrally planned economy, Soviet style, complete with Five-Year Plans and other dicta from on high. But nothing could be less like the old Soviet image of long lines and shops empty of consumer goods than the buzzing streets of Syria's cities, veritable temples to small-scale capitalism. Little shops and businesses, handed down from father to son, are jammed into every possible spot, each with its presiding boss bustling around, brewing coffee, and doing deals in the dark recesses behind the goods, the closest thing these tiny emporia have to a backroom.

Leading off at angles from the souqs are the khans that functioned as warehouses and caravanserais. Many of them continue to be used today, though nowadays little trucks and the occasional donkey are parked there rather than the camels for which the spaces were originally designed back in the seventeenth and eighteenth centuries. The central courtyard is the camel area, used—still used—for unloading goods and organizing storage. The upper stories have offices for the merchants and bedrooms for those who have transported the goods. Many of those no longer in use are lined with shops, like the 1609 Khan al-Jumruk or Customs Khan. The most spectacular of Damascus's khans, now kept open purely as a tourist attraction, is the eighteenth-century, nine-domed Khan Asad Pasha (plate 4), in which, as historian and antiquarian Ross Burns has judged, "The Damascus flair for covering the entire central courtyard with domes reached its most spectacular development."

. . . the *khan* develops the concept of the domed courtyard to cathedral-like proportions. The domes soar on four huge pillars, the central space actually uncovered above its pendentives as its planners probably intended. The sun penetrates the courtyard with dramatic effect; the receding volumes around the central dome of pure light almost take the breath away with their play on simple themes of light and shade, repetition of basic shapes and the uncompromising use of traditional Damascus banded masonry. This is the great masterpiece of Ottoman Damascus . . . As the witness to the power of the *a'yans* [Ottoman notables], it hides magnificently the feet of clay on which their rule was based.[7]

The architecture is so exalted it's hard to associate with the commercial business of the khan, and what Burns doesn't mention is that the geometrical perspectives rearrange themselves with mathematical perfection as you ascend to the upper story where the counting houses and dormitories would have been. Peter, an architectural photographer by profession, became obsessed with trying to capture the receding and multiplying vistas (fig. 14). Many visitors have remarked on the similarity of its bold, black-and-white-banded décor to that of Italian churches, and this is not surprising since the Italians, particularly the Venetian merchants, were in continual contact with their eastern counterparts. Cultural exchange was inevitable.

Straight Street, which runs east-west across the whole breadth of Damascus's Old City, shows the city's evolution in microcosm. The street has biblical antecedents as the place where St. Paul—at that time the proselytizing Jew, Saul of Tarsus—took refuge after he was blinded by divine revelation while on his way to Damascus to persecute Christians. "Arise," the Lord told the Damascene Christian Ananias, "and go into the street which is called Straight, and enquire in the house of Judas for one called Saul, of Tarsus: for behold, he prayeth . . ." (Acts 9:11). Entering the house, Ananias laid hands on the blind man,

"And immediately there fell from his eyes as it had been scales: and he received sight forthwith, and arose, and was baptized." Mark Twain had some fun with the name. "The street called Straight," he wrote after his visit to Damascus described in *The Innocents Abroad*, "is straighter than a corkscrew but not as straight as a rainbow. St. Luke is careful not to commit himself; he does not say it is the street which *is* straight, but 'the street which is *called* Straight.' It is a fine piece of irony; it is the only facetious remark in the Bible, I believe."[8] Still, by medieval standards—and Straight Street is now essentially medieval in character—it *is* straight, very straight, a trait it owes to its classical antecedents. After Syria's conquest by Alexander the Great in 333 B.C., the new Greek masters of Damascus imposed upon it the same grid pattern they gave to other cities newly under their rule, such as Apamea, Aleppo, and Latakia (now Syria's major outlet to the Mediterranean). This Hippodamian grid, as it was called—named for its originator, the fifth-century B.C. Greek city planner Hippodamus of Miletus—eventually morphed under the Roman Empire into a specifically Roman celebration of symmetry, display, urban planning, and central authority, with Straight Street, Via Recta, transformed into the city's *decumanus maximus*, the principal east-west artery.

Looking at it today, it's hard to believe that Straight Street was once a wide, classical thoroughfare with imposing colonnades rising on either side, just the kind of thing we can still see in the ruins of Palmyra and Apamea. As the centuries passed, the stores and workshops in the shelter of the colonnades encroached farther and farther into the street itself, while in post-classical times the Corinthian columns crumbled away, never to be replaced. Straight Street is now so narrow that we had to press ourselves against the shopfronts to keep from being pulverized by the passing traffic. In Europe the locals would have manufactured clever little automobiles to maneuver such spaces, but Syria, like Cuba, contains a surprising number of very old American cars, lumbering behemoths eminently unsuited to these narrow precincts. Remains of classical columns that were never cleared away have now been put to use as barriers to prevent cars from climbing up onto the narrow sidewalks. Other traces of the ancient world still stand, sometimes looking very odd amid the bustling shops with their overhanging Ottoman-era porches and sagging façades (fig. 15). The theater built there by Herod the Great no longer exists, but a lovely Roman arch still stands, for no apparent reason, halfway down the street, impeding traffic even further (fig. 16). Bits of columns lie piled hugger-mugger by the side of the road.

The dignity and visual unity aspired to by the classical city planners has vanished, and Old Damascus is now an amalgam of styles, a monument to accretion and agglutination. Bab Sharqi, the Eastern Gate at the end of Straight Street, is a perfect example of this syndrome, a rather bizarre architectural mishmash consisting of a triple Roman gate with a medieval mosque precariously perched atop one side. It has seen plenty of history. This is the gate through which Khalid ibn al-Walid, the Arab conqueror of Christian Damascus, entered the city in 635. Half a millennium later it served as the entryway for Muslim reinforcements who helped fight off the ill-conceived and ill-fated Second Crusade, whose leaders, Louis VII of France and Conrad III of Germany, insanely targeted the one and only Muslim city that had always been their staunch ally—Damascus. Nearby, along the ancient city walls, is the spot where St. Paul was lowered out of the city in a basket to escape the vengeful Jews, angry at his defection and his preaching of the Christian heresy. Guides will claim to show you the exact spot, but no one really knows where it is. The house of Ananias is still there though, or at least its catacomb-like basement—as Mark Twain said, "There is small question that a part of the original house is there still; it is an old room twelve or fifteen feet underground, and its masonry is evidently ancient. If Ananias did not live there in St. Paul's time, somebody else did, which is just as well."[9] The basement is still a draw for Christian pilgrims. The day we visited, a group of Danish Lutherans had convened in the gloom, praying and singing hymns in polite, quavering Protestant tones.

Going west from Bab Sharqi along Straight Street, we passed through the Christian quarter, as thoroughly Christian today as it was a millennium ago, alive with Greek and Armenian merchants and businessmen. It amused us to stroll through the area on a Friday, the Muslim day of prayer, and see all these fellows rather ostentatiously playing cards and shaking dice at the ubiquitous little tables set up in front of every shop. They all drink tea or maybe something stronger, for many of the cavernous shops of the Christian quarter sell liquor, in greater quantity than a single neighborhood should require; this leads to the inevitable conclusion that they must be patronized by Muslims as well as Christians, despite the Koranic injunction against alcohol. Islamic history, like the Christian variety, has alternated between looser times and more puritanical ones, and in the Umayyad and Abbasid eras prohibition seems to have been no more effective than it was in 1920s America. There was even a tradition in early Islam of the poetic celebration of wine: here is the poet Akhtal, for instance, writing at the beginning of the Umayyad period (in a beautiful translation by C. G. Tuetey):

Many's the fellow worth his draught
in gold, good company, never ajar,
whom I joined in wine when the cock had crowed
and the night-long caravans drew to a halt;
wine of 'Ana, where gliding by
the Euphrates draws its rolling wave;
three years under lock, it had shed its heat
and, mellowing, sunk to half the jar
which a Greek-tongued jack had filled to the brim
and decked with leaves of laurel and vine;
fair, neither black, of humble earth,
nor ruddy, from overconcern with the hearth;
dressed in a quivering gossamer gown
and a skin-tight bodice of fiber and tar;
golden, deepening to amber with time
confined in a vault among gardens and streams;

a virgin whose charms no sailor had seen
till unveiled in a shop for a gold dinar . . .[10]

But in later centuries the Prophet's order was taken more seriously. An amusing pointer I found in a 1926 primer called *Colloquial Arabic*, by one De Lacy O'Leary, advises Western travelers that it is best to pose as a teetotaler among Muslims, for since they do not drink wine "it is a great relief when they find that you do not expect any to be procured for you. If a Muslim, himself a strict abstainer, sends for spirits or beer for you, you are likely to get some abomination decocted by a Greek trader, and your well-intentioned host will wonder why you find it so hard to finish what he took no little trouble to procure. When you find men accustomed to drink spirits you may generally suspect that they are not the most reputable members of the community."[11] This advice still holds good, I think, though Syrian friends informed us that a good deal of alcohol abuse goes on behind closed doors.

Christians have traditionally acted as bootleggers here: in the Middle Ages monks, in particular, were expert winemakers and monasteries often provided not only drink but also loose women, to Muslims as well as Christians. This pattern seems not to have changed much. Booze flows freely throughout the Christian quarter. Even the proprietor of the internet café we frequented every few days would sometimes bring out a bottle of his rather noxious homemade wine and proudly serve it up for his clients.

Another facet of city life that displays remarkable continuity is the habit of going to the public baths, the *hammams*. Many of these hammams have been in continuous operation since the Middle Ages—not as tourist destinations, though tourists are certainly welcomed, but as the same oases of refreshment and relaxation they have always been. I noticed one, the Hammam al-Malik al-Zahir in Damascus, that had been open since 985 A.D., and in it you can have a treatment that has probably changed very little in the last thousand years (though I chose not to, having undergone the ordeal in Istanbul and decided that being slapped around by a bare-breasted Amazon was not my idea of fun). The Arab hammam is a direct descendant of the Roman *thermae*, and its continued use since antiquity displays a historical continuity that is almost unheard of in the West, where the so-called Dark Ages interrupted the steady dissemination of classical tradition.

What you see when you enter the hammam is a peculiarly Arab and Islamic adaptation of the Roman thermae. The bathing habit spread throughout the Roman Empire, with enormous central bath complexes being built in urban areas, examples of which can still be seen in Rome, at the Baths of Caracalla for instance, and at the city of Bath in England. But the breakup of the empire and the loss of its expertise in plumbing and engineering plunged Western Europe not only into darkness but also into filth: the habit of regular bathing died, not to be resurrected until the twentieth century. Even as late as the 1970s, I can remember trips to Europe where I was practically felled by the wafts of B.O.

This did not happen in the Islamic caliphate, Rome's eastern successor state, largely because the Prophet promoted bathing and even required it of his followers for ritual religious purposes. Cleanliness became a theological virtue; rulers and nabobs throughout the Middle East endowed public baths just as they endowed mosques or *madrasas*, but they also had extensive private ones as well, and no palace is without one. Their remains, all remarkably similar, can be seen in every major Arab fortress including the citadel of Aleppo, and even inside the great Crusader castles that were later retaken by the Arabs.

The hypocaust heating system was retained by the Arabs, as was the basic Roman sequence of proceeding through rooms of different temperatures—*frigidarium, tepidarium, caldarium*—and there were a few added luxuries, like being able to receive a massage in the hot room (*harara*) (fig. 17) or getting one's feet scrubbed. Modeled on the Roman *apodyterium* is the pleasing Arab anteroom where patrons, having deposited their street clothes in little niches, sit wrapped in towels, drink tea, and gossip. There, they are given wooden sandals to wear into the bath—the same sandals the Romans wore in their baths, and the same that modern Syrian hotels provide for their guests. Just as there is a standard prototype for the Roman bath, there is one for the hammam as well. Mosaic pavements, marble-lined walls, rooms arranged in maze-like sinuosity to keep the steam from blowing away, and most distinctively, an inner chamber topped by a dome studded with tiny round windows of variously-colored glass, which let in just enough sun to maintain an intimate, drowsy half-light, so that the ablutions take on a quasi-religious significance. As an element of Muslim ritual, bathing might be considered a religious experience, but it is also intensely social. Then again, so is the mosque. Like the mosque, the hammam is a meeting place, a locus for cementing social ties and making deals, and even a party space, particularly for women, who still continue the ancient tradition of having bridal parties in the hammam—occasions a bit like our bridal showers, where older and more experienced women take stock of the potential bride and help prepare her for marriage.

Personal cleanliness still seems almost a fixation, and one of the country's most popular products is the olive oil soap made and sold in Aleppo. Washing with olive oil is another local habit that dates back to the Romans, who poured the liquid onto their bodies and then removed it with a scraper. Nowadays the oil is incorporated into soap, and we found on a visit to old-town Aleppo's Jubeili Soap Factory that it is still being made exactly as it was two or three hundred years ago. Mr. Jubeili took us through his eighteenth-century factory, where the olive oil is cooked up with a caustic soda over high heat, with laurel and *ghar* added at the end to lend fragrance and health-giving properties. After being cooked the substance is poured right onto the floor to dry, then cut into rough cubes, stamped with a rather elegant maker's mark, and arranged into pyramids to dry for several months (fig. 18); after that, they are "aged" much like cheeses. The older the soap, the better it is supposed to be; Mr. Jubeili presented Arthur, who took a great interest in the procedure, with a fifty-year-old cake of it, something very special indeed.

There can be no doubt that one of the barriers to mutual understanding between the West and the Arab world is that each side perceives the other as being dirty. Islam makes much of personal cleanliness, requiring two sorts of ritual ablutions: *wudu*, a partial ablution, to be performed after various "unclean" events such as the discharge of body fluids or becoming intoxicated; and *ghusl* or full-body ablution, done after sex, childbirth, and other physical extremities. Washing of hands and feet is also done at the mosque before praying. Cleanliness is thus a religious duty as well as a social one. Westerners, who cheerfully devour polluted animals such as pigs, use their left hands at table, and fondle filthy dogs at will, are thought to be deficient in this important department. How grotesque the stinking, unbathed Crusaders must have seemed!

But driving outside of the cities and through Syria's frequently beautiful countryside left me with the impression that this stress on cleanliness is mostly confined to the human body, for quantities of rubbish are strewn along roadsides everywhere, with a special emphasis on plastic bags, surely one of the most dreadful of twentieth-century inventions. In fact there are so many of them in proportion to the rest of the trash that their presence seems almost purposeful, as though some didactic conceptual artist had created the vistas to emphasize the plastic bag as a particular symbol of environmental degradation. There have been recent efforts by volunteer organizations to persuade shoppers to bring canvas bags to stores, and some people are beginning to change their habits; but it would appear that without a nationwide governmental ban on the things very little headway can be made.

The question of why this unsightliness is culturally acceptable in nice neighborhoods of Syria, as it would certainly not be in similar places in the West, is a puzzle. Surely in such a community-minded culture as Islam, a general clean-up effort would not be impossible. Such campaigns have proved very successful when it comes to tree planting, among other projects. So why doesn't it happen? Is it that the emphasis on cleanliness is strictly a personal one? Are we supposed to ignore outward schmutz and concentrate on inner purity?

There seemed to me a connection here with the traditional houses of the cities' old neighborhoods: closed off from the street by high walls, these would be deliberately left looking crummy on the outside, so as to fool thieves and tax collectors. The foyer, too, would be poor and dirty. But once inside the house, in the great court with its central fountain, its trees of citrus and jasmine, its enormous cushioned *iwan* with marble inlay, *ablaq*, and precious stones, the visitor would be overwhelmed with *luxe, charme et volupté* (fig. 19). The inner, private world is cultivated with infinite care, while the public one is left alone.

An English visitor of the early nineteenth century remarked on the custom with interest:

> Not a year passes that a pasha or governor does not lay violent hands on some rich man, whether Turk or Nazarene. Excuses are never wanting . . . To such as have imprudently made a display of their riches the ransom will be proportionally high. They have, therefore, no other means of avoiding similar difficulties than by carefully hiding what they possess . . . It is obvious to every traveler in Turkey [i.e., the Ottoman Empire] how much the extreme of indigence is affected in the dress and houses of rich individuals. The receiving apartment of a Christian, more especially when visited by a Turk, is generally the hall of his house, sometimes a bench at his door, where everything intentionally indicates poverty: whilst a Turk pursues the same course towards everybody. Relatives and intimate friends alone see the interior of each other's houses, and it is before these only that a person displays his smart pipes, his pelisses, his shawls, and his rich silks; so that, in the most tranquil state of such a government, every possible caution is necessary to escape the invidious eyes of oppressive masters.[12]

This way of doing business would seem to harmonize with the Muslim feeling for privacy and the urge to keep personal, family life separate from public existence. Houses of the Ottoman era are divided into *salamlek*, where guests are entertained, *khadamlek*, or servants' quarters, and *haramlek*, quarters exclusively used by the family, just as many restaurants even now have "family" rooms separated off from the public dining room.

It is hard to imagine a style of building more exquisitely suited to the hot, dry climate of the Arab world than this domestic architecture, which reached its peak in the seventeenth and eighteenth centuries. The thick walls cooled every room in summer; the central courtyard, open to the sky but densely planted with fragrant trees and freshened by a flowing fountain, contains a framed iwan, shaded from summer sun and protected from autumn winds, in which the family could recline on cushions.

Private as these houses were, they nevertheless reveal a peculiarly Eastern variety of conspicuous consumption, and even the shabbiest of the grand old palaces gives us a glimpse of just how very rich the Damascus and Aleppo merchants must have been in their heyday. The intricate inlay work would have required the labor of many, many craftsmen, and skilled ones at that. Floors and walls are inlaid with marble, precious stones, and decorative stonework. The rooms opening off the courtyards have beams and wooden ceilings, *ajami* (plate 5) delicately painted with flowers and fruit, much of which work markedly resembles the rococo decorative painting that was being produced in France during the same era.

In a fit of modern perversity, Syria's richest citizens during the late twentieth century deserted the Old Cities for modern apartments and villas on the outskirts of towns. These are not only hideous but are stunningly unsuited to the desert climate, and indeed are only livable at all thanks to air conditioning. For decades the lovely old houses were allowed to decay, and it is only recently that a few preservationists, including the Aga Khan Trust and the Mudiriyat Dimashq Al-Qadima (Council for Old Damascus), have stepped in to save some of them from ruin.

And then there are the entrepreneurs, who have finally hit on the obvious idea of turning these beautiful old houses into boutique hotels: with their big public spaces, two-or-three-story open courtyards, and warrens of smaller rooms designed for large extended families, they have turned out to be ideally suited for it. Catherine and I met Mr. Hadad while wandering by his *beit* (the Arabic word for house) in the Christian quarter. It was undergoing a massive facelift and we peered through the gate to get a better look; noticing us, he invited us in to show it all off. The house had been in his family for many generations, he told us; he was now turning it into a hotel, to be open for business in just a few weeks' time. Workmen were rushing about, dust was swirling, and craftsmen were restoring the ablaq and inlay work meticulously. This was a major overhaul, very expensive, and I reflected that Mr. Hadad was lucky to have the funds for this kind of restoration. It made a poignant contrast with the Dahdah Palace, a decayed but still gracious beit in the old Jewish quarter that we had visited the day before.

The lady of that house, a Christian, had come as a bride from Beirut in the 1950s, marrying into the once-prosperous Dahdah family. Now she was the very archetype of the distressed gentlewoman: the family home was literally crumbling around her, the ablaq corroding and the dust working its way into every crevice. A giant pine tree in the courtyard had fallen down, pulling up quantities of paving stones; missing mosaic tiles left blank spaces along the walls. Our hostess complained that craftsmen no longer knew how to do these things and simply painted in missing stones or tiles rather than replacing them. Having just seen Mr. Hadad's meticulous restoration job, we knew this to be demonstrably untrue. The lady simply lacked the funds. She and her daughter were reduced to selling a few antiques and handmade objects in the beit's reception room, a hopeless endeavor since they did not signpost their house as a tourist destination and few people know about it. Looking around, it was easy to see that the remnants of the Dahdah family would soon have to leave their degenerating pile. Perhaps the Dahdah Palace's next owners will restore it with the same energy and bankroll Mr. Hadad is lavishing on his beit. Or perhaps it will end up like the hundreds of other hopelessly decayed beits in old Damascus.

The queen of all the beits is the Azem Palace, a great house built in the mid-eighteenth century by Asa'd al-Azem, at that time the Ottoman governor of Damascus. Now open to the public as the Museum of the Arts and Popular Traditions, it is the culmination of the long tradition of Damascene domestic architecture. The courtyard is dense with lemon, orange, uglifruit (so large and heavy it seems it could hardly stay on the bough), jasmine, and cypress; fountains flow constantly, with the sound of running water audible everywhere. This architecture is designed to be multi-dimensional, engaging the senses of sight, hearing, touch, and scent simultaneously. Water signifies renewal, refreshment, fertility, purification, and creation; green, the color of all these trees, is also the color of the Prophet. Such gardens in the middle of cities have spiritual as well as functional, curative properties.

Like the rulers of Mecca and Medina in what is now Saudi Arabia, whose authority depended on their ability to guard the Holy Places and make them available to pilgrims, the rulers of Damascus—men like Asa'd al-Azem—derived their authority from their control of the Hajj, which assembled annually at Damascus to prepare for the six-week journey across the desert to Mecca. From 1708, the Ottoman governors of Damascus were personally responsible for escorting the caravan to the Hijaz and protecting it from marauding tribesmen. Every year some 30,000 pilgrims gathered in the Midan quarter to join the caravan, and this process went on into and through the nineteenth century:

> Every balcony and window overlooking the route was packed with sightseers . . . All around them was the sound of bands playing 'wild and wailing music,' and street vendors, the sweetmeat-sellers, carpet-sellers, water-carriers, all vying with each other to advertise their wares. As the

procession approached, a deathly silence fell as thousands of pilgrims, from the opulent court of the emir, wali and mushir in their golden palanquins, to the military escort and Bedouins who would protect and police the massive caravan, down to the poorest pilgrim, filed through the gates of the city.[13]

This must have called for a large open space, and in fact the word *midan* signifies open space, or field. But there are no traces of that now, the commercial businesses having grown until the quarter has been swallowed up into a maze of streets. Midan Street itself is a favorite spot for late-night and early-morning dining, with restaurants open all night long and food stalls doing a brisk business around the clock. A number of these specialize in delicacies I couldn't quite bring myself to try, even in the interests of multicultural experience—items like offal, sheep testicles, and something bearing the sinister name of "Jew's mallow"— but the arrangements of cheese, olives, and other "deli foods" on display are works of art. Moseying along Midan Street the day before Eid, watching the locals shopping for their holiday feasts, we saw sweets piled in artful pyramids, heaps of cakes and pancakes, pistachio-studded pastries. Live sheep and turkeys lurked in alleyways, all too clearly waiting to be served up at festive tables on the morrow.

During the early twentieth century the camel caravans to Mecca gave way to more modern forms of transport. The Ottoman sultan Abdul Hamid, who espoused a Pan-Islamic policy and tried to revive the caliphate to underpin his own religious legitimacy, conceived the idea of a Hijaz railway for pilgrims, linking Istanbul to Medina with stops in Damascus and Aleppo. The three-million-pound price tag for this engineering feat was partially paid for by contributions from Muslims around the world, and its financial set-up was that of a *waqf*, which is a Muslim religious endowment—something like an American nonprofit foundation. The 810-mile line between Damascus and Medina was completed, but the building of the extended line to Mecca was interrupted by the outbreak of World War I. The Turks used the railway for wartime transport; it was this line that Lawrence and his Arab guerrillas kept blowing up during the war.

Damascus's 1913 Hijaz Station still stands, a magnificent specimen of Orientalist-Imperial architecture and a monument to a world that was to disappear almost the moment it was built (fig. 20). A World War I–era steam engine is displayed outside. Inside, the unreconstructed waiting room—how commodious train stations all over the world were, up until the architectural depredations of the 1960s!—has been turned into a bookshop, of all things. As so often in Syria, I was shocked by how little advantage had been taken of a site's potential for tourism. A smart restaurant or café would be a hit in this richly nostalgic setting. Instead there are a few scruffy books, a few desultory book-buyers.

Nowadays the hajj traffic has moved from midan and railway station to airport. The current yearly influx of some three million pilgrims into the Hijaz would have flummoxed even the sophisticated Ottoman bureaucracy, and while Damascus still handles a lot of the traffic, the city functions more as a way station than a rally-point for the journey. My family and I encountered a large crowd of hajjis at 2:00 A.M. in the Damascus airport, en route from Baghdad to Medina. It was a mostly elderly crowd and extremely friendly; as always with Iraqis I hesitated before revealing my nationality, but their good humor seemed unshakeable. Evie and Lizzy, at this time, were addicted to a card game called Fan-Tan and as they sat on the floor playing it several of the hajjis joined them, clustering round and suggesting which cards they ought to play. Many of them wanted their pictures taken with us, and all in all they seemed to be in high holiday spirits, as though they were embarking on a great worldly as well as spiritual adventure. Having seen pictures of the horrendous crowds that now surround the *kabaa* at hajj time, I felt sad that the journey has become so prosaic and uncomfortable; all these jolly folks deserved a jollier trip, as I imagine the hajj must have been in the days of camels and even of the Hijaz Railway. It's too bad that the hajj has never had its Chaucer, for there must surely be some very wonderful tales to be told.

In the West, we have been educated to see the mainstream of civilization (except for a few early exceptions like the Egyptians, the Sumerians, and of course the Israelites) as a Western affair. It started with Greece, which passed the torch to Rome. Then there were those unfortunate Dark Ages. Before too many centuries had passed, though, the lamp of civilization once more flickered alight, thanks to the gallant monks who kept learning alive in their remote monasteries. The intellectual riches of antiquity were recaptured by the Renaissance, which paved the way to modern enlightenment, scientific rationalism, and our world leadership. We see the Arab world as having gone in an entirely different direction, rejecting the humanism implicit in the Greco-Roman heritage to embrace a mindless, authoritarian way of life.

Here, all this stands revealed as nonsense. The Syrians, like the modern Greeks, Italians, Lebanese, and Palestinians, are direct heirs to the classical world. Their ancestors walked the classically laid-out streets of Apamea and Palmyra. They worshiped at the Byzantine churches, which have also been assiduously preserved. Islam is a product of Christianity, which in turn is a product not only of Judaism but of the Neo-Platonism that flourished in ancient Syria as well as in Athens. As for the Dark Ages, the name is simply a Western convention, perhaps deriving from an unwillingness to admit that those years comprised the great period of Islamic ascendancy, when the Arab world, anything but dark, was at the height of its civilization and the Mediterranean was a mere Arab pond.

These facts have not escaped observant students of the region. William Dalrymple has pointed out the deep religious continuity that survived through pagan, Christian, and Muslim dispensations:

Today the West often views Islam as a civilization very different from and indeed innately hostile to Christian-

ity. Only when you travel in Christianity's Eastern home-
lands do you realize how closely the two religions are really
linked. For the former grew directly out of the latter and
still, to this day, embodies many aspects and practices of
the early Christian world now lost in Christianity's modern Western incarnation. When the early Byzantines were
first confronted by the Prophet's armies, they assumed that
Islam was merely a heretical form of Christianity, and in
many ways they were not so far wrong: Islam accepts much
of the Old and New Testaments, and venerates both Jesus
and the ancient Jewish prophets.

Certainly if John Moschos [a Byzantine monk] were to
come back today it is likely that he would find much more
that was familiar in the practices of a modern Muslim Sufi
than he would with those of, say, a contemporary American
Evangelical. Yet this simple truth has been lost by our tendency to think of Christianity as a Western religion rather
than the Oriental faith it actually is.[14]

These observations go not only for religion but for architecture, philosophy, art, cuisine—so many aspects of life. Greco-
Roman culture lives on among its descendants in the eastern
Mediterranean as clearly as it does in the West—and it is far
more visible in contemporary Damascus than it is in, let us say,
contemporary New York or Los Angeles.

Figure 1. People-watching at the Aleppo Citadel.

Figure 2. Damascus propylaeum.

Figure 3 (ABOVE). *Treasury in the Umayyad Mosque.*

Figure 4 (LEFT). *The Nawfara Café.*

Figure 5 (ABOVE). *Tea-boy at the Nawfara.*

Figure 6 (RIGHT). *Tea-vendor in the Hamadiye souq.*

Figure 7. Bakdash, Damascus souq.

Figure 8. Spice market.

Figure 9. A lingerie shop in the Hamadiye souq.

Figure 10. Boy in the souq.

Figure 11. Transportation in the Aleppo souq.

Figure 12. Laden donkey.

Figure 13 (ABOVE). *A public fountain in the souq.*

Figure 14 (RIGHT). *Vista from inside the Azem Pasha Khan.*

Figure 15 (LEFT).
Damascus street scene.

Figure 16 (BELOW).
*The Roman arch in
Straight Street.*

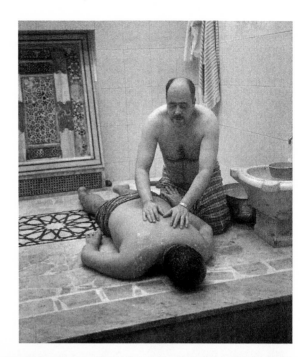

Figure 17 (RIGHT).
Inside a hammam.

Figure 18 (BELOW).
*Soap in the Jubeili
factory, Aleppo.*

67

Figure 19. Interior courtyard.

Figure 20. The Hijaz Station.

3 ❖ *Ruins*

From one end of Syria to the other the sanctuaries
blend and merge, ruin on ruin, each carrying forward some of its character and style into the next
metamorphosis. The Roman temples become
Byzantine churches, with Greek-Oriental ornament; they develop in style right up to the Arab
invasion, till such late sixth-century buildings as
Kalb Lozeh among the mountains of Barisha are
nearly Romanesque. The Arabs either doomed or
destroyed them; in either case they stand now in
ruin, tranquil and harmonious, a part of the wild
landscape in which they seem natural growths,
like the olive trees.

—Rose Macaulay, *Pleasure of Ruins*

Yes, there are glorious ruins. And few of them are
more glorious than the Baron Hotel in Aleppo, which
we made our headquarters for our travels around
the northern part of the country. Now a seedy relic
of Empire, the kind of place at which a down-at-heel
Old Etonian in a Graham Greene novel might fetch
up, the Baron possesses a heady aura of past grandeur
(fig. 21). Its solid Edwardian architecture, enhanced
by bold Orientalist flourishes, recalls an era when the
clients of luxury hotels expected value for money—in
a distinct contrast to the Ian Schrager-style boutique

hotels of today, where the hoteliers lay on lots of hip little extras to keep you from noticing how minuscule the rooms are. There is nothing remotely hip about the Baron. It is a noble wreck.

It clings to its place in history. In 1919 King Faisal declared the independence of Syria from this very balcony, to cheering crowds below—a little prematurely, as it turned out. T. E. Lawrence's bar bill is framed and enshrined in the lounge. Charles Lindbergh's bedroom has been kept pretty much as it was (but more run down); so has the room in which Agatha Christie began *Murder on the Orient Express* (the opening scene of the book takes place on the Aleppo railway platform). The hotel's guest book, now kept in a bank vault, is famous: it contains the signatures, among others, of Kemal Atatürk, David Rockefeller, Prince Peter and Princess Eugenie of Greece, Maria Teresa de Borbón, General Auchinleck, the Duchess of Westminster, Lady Mountbatten, Field Marshal Lord Slim, Patrick Leigh Fermor, Lord Hore-Belisha, Queen Ingrid of Denmark, and Dr. Schacht, the Nazis' banker. In the front hall, alongside a pre–World War II–era archaeological map of Syria, there is a poignant reminder of former splendors in the form of a poster, circa 1930:

HOTEL BARON
l'Unique Hotel de 1 ière Classe à Alep
Chauffage Central Partout
Confort Parfait   Situation Unique
le Seul Recommandé par
les Agences de Tourisme

Outside the front door are medallions of membership in the Touring Club von Deutschland, the Touring Club d'Italia, and the International Touring Club—though I doubted that these organizations still direct their members toward the Baron.

Muhammed Four disapproved of our putting up there. "We do not recommend it to our clients any longer," he announced.

"Why not?" I wondered. "It looked fine to me when we visited it in April."

"It is very run down, no one spends any money to keep the place up. Also, the people who run it are too materialistic," he said—cryptically, for isn't the whole purpose of running a hotel to make money? Later Catherine, who is Jewish, surmised that "materialistic" might prove to be a coded way of saying "Jewish," but it turned out that the Mazloumian family who have run the Baron for many years were Armenian Christians. Then I thought "materialistic" might be a coded way of saying "Christian." But Mylène, herself an Armenian Catholic, didn't approve of the Mazloumians any more than Muhammed did. "The first thing they will ask you is if you want to change money," she predicted, "even before they say 'Welcome.'"

This did not prove to be the case. In fact they had a sign ostentatiously displayed right in front of the reception desk:

IF ANY MEMBER OF STAFF OFFERS
TO CHANGE MONEY FOR YOU,
PLEASE NOTIFY THE MANAGEMENT
AT ONCE, BECAUSE THIS IS AGAINST
THE LAWS OF OUR COUNTRY.

I didn't quite dare challenge this uncompromising attitude. In any case, I often wondered what Syria's myriad illegal money-changers get out of the deal, for the rate they offer is usually pretty much the official exchange rate. You would have to exchange several thousand dollars before they made a significant profit. I did not try this at the Baron, though the Mazloumians went out of their way to be helpful in whatever way they could. The place's general factotum, Mr. Walid, a Levantine fixer of the old school, can find you a driver, get your laundry done, or help get your visa renewed. He haunts the corridors of the Baron showing off to anyone who will look a sheaf of letters recommending his services.

We found the place picturesque, with its wide halls, spacious foyers, and large if shabby public rooms, including a television room furnished with "mod" pink chairs, incongruous jetsam of the 1960s. The wide stone staircase is framed by a Moorish-style archway; there are heavy oak doors, floors covered in Turkish-style tiles, whitewashed walls. In the front hall stands a 1940s-era telephone kiosk, still functioning as such; a 1950s poster proclaims BOAC a world leader in jet travel. The bedrooms, though a bit tattered, are big and comfortable, and we were even provided with a plug for the bathtub, a rare commodity in Syrian hotels. The bar would be a great bar anywhere; in Syria, it is unique. Big scuffed leather chairs arranged in cozy corners, faded rugs, old Johnnie Walker cut-out ads on the walls. A motley collection of locals and hotel guests prop up the bar. The barman looked like a relic of the Raj in his own right, a tall, dignified man who kept an eagle eye on the level of his clients' glasses and was always prompt with the refills.

The front of the building and the balcony where Faisal made his speech could use a good power wash, but it is still an impressive structure and must have been a beauty in 1911, when it was built. When Lawrence stayed at the hotel before the First World War, he reported that from its balcony, he could shoot ducks into the marshy wilderness that surrounded it. Now, less than a century later, the place has been engulfed by a bustling urban scene complete with hooting traffic, street hawkers, and two neighboring cinemas, one showing kung-fu films, the other soft-core porn. The quarter is a favorite haunt of Russian prostitutes, still plying their trade two decades after the departure of Syria's Soviet patrons.

But the neighborhood offers compensations. The street leading from the hotel to the Old City, the Sharia al-Baron, contains a string of pleasant and inexpensive restaurants whose proprietors call out invitingly to passersby; one of these establishments is reputed to have cooked the world's longest shish kebab, making it into the Guinness book of records. We tried several of these spots during our stay in the city, sampling the special Aleppan kebabs with cherry sauce, lamb with eggplant, something listed as Ardy Soaky Salad (you can guess what it is if you try), and the first-rate Syrian beer, Barada, but passing up such dubious delicacies as Stikboofer, Climary, Shocolat mou, and Shempania Bottle. Better yet, down the cross street was a falafel stand to beat all falafel stands. For about a dollar you buy a poker chip from a young man outside the store, then exchange it inside for a cone of pita which they fill with falafel and "the works," if you want that much: yogurt, mint, tomato, cilantro, onion, and hot peppers. As you exit you pay your respects to an ancient gentleman swathed in white robes. He asked us where we were from, and I answered "America." He smiled. "I escaped from Hitler," he said simply. Could he be one of Syria's last, elusive Jews?

The Baron is a ruin, yes. What are the alternatives, here in Aleppo? There are countless very decent hotels catering to the locals and to the backpacking trade. One hostelry in the neighborhood of the Baron had a rather charming poster, advertising the hotel's

> Quite Feelings
> Conditional Rooms
> Hot Bathrooms

This seemed tempting, and I thought I might try it on a future trip. For the better-off traveler there is a monstrous, glistening Sheraton, as big as the Pyramid of Cheops and just about as inviting. Isolated in solitary splendor from the urban throng, it reposes behind what actually seems to be a moat. But the top choices for financially flush Westerners are the boutique hotels, extremely pretty and comfortable, in remodeled, traditional beits in the Jdeideh quarter. These seventeenth- and eighteenth-century houses were probably once ruins themselves, looking something like Damascus's decrepit Dahdah Palace. Over the past few years they have been given tasteful facelifts, with guest rooms and suites rather than haramlek quarters now opening out from the central courtyard and its fountains and citrus trees. Some of them, like the Yasmeen d'Alep, are very high-end indeed, and one, the Mansouriya Palace, contains a beautiful and greatly tempting spa and Turkish bath complex. The rooms have been so tarted up that they have passed from the luxuri-ous over the edge into kitsch, with themed suites like "the Byz-antine" (heavy on the gold!), "the Hittite," and "the Bedouin." Impressive, but by and large, and even without considering the difference in price, we preferred the ruined Baron.

Many people have come up with lists of the Seven Wonders of the World, from Herodotus in the fifth century B.C. to the edi-tors of *USA Today* in the twentieth, but none of these, so far as I can discover, have included the ruins of Palmyra in the Syr-ian desert. Strange, because everyone I know who has seen this sight has it near the top of his list: a full-scale Roman-era city, sacked and deserted in the third century, which has moldered away unmolested through the intervening centuries. There is nothing comparable in Europe; in all the world, perhaps only Leptis Magna in Libya can come close. The great ruins of Rome and Athens have been altered by millennia of accretion and re-building; Agrigento has nothing like Palmyra's scale; Apamea, in western Syria, lacks the high drama of its desert setting. Even Ephesus cannot boast a situation as spectacular as Palmyra's, with its golden litter of classically laid-out streets, buildings, and colonnades spread across the endless desert sands, its great Tem-ple of Bel, its weird tomb towers on the nearby hillside, and the imposing medieval castle looming over the scene on its sheer promontory (fig. 22).

Palmyra (a Greek name; its Semitic version is Tadmor) has inspired many a case of raging *Ruinenlust*. It was while gazing at its remains that the nobleman Constantin-François de Volney, exiled from Revolutionary France in 1791, was moved to write his influential work of historical philosophy *The Ruins, or Medi-tation on the Revolutions of Empires*. "After a walk of three quarters of an hour along these ruins," he wrote in his first chapter:

> I entered the enclosure of a vast edifice, which had formerly been a temple dedicated to the sun: and I accepted the hos-pitality of some very poor Arabian peasants, who had estab-

lished their huts in the very area of the temple . . . Here, said I to myself, an opulent city once flourished; this was the seat of a powerful empire . . . And now a mournful skeleton is all that subsists of this opulent city, and nothing remains of its powerful government but a vain and obscure remembrance! To the tumultuous throng which crowded under these porticoes, the solitude of death has succeeded. The silence of the tomb is substituted for the hum of polite places. The opulence of a commercial city is changed into hideous poverty. The palaces of kings are become the receptacle of deer, and unclean reptiles inhabit the sanctuary of the gods. What glory is here eclipsed, and how many labors are annihilated! Thus perish the works of men, and thus do nations and empires vanish away![1]

The place has also inspired any amount of hack poetry. Here is Thomas Love Peacock, for instance, writing in 1806:

> 'Mid SYRIA's barren world of sand,
>   Where THADMOR's marble wastes expand,
> Where DESOLATION, on the blasted plain,
>   Has fix'd his adamantine throne,
>   I mark, in silence and alone,
>   His melancholy reign.
> These silent wrecks, more eloquent than speech,
>   Full many a tale of awful note impart;
> Truths more sublime than bard or sage can teach
>   This pomp of ruin presses on the heart.
>   Whence rose that dim, mysterious sound,
>   That breath'd in hollow murmurs round?
>   As sweeps the gale
>   Along the vale,
>   Where many a mould'ring tomb is spread,
>   Awe-struck, I hear,
>   In fancy's ear,
>   The voices of th' illustrious dead:

As slow they pass along, they seem to sigh,
'Man, and the works of man, are only born to die!'

This is not a feeble imitation of Shelley's "Ozymandias," as one might think, but its precursor: Ruinenlust was so much a part of the Romantic mental picture that such tropes were commonplace. All this was spurred, no doubt, by the birth of archaeology, a science that did not get underway until the eighteenth century and whose startling, revelatory discoveries must have done much to reinforce the Romantic movement's fascination with ruins. The engraver Robert Wood's visit to Palmyra in the early 1750s with his colleagues James Dawkins and Giovanni Battista Borra was pivotal, for at that time the journey was an arduous, expensive, and very dangerous affair, requiring nine days on camel-back across the desert under an escort of armed Bedouins; marauding tribes posed a very real threat to travelers right up into the twentieth century. A few intrepid Europeans had already ventured there; but it was not until the appearance of Wood's mammoth book of engravings, *The Ruins of Palmyra*, that the romance of the ruined desert city made its impact on the Western psyche. There quickly arose a craze for all things Palmyrene, with Palmyrene decorative motifs brought into countless pieces of the neoclassical architecture and design that was *à la mode* at that time. "Of all the works that distinguish this age," rhapsodized Horace Walpole, "none perhaps excel [Robert Wood's] beautiful editions of Baalbeck and Palmyra." The Adam brothers, the Scottish architects who spearheaded the classical revival in England and America, adapted Palmyrene design in their work, and plate XVIII in Wood's volume, "Eagle Decorating Ancient Roman Temple," was even incorporated into the Seal of the United States.

Palmyra owes its importance to its large oasis watered by underground springs, and to the fact that it lies on the trade route between the Mediterranean and the East; it was settled as early as the third millennium B.C. The desert city's innate romanticism has always been intensified by what we know of its most famous ruler, Queen Zenobia (Bat-Zabbai in the Palmyrene Aramaic dialect she would have spoken). The daughter of a Palmyrene general, Zenobia was born in about 241 A.D., when the city had been part of the Roman Empire for nearly two centuries. She achieved prominence by marrying Septimius Odenathus, Rome's client-king of Palmyra, who had earned great favor in Rome through the feat of repulsing the Persians from his kingdom in the 260s and pursuing them all the way back to their capital at Ctesiphon. The Persians posed a major threat to the empire at that time: only a few years earlier they had captured the emperor Valerian and let their cavalry use him, so it is said, as a human mounting block before brutally putting him to death. Odenathus, then, was a hero, and was given the titles *dux Romanorum* and *restitutor totius Orientis*, but he himself was murdered along with his elder son shortly thereafter in a dynastic feud. He was succeeded by his younger son, Wahballath, with Zenobia acting as regent.

Zenobia was not content to fight Rome's battles. She fought for herself, and for her son. Two years after assuming power she attacked Palestine, then Anatolia, then, most boldly of all, Egypt—the source of about one-third of Rome's grain supply. The new emperor, Aurelian, was outraged, especially when Zenobia began producing coins at the mints she had captured at Alexandria and Antioch, coins that arrogantly depicted her son and Aurelian as equal rulers of East and West. Pretty soon she was leaving Aurelian off altogether and adding her own portrait to that of Wahballath. Throughout the millennia, coins have been a potent medium for the assertion of personal power, and this gesture of Zenobia's was interpreted, correctly, as open rebellion against Rome. (A Zenobia coin, by the way, can still be seen at the Palmyra museum; it is a rare and valuable but ugly object, greatly outshone in beauty by the more common silver drachma of Alexander the Great—or "Alexander the Makdonean," as the museum's text panel would have it. It would no doubt afford Zenobia infinite gratification to know that now, nearly two thousand years after her death, her portrait appears on the Syrian 500-pound note.)

Leading the Roman armies himself, Aurelian rode eastward and retook Anatolia and Antioch, then attacked Emesa (modern Homs) and finally Palmyra, from which the fleeing Zenobia was captured as she attempted to cross the Euphrates. The story goes that she was taken back to Rome for a starring role in Aurelian's triumph. Later historians have thought that this might be a fabrication, but it makes far too colorful a tale to ignore:

> It is not without advantage to know what manner of triumph Aurelian had, for it was a most brilliant spectacle. There were three royal chariots, of which the first, carefully wrought and adorned with silver and gold and jewels, had belonged to Odenathus, the second, also wrought with similar care, had been given to Aurelian by the king of the Persians, and the third Zenobia had made for herself, hoping in it to visit the city of Rome. And this hope was not unfulfilled; for she did, indeed, enter the city in it, but vanquished and led in triumph. There was also another chariot, drawn by four stags and said to have once belonged to the king of the Goths. In this—so many have handed down to memory—Aurelian rode up to the Capitol, purposing there to slay the stags, which he had captured along with this chariot and then vowed, it was said, to Jupiter Best and Greatest. There advanced, moreover, twenty elephants, and two hundred tamed beasts of divers kinds from Libya and Palestine, which Aurelian at once presented to private citizens, that the privy purse might not be burdened with the cost of their food; furthermore, there were led along in order four tigers and also giraffes and elks and other such animals, also eight hundred pairs of gladiators besides the captives from the barbarian tribes . . .
>
> And there came Zenobia, too, decked with jewels and in golden chains, the weight of which was borne by others. There were carried aloft golden crowns presented by all the cities, made known by placards carried aloft.[2]

No one is quite sure what happened to the doughty queen next, but the most attractive theory has it that Aurelian was not as vindictive as he might have been, and that he made her the gift of a villa in Tivoli, where she lived out the rest of her life, marrying and bearing more children. Aurelian ordered the rebuilding of the Temple of the Sun at Palmyra and the construction of a new Temple of the Sun at Rome as well. The city of Palmyra was remilitarized by the triumphant Romans, especially under the Emperor Diocletian, who enlarged its military camp and built extensive baths over what had once been Zenobia's palace. Its importance as a caravan center dwindled under Roman rule, but the city continued to have some limited strategic importance: Justinian rebuilt its walls during the Byzantine era and a fortified citadel, the present Qalaat Shirkuh that hangs so imposingly over the ruins, was built by a thirteenth-century Ayyubid ruler and refortified three centuries later (fig. 23). Tamerlane sacked what remained of the city in 1400, but its glory days were already over. By Ottoman times it had degenerated into a mere village, with peasants living very basic lives camped among the magnificent detritus.

Needless to say, Zenobia has proved an irresistible figure of romance from her own day to ours. As with Britain's Boudicaa, the combination of strength, chutzpah, and sex appeal is fatally attractive. She has been the subject of four operas (including one by the great Rossini), a play and even, as recently as 2007, a Lebanese musical. She makes an appearance in Boccaccio's fourteenth-century *On Famous Women*, an excerpt of which Chaucer translated and inserted into "The Monk's Tale" in his *Canterbury Tales*. Chaucer's lines stress the queen's physical stamina and chastity—a sexually provocative mixture, then as ever:

> Cenobia, of Palymerie queene,
> As writen Persiens of hir noblesse,
> So worthy was in armes and so keene
> That no wight passed hire in hardynesse,

Ne in lynage, nor in oother gentillesse.
Of kynges blood of Perce is she descended—
I seye nat that she hadde moost fairnesse,
But of hir shape she myghte nat been amended.

From hire childhede I fynde that she fledde
Office of wommen, and to wode she wente,
And many a wilde hertes blood she shedde
With arwes brode that she to hem sente.
She was so swift that she anon hem hente.
And whan that she was elder, she wolde kille
Leouns, leopardes, and beres al torente,
And in hir armes weelde hem at hir wille.

And as for her marital relations with Odenathus:

>   . . . she wolde nevere assente
> By no wey that he sholde by hire lye
> But ones, for it was hir pleyn entente
> To have a child the world to multiplye.
> And also soone as that she myghte espye
> That she was nat with childe with that dede,
> Thanne wolde she suffer hym doon his fantasye
> Eftsoone and not but oones, out of drede.

Hot stuff indeed. Chaucer respected Zenobia's honor and re-
frained from the kind of frank lubricity of which he was capable. The American pulpmeister Alexander Baron, writing on the
same subject in 1956, showed no such refined taste. His *Queen
of the East*, a novelized bio of Zenobia, is an outrageous example
of Orientalist soft-core, the sort of thing the late Edward Said
made an entire career out of deploring. Here is his Zenobia at
her ablutions:

> Her foot and her dark, gleaming shoulders sank again
> into the water. Zenobia liked her evening bath hot. The

steam rose around her, powerfully scented with cassia. Two of her bath slaves crouched on the steps of the sunken pool. Two more waited by a massage couch. They were Indian girls, naked like herself in the steam, copper-dark, dainty as gazelles, their eyes bright and eager . . .

Naked, she looked a docile, passive creature, soft, sensual, sleek as satin, the breasts large and proudly firm, the small waist accentuated by full haunches, a golden sheen upon the skin. She might have been an odalisque sister to the clothed Zenobia whom the world knew. She lay on the couch and the girls worked on her flesh with firm, cunning fingers, touching her armpits with the depilatory sap of the white vine and anointing her skin with sweet spikenard. They dressed her in loincloth and brassiere, white blouse and loose red Persian trousers, and put Persian slippers of soft red leather on her feet. She stood up, soft and small, and went into her dressing room . . .

. . . Zenobia surveyed herself with satisfaction in the oval mirror and imagined the effect of her entry upon the envoy. It was twice a pleasure to keep a man waiting when he was a Roman . . .

She was ready. The nubile little animal that had emerged from the bath was hidden. Looking at her from the mirror was the public Zenobia, a woman, yes, armed with beauty, but bold and haughty as a man. She went out to meet the Romans.[3]

Men have been titillated by Zenobia; women have often identified with her. One of the preeminent lunatics of the nineteenth century, Lady Hester Stanhope, determined to become the first European woman to make the journey to Palmyra. Lady Hester had been a famous society hostess and wit in London, where she presided over the home and salon of her uncle, Prime Minister William Pitt the Younger. After his death she was launched on the world with a stipend from a grateful nation, and she headed eastward in 1810 with an entourage that included a macho lover some fifteen years her junior and her personal physician, Charles Lewis Meryon, who wrote up their extraordinary travel tales for posterity. In Syria Lady Hester mistook the common courtesy of the locals for veneration of herself, heightening her already exaggerated delusions of grandeur:

> All I can say about myself sounds like conceit; but others could tell you I am the oracle of the Arabs, and the darling of all the troops, who seem to think that I am a deity because I can *ride*, and because I wear arms; and the fanatics all bow before me, because the Dervishes think me a wonder, and have given me a piece of Mahomet's tomb, and I have won the heart of the pasha by a letter I wrote him from Dayr el Kamer . . . I was even admitted into the library of the famous mosque, and fumbled over the books at pleasure—books that no Christian dare touch, or even cast his eyes upon.[4]

During her travels in the Levant Lady Hester came to believe that she was on a supernatural mission: she was destined to become the bride of a new messiah, the harbinger of an apocalyptic new age in the East. She dressed in Arab men's clothes, took to smoking a nargileh, and demanded, with even more than the usual arrogance of the English upper classes of her day, audiences with the major sheikhs and notables in every city she visited. At length she settled on the idea of visiting Palmyra, an irresistible challenge to someone of her grandiose disposition. The visit was, to her, a triumph, and for the rest of her life she believed she had been crowned Queen of the Desert there, and worshiped almost as a goddess.

Here is her account of the great day as dictated to her Boswell, Dr. Meryon:

> The chief and about 300 people came out about two hours' distance to meet us. He and a few of the grandees were upon Arab mares, and dressed rather more to imitate Turks than Arabs, with silk shawls and large silk turbans. The men, at

least many of them, had their whole bodies naked, except a pestimal or petticoat studded or ornamented with leather, blackamoors' teeth, beads, and strange sorts of things that you see on the stage. They were armed with matchlocks, and guns, all surrounding me, and firing in my face, with most dreadful shouts and savage music and dances. They played all sorts of antics, till we arrived at the triumphal arch at Palmyra. The inhabitants were arranged in the most picturesque manner of the different columns leading to the Temple of the Sun. The space before the arch was occupied with dancing girls, most fancifully and elegantly dressed, and beautiful children placed upon the projecting parts of the pillars with garlands of flowers. One, suspended over the arch, held a wreath over my head. After having stopped a few minutes, the procession continued: the dancing girls immediately surrounded me. The lancemen took the lead, followed by the poets from the banks of the Euphrates, singing complimentary odes, and playing upon various Arabian instruments. A tribe of hale Palmyrenes brought up the rear, when we took up our habitation in the Temple of the Sun, and remained there a week.[5]

The Temple of Bel today is still in remarkably good repair, having been restored during the Arab and Ottoman periods. It is simply enormous, second only to the Temple of Jupiter at Baalbek in Lebanon as the greatest of Syro-Phoenician temples. Like so many religious structures in Syria it was constructed and reworked over the course of centuries: first the Bronze Age site, then the Hellenistic temple, then the Roman era religious complex we see today, which was begun on a massive scale in the age of Augustus, completed in the Antonine era and periodically tweaked thereafter by the Arabs and Turks. Greek, Roman, Eastern: the various styles and traditions meld into a distinctly Palmyrene unity.

We came upon our guide in a characteristically Syrian manner: over literature. A distinguished-looking man in his late fifties, Safwan approached us as we sat among the ruins. We told him we were not interested; that day, we preferred to wander on our own. He took the rebuff with good grace and stayed to chat with us. When he heard that Catherine's husband was Irish, he began enthusing over George Bernard Shaw, quoting *Arms and the Man*, of all things. After twenty minutes of such talk it occurred to us that he was likely to be an excellent guide, and we hired him for the morning.

He *was* an excellent guide, knowledgeable and unhurried, and like all the guides we had in Syria he responded warmly to a little bit of informed interest. Yet there was something sad about him, a quiet desperation we found in many of the over-educated, under-employed men in this country. They know so much, have studied so deeply, yet have so few ways of creating a livelihood out of their cultural capital. If the bureau of tourism would only focus on exploiting its cultural heritage, men like Safwan would be highly valued and well recompensed, but as it is they can hardly scrape out a living. We were not surprised to learn that Safwan owned an antique shop in the town of Palmyra, and he invited us there that evening. It was a very decent place, with genuine antiques and genuine bargains: but where were the eager shoppers? We seemed to have been the only tourists to visit the place in days. Safwan and his partner, dignified, patriarchal figures, were reduced to practically begging us to buy—a situation that can only have been embarrassing.

In the ruins, Safwan showed us things we might never have noticed on our own. Armed with a little mirror, he caught the sun's reflections and used it as a pointer, indicating decorative features high on friezes or hidden under pieces of masonry— repeated motifs such as pomegranates, pinecones, palm trees, grapes, figs, olive leaves, and egg-and-dart (fig. 24). Inscriptions are bilingual, in Greek and Palmyrene, a local variant of Aramaic with a distinctive curly script. There are visible remains of Byzantine Christian frescoes in the inner *cella* of the ancient temple as well as later, Muslim decorations. At the intersection of the ancient city's two great thoroughfares is the Tetrapylon, a great platform on which stand four groups of four columns—a structure that seems to have functioned much like a modern traffic roundabout (fig. 25).

Like the Adam brothers before us, we fell in love with the Palmyrene intermixture of East with West, classical with Oriental. The great tomb temples rising out of the sandy wastes looked a little Egyptian and a little Persian and not quite classical, though they were built during the Roman era (fig. 26): inside, the burial system consisted of story upon story of tombs, slid into the walls in what Ross Burns has likened to filing cabinets—a pragmatic marriage of aesthetics and engineering. The underground tombs, or *hypogea*, recall Etruscan burial sites at Tarquinia, with stairs going underground and opening out into spacious corridors and galleries. The limestone statues of the dead recline in a fashion similar to the depictions of the Etruscan deceased, but they have a far more distant and otherworldly—more Eastern—expression. In place of the lively, social visages of the Etruscan dead, these Palmyrenes fix their gazes toward eternity (fig. 27).

The Hypogeum of the Three Brothers is decorated with classical frescoes: Achilles in feminine dress, hiding among the daughters of Lycomedes to escape his foretold death in the Trojan War, and the adolescent cupbearer Ganymede being carried off by an eagle to Zeus. It occurred to us that all this subject matter was just a little bit gay. Perhaps there was a gay subculture here in Roman times? But all the literature we could find on the subject merely stated that these images were symbols of the soul's transportation to the hereafter. Well, maybe; maybe not.

Over fifty of these hypogea have been unearthed (one of the most famous, the so-called Hypogeum of Artaban, by engineers digging the oil pipeline between Iraq and the Syrian coast). Dozens more remain to be explored. There are enough sites in this country to keep archaeologists busy for generations. The estimate is that fifty percent of Palmyra still remains to be excavated, and a whopping ninety percent at Bosra. Sometimes new discoveries are simply buried again, for there is not enough space in the museums to accommodate the finds, and they are safer from thieves and the weather buried underground than they would be if exposed to general view.

It is late in the day with the sun going down, and Catherine and I stroll out to Diocletian's camp, reveling in the afternoon peace. The weathered limestone columns turn from pink to gold in the shifting light. A young camel driver comes up to us, trying to interest us in a ride, but we're not in the mood to spend money— and I don't relish the prospect of looking as gringoesque as the group of Germans I saw on these same camels earlier in the afternoon. Discouraged, he wanders off to pursue a lone young Englishwoman, who also seems disinclined for a ride: "I'm afraid of camels," she tells him. Unpersuaded, he tags along after her.

We wander off to the Temple of the Standards, with its great staircase so melted away by weathering as to appear almost liquefied. To me it looks like a giant drip castle, but Catherine compares it to the wavering Sea of Steps in Wells Cathedral.

A little girl, one of a family of children desultorily trying to sell scarves to the very few tourists who come along, asks us for a *caramela*. The only thing we have approaching a caramela are some dire Syrian cough drops, whose ingredients, we have noticed, include "nourishing colors." We give her one of these. Too polite to reject it, she pops it in her mouth dubiously.

As we walk back to the Roman camp, we see an absurdly romantic sight: a boy on an Arabian horse, practicing what appear to be dressage movements. The sun is heading down toward the horizon. We notice that the young camel driver has finally succeeded in snagging his English girl. The two of them are now sitting on a blanket with his mother and little sister—the *caramela* child—drinking tea and smiling when their language skills fail them. A pastoral scene (fig. 28).

Modern Palmyra—created by the *Service des antiquités* under the French Mandate in the late 1920s for the Arab villagers whose habitations were being cleared out of the ruins by the excavators—is a fly-blown little burg, just exactly like the godforsaken

Figure 21. The Baron Hotel.

Figure 22. Vista of Palmyra with castle in background.

Figure 23. Qalaat Shirkuh.

Figure 24. Palmyrene sculptural detail.

Figure 25. The Tetrapylon.

Figure 26 (LEFT).
*A tomb tower
at Palmyra.*

Figure 27 (BELOW).
*Palmyrene tomb
sculpture, Damascus
Museum.*

every shape and color—yellow, brown, golden;
thered; some plain, some stuffed with almonds
ue made by Abed's mother into a smooth date
read on toast (fig. 30). Other shops displayed
ncured olives in blinding hues of green. All
ed past our windows as we finally drove out of
poulevard of boxy, cheap houses and past a lone
ue greatness, a single Roman column looking
of this seedy modern thoroughfare.

ites—"The Cradele of Civilization" as one of
l it—and the eastern edge, give or take a bit,
pire. For centuries West and East, Roman and
and Persian duked it out here. Today it still
it border, for only a few miles beyond is the

of the river, cutting across the dusty provin-
ez-Zor, was a bit of a surprise because it looks
it does in books and pictures, oozing along
at, gray, green, greasy Limpopo, bedizened
ogged with huge, fifteen-foot reeds, bordered
covered with the date palms made familiar
a art, their fronds standing up at forty-five-
the trunks. At Deir, the Euphrates is filled
but it's hard to see much of them because of
reeds. The overall effect is soft and painterly,
s a muddy, mellow smell. I imagined it might
the summer, but in November there's just a
Coots float along the water's surface, row-
rs, and old men drop their fishing lines along

nd an elegant little suspension bridge for pe-
rom 1931, courtesy of the French. It's a favor-
en and for *flâneurs* of every sort. This was the
r; when Gertrude Bell came by in 1911, there
ry, which not everyone could afford. She must

Figure 28. Palmyra.

Figure 29. Palmyra town.

Figure 30. A Palmyra date shop.

Texas town in *The* \
much of *dolce far nie* \
else to *far* (fig. 29). \
boys roam about, \
gines they rev dram \
a small establishme \
frolicsome French \
stuck in the elevate \
with Donald Duck

There were two \
one Christian. The \
young man who m \
coffee. We soon g \
break there, also er \
gratis, "for hospita \
of the more upscal \
best view of the r \
the gathering moo \
nice bottled water \
nate English name \
Christian joint ne \
beer. Generally a j \
evening chill. Cat \
by, occasionally ju

As in all hick \
with almost inde \
arrival the Palmy \
café proprietors \
and the gentle yo \
taurant—which \
traditional Palmy \
ger—would cross

It was Novem \
were laden with \
dates hanging fr \
named Abed who

fantastic variety \
some fat, some \
or pistachios; sc \
"honey" to be s \
great baskets of \
these colors blu \
Palmyra, down \
survivor of anti \
lost in the midd

On to the Euph \
the road signs h \
of the Roman E \
Parthian, Roma \
marks a significa \
chaos of Iraq.

Our first vie \
cial town of Dei \
so *exactly* the wa \
like Kipling's g \
and sometimes c \
by muddy banks \
by Mesopotamia \
degree angles to \
with little islands \
the all-obscuring \
and the river em \
get pretty rank i \
nice river-y odo \
boats ply the wat \
the banks.

At Deir we fo \
destrians, dating \
ite spot for fisher \
first bridge at De \
was still only a fe

Figure 28. Palmyra.

Figure 29. Palmyra town.

Figure 30. A Palmyra date shop.

Texas town in *The Last Picture Show*. It has a similar air, not so much of *dolce far niente*, but of *far niente* because there is nothing else to *far* (fig. 29). As in small towns everywhere, bored teenage boys roam about, many of them on little motorbikes whose engines they rev dramatically. We put up at the Tetrapylon Hotel, a small establishment whose only other guests were a group of frolicsome French tourists who roared with laughter when I got stuck in the elevator. The twin beds in our room were made up with Donald Duck blankets.

There were two cafés on the main *piazza*, one Muslim and one Christian. The Muslim place was run by a plump, smiling young man who made a mean cup of cardamom-flavored Arab coffee. We soon got in the habit of taking our mid-morning break there, also enjoying the plate of Palmyra dates he included gratis, "for hospitality." Sundown would find us on the terrace of the more upscale Hotel Zenobia, strategically situated for the best view of the ruins in the rays of the setting sun and, later, the gathering moonlight, enjoying a glass of wine or some of the nice bottled water sold all over the country under the unfortunate English name of "Drekish." At night we would repair to the Christian joint next door, whose wiry, vigorous proprietor sold beer. Generally a jolly crowd gathered there, enjoying a jar in the evening chill. Cats, indulged everywhere in Syria, would stroll by, occasionally jumping into our laps or even onto the table.

As in all hick towns, outsiders become part of the furniture with almost indecent speed. Not twenty-four hours after our arrival the Palmyrenes started to recognize and greet us. The café proprietors would place our "regular" order in front of us, and the gentle young man who ran the nearby Casa Mia restaurant—which was not Italian, curiously enough, but served traditional Palmyra cuisine including stewed camel meat in ginger—would cross the street to wish us good morning.

It was November, and the date palms throughout the oasis were laden with fruit. Every shop in Palmyra had branches of dates hanging from the eaves. Our favorite shopkeeper, a boy named Abed who looked no more than nineteen or twenty, sold a fantastic variety of every shape and color—yellow, brown, golden; some fat, some withered; some plain, some stuffed with almonds or pistachios; some made by Abed's mother into a smooth date "honey" to be spread on toast (fig. 30). Other shops displayed great baskets of uncured olives in blinding hues of green. All these colors blurred past our windows as we finally drove out of Palmyra, down a boulevard of boxy, cheap houses and past a lone survivor of antique greatness, a single Roman column looking lost in the middle of this seedy modern thoroughfare.

On to the Euphrates—"The Cradele of Civilization" as one of the road signs had it—and the eastern edge, give or take a bit, of the Roman Empire. For centuries West and East, Roman and Parthian, Roman and Persian duked it out here. Today it still marks a significant border, for only a few miles beyond is the chaos of Iraq.

Our first view of the river, cutting across the dusty provincial town of Deir ez-Zor, was a bit of a surprise because it looks so *exactly* the way it does in books and pictures, oozing along like Kipling's great, gray, green, greasy Limpopo, bedizened and sometimes clogged with huge, fifteen-foot reeds, bordered by muddy banks covered with the date palms made familiar by Mesopotamian art, their fronds standing up at forty-five-degree angles to the trunks. At Deir, the Euphrates is filled with little islands, but it's hard to see much of them because of the all-obscuring reeds. The overall effect is soft and painterly, and the river emits a muddy, mellow smell. I imagined it might get pretty rank in the summer, but in November there's just a nice river-y odor. Coots float along the water's surface, rowboats ply the waters, and old men drop their fishing lines along the banks.

At Deir we found an elegant little suspension bridge for pedestrians, dating from 1931, courtesy of the French. It's a favorite spot for fishermen and for *flâneurs* of every sort. This was the first bridge at Deir; when Gertrude Bell came by in 1911, there was still only a ferry, which not everyone could afford. She must have been one of the last to witness the immemorial method of crossing the Euphrates by way of an inflated goatskin—a process that can actually be seen on the ancient Assyrian bas-reliefs in the British Museum. "You blow out your goat-skin by the river's edge," Bell recorded, "roll up your cloak and place it upon your head, tuck your shirt into your waistcloth and so embark, with your arms resting upon the skin and your legs swimming in the water. The current carries you down, and you make what progress you can athwart it. On the further side you have only to wring out your shirt, don your cloak and deflate your goat-skin, and all is done."[6]

Deir ez-Zor was the first place in Syria where I felt truly exotic, a subject of scrutiny and even amusement. At every other spot we had been to, tourists were taken for granted and even American tourists were not too surprising. Here, people seemed astonished to see us; heads turned. It was the first place, too, where no one, *no one*, spoke English. Deir is small and it's not easy to get lost there, but Catherine and I managed to do so, and when we tried to ask directions back to our hotel, we were met with total incomprehension. I suppose we should have written down the name of our street, but I was mindful of my friend who tried this in Moscow, only to discover that she had copied down the words for "One Way Street."

Still, with or without any common language we met with the usual Syrian courtesy. Three old men seated on plastic seats in the street, drinking tea, invited us to join them. At lunch, we stood in line to buy little lamb pizzas that were being cooked on a clay oven of ancient design, an object that looked as though it came right out of a prehistoric tell. The bartender from the dingy-looking joint next door hated to see two foreign ladies having to line up: he hollered at the pizza man for not serving us ahead of the other customers, hustled us into his bar where he seated us at a table, and lined up for our pizzas himself, refusing to take any payment for the tea and Drekish water he brought to our table. A sign on his door said "Well Come," and I did feel very welcomed that day.

There is no very good reason to come to Deir except to use it as a jumping-off spot to see the archaeological sites along the Euphrates, and to go to the absolutely top-notch museum, which has few visitors, alas, though it is chock full of treasures from the archaeological excavations at nearby Mari, Dura Europos, Tell Brak, Tell Bouqras, Tell Mashnaqa, and Tell Leilan, where eight hundred Old Babylonian tablets were recently discovered. As at Damascus, where the world's first alphabet, carved on a cuneiform tablet from Ugarit, and the world's first musical note are displayed almost casually in back rooms, one is astounded by the riches here. Among other prizes is a tiny clay head of a male figure, about one inch in height, that is supposed to be the first lifelike expressive impression history has to offer of a human head and face. This dates from about 6000 B.C.; there are also models of hares, hedgehogs, tortoises, and bulls, equally lively and expressive, from the same period. The material predating 1000 B.C. is so copious and of such high quality that we scarcely had energy to look at the more recent works.

This was too bad, because the Deir ez-Zor Museum is well designed and cleverly laid out, far more so than Syria's other museums, which in spite of their quantity of treasures are haphazardly arranged and do not exhibit the works to their best advantage. The Deir designer even felt free to express a sense of humor, for when it came to building a panorama depicting a modern Syrian scene he (or she) recreated an utterly banal small-town street corner complete with beat-up radio, plastic chairs, and dangerously overloaded wiring. This is truly witty, but who sees it? Our hosts at the museum asked us to sign the guestbook, and we noticed while doing so that we were the first visitors they had had in days.

Some of the most famous archaeological sites can be disappointing, for the best of their contents have been carted away to museums and research institutions and only the foundations of the ancient buildings, or at best the walls, remain to be seen. Mari, for instance: a fabled ancient Mesopotamian city discovered in 1935 with its palace, temples, and archive of 15,000 cuneiform tablets relatively unharmed. In the words of one of its

French excavators, "Mari's richness in the materials of daily life and in art objects has contributed to its renown: no other site of the Near East has offered up as many statuettes of exceptional quality, and it provides the only evidence of the existence of a tradition of large mural painting at that time."[7] Mari's artistic treasures were carried away to the Louvre and the Damascus and Aleppo Museums, its archive taken to be deciphered by scholars. The beautiful frescoes of its second millennium Palace of Zimri-Lim, sacked in 1760 B.C. by Hammurabi of Babylon (author of the famous law code) now grace the museum at Deir. We were very excited about visiting Mari—but what did we find there? Nothing (to our admittedly untrained eyes) but a giant mud pie. We could walk around it; we could try, try—in vain—to mentally recreate the ancient city according to the maps and charts provided; but it was a pointless exercise. Mud, mud, and more mud; that was all we took in.

Dura Europos was slightly more satisfactory, but only because many of its walls still stand, and because of its gorgeous situation high on a bluff above the Euphrates. It was for centuries the eastern outpost of the Roman Empire. Built on a massive scale—its citadel is still an imposing sight—it has mud-built walls that look perilously propped up in places. One can reach in and pull hunks of straw and dust right out.

Dura's plentiful artifacts have now dispersed, and one must go to the Louvre, the Yale University Art Gallery, and the Damascus Museum to find them. But the site was of interest to me because I had just read the enchanting book about it by Clark Hopkins, the Yale archaeologist who as a young man was present at the momentous discoveries made at this site. Reading Hopkins's 1979 *Discovery of Dura-Europos*, written more than forty years after the events he described, I was reminded of Agatha Christie's *Come, Tell Me How You Live*, an account of the archaeological digs in Syria and Lebanon she participated in at the side of her husband. Hopkins's book is even better, though, thanks to his expertise in the subject, and his personal touches about life on this dig during the eight seasons he spent there, from

1928 to 1935, are especially amusing. I loved his description of Christmas at Dura, with the archaeologists dining on turkey, mince pie, tiny local tomatoes, and champagne while listening to the popular new records sent from home: "You're Not the Only Oyster in the Stew" and "O.K., Toots." Hopkins is especially good on day-to-day life "in the field," including the petty rivalries and jealousies that Christie brought so brilliantly to life in her mystery novel *Murder in Mesopotamia*, based on her experiences at Sir Leonard Woolley's dig at Ur.

The 1920s and 30s were great times for archaeology in the region, with French officials under the Mandate leading the *Service des antiquités* in a valiant effort to begin systematic excavation of the country's many untouched sites. Concurrently with the Yale work at Dura, the French were at Byblos, Princeton was at Antioch, and joint French-Syrian teams were working at Palmyra and Baalbek. Digging had been undertaken at Dura after British soldiers came across some unusual ancient paintings there in 1920. They had summoned the famous archaeologist James Henry Breasted of the University of Chicago, who was then working at a site on the upper Tigris, to come and have a look. As Breasted recollected the magic moment:

> Descending from the car, General Cunningham led the way over the rubbish piles commonly found in such ruins and around a jutting corner of massive masonry. Suddenly there rose before us a high wall covered with an imposing painting in many colors depicting a life-size group of eleven persons engaged in worship . . . It was a startling revelation of the fact that in this deserted stronghold we were standing in a home of ancient Syrian civilization completely lost to the western world for sixteen centuries . . . We had before us the easternmost Romans ever found on the Euphrates or anywhere else for that matter.[8]

Based on this one glimpse on this one day, Breasted produced a small book, *Oriental Forerunners of Byzantine Painting*.

The conclusions he drew had interesting implications not only for history but for the history of art and aesthetics, and inspired the French and subsequently the Yale teams to explore there. Aside from what Breasted had seen, they could be fairly sure of interesting finds. The city had been founded around 300 B.C. by Seleucus I Nikator, Alexander the Great's erstwhile general and the founder of the Seleucid Empire. It had remained under Hellenistic rule for nearly two centuries, one of a group of military colonies designed to secure Seleucid control of the Euphrates. (*Dura* is a Semitic word for fortress; *Europos* is the name of Seleucus's home town in Macedonia.) Dura was taken by the Parthians in the late second century B.C. and the Romans incorporated the region into their empire a century later, though Dura remained essentially a Parthian city; for as in the north of England, where the Emperor Hadrian finally gave up the fight against the native tribes and built a wall, the Euphrates region was a distant border, or *limes*, almost impossible for the empire to control. It was not until 164 A.D. that Rome took direct control of Dura. In 211 it was made an official colony and expanded to accommodate a garrison, becoming an important military outpost. In 256 it fell, finally, to the Sassanian Persians and was never revived.

What made the excavations at Dura so extraordinary was the variety of religious structures uncovered by the startled archaeologists, for this far-off outpost typified the religious syncretism for which Syria was famous over the course of many centuries. There were pagan temples, of course: the origins of the city were Greek, and Greek culture persisted throughout the Parthian era. The archaeologists discovered temples to Zeus Theos, Adonis, Artemis, Zeus Kyrios, Hadad, Atargatis (the "Syrian Goddess," of whom more in chapter four), and Zeus Megistos, as might be expected. There was also a temple to the Palmyrene gods, for numerous Palmyrene traders lived in ancient Dura and wished to worship their own deities. More surprising, to the archaeologist, was the presence of a Christian house church, adorned extensively with murals—the earliest example, as it turned out, of a Christian place of worship to be found anywhere in Syria. Hopkins describes it:

> Our camp was awestruck by the extraordinary preservation of Christian murals dated more than three-quarters of a century before Constantine had recognized Christianity in 312. The scenes were small, but they were unmistakable. It is true that compared with the paintings in the Temple of the Palmyrene Gods they were sketchy and amateurish, but that little mattered, for they were Christian! . . .
>
> Christian communities, whose central places of worship we know only from literary sources, spread and grew even in the third century, this dark period in the history of Rome. Pictorial remains had been preserved only in the Christian catacombs of Rome or in small, often cryptic chance finds . . .
>
> In any case, it seems almost a miracle that the Dura meeting house was preserved to give us a glimpse of a Christian community in the mid-third century. We have contemporary Christian painting only in the catacombs. While the private house as meeting place and church as such was continually mentioned in the early Church Fathers, the house at Dura is our sole archaeological representative for three centuries of houses dedicated to Christian use.[9]

The chapel was dated to between 232 and 256. Hopkins favored the earlier date, which would make its establishment fall within the reign of the religiously tolerant Alexander Severus. Otherwise it would be hard to account for the fact that the building does not seem to have been a secret one.

The diggers at Dura were thrilled with their find, but to their disappointment the outside world did not seem to be as thunderstruck. The Yale archaeologist Michael Rostovtzeff, who was directing the dig (and wrote an excellent popular book about Dura and Palmyra, the 1932 *Caravan Cities*), complained that only scholars seemed to be interested, while the Christian clergy paid hardly any attention to the significance of the find. The Jews, Rostovtzeff said, were much more interested in their own history and cared more about the conservation of their monuments than the Christians did. "Find a synagogue," he predicted, "and we shall gain the acclaim which such startling discoveries really deserve."[10]

Not that he seriously expected a synagogue to turn up. But sometimes prayers are answered. As Clark Hopkins remembered it:

> Once, when I was involved in a train wreck, I had no recollection of the moment between the shock when I was thrown from my seat and when I began to pick myself up from the bottom of the overturned car. So it was at Dura. All I can remember is the sudden shock and then the astonishment, the disbelief, as painting after painting came into view . . .
>
> A casual passerby witnessing the paintings suddenly emerging from the earth would have been astonished. If he had been a Classical archaeologist, with the knowledge of how few paintings had survived from Classical times, he would have been that much more amazed. But if he were a biblical scholar or a student of ancient art and were told that the building was a synagogue and the paintings were scenes from the Old Testament, he simply would not have believed it. It could not be; there was absolutely no precedent, nor could there be any. The stern injunction in the Ten Commandments against the making of graven images would be sufficient to prove him right.
>
> If, finally, this passerby had been in my shoes, the director of the excavations, responsible for the success of the expedition, and the one who would be credited most with its achievements, then the discovery of the Synagogue that day would be like a page from the Arabian nights. Aladdin's lamp had been rubbed, and suddenly from the dry, brown, bare desert, had appeared paintings, not just one nor

a panel nor a wall, but a whole building of scene after scene, all drawn from the Old Testament in a way never dreamed of before.[11]

There is nothing like this representational painting in all of Jewish art: the Dura Synagogue frescoes are still unique, and have provided much food for thought on the connections between Greco-Roman art and the subsequent iconography of the Byzantine period. According to the original agreement, Yale was to get these synagogue murals, just as they got those from the Christian chapel. But the Syrians tenaciously and wisely clung to them. They are now the most prized objects in the Damascus Museum, where the synagogue has been reconstructed just as it would have looked, the murals placed in their original positions on the walls. Brightly colored and somewhat naïf in style, they show, in a fetching combination of Eastern and Western styles, a number of Old Testament scenes that have not made it into the Christian art with which we are familiar: Moses striking the rock with his staff for water (the Dura artists depict the twelve resulting streams coming out like a maypole of waving ribbons), or the Ark of the Covenant being drawn by two cows before Dagon's destroyed temple.

But even this was not all. The Belgian archaeologist Franz Cumont, a member of the first French team that had excavated at Dura in 1922, expressed a wish to go back for a visit but said, jokingly, that he was getting too old for desert travel and would only go if they found a temple of Mithra. And then—yes—a Mithraic temple was dug up. The structure itself was not spectacular, and Hopkins admitted that it seemed an anticlimax—until, that is:

we realize that the Persian religion was the third great monotheistic religion at Dura. It was the great rival of Christianity in the third century, and it played a most important role as the background of Islam—growing up under Persian control, but linked with the West—and especially belonging to the Arabian peninsula, close to Palestine, under the Persians. Astounding at Dura in the third century is that we have in this outpost sacred buildings of the three great religions preserved almost side by side.[12]

Here in this not-very-large community four religious systems existed simultaneously and apparently in harmony: the pagan, the Mithraic, the Judaic, and the Christian.

With the loss of Dura, the Romans gave up their push across the river. When Justinian came to beef up the Euphrates fortifications more than two centuries later, he moved his center of operations northward, to Halebiye (in ancient times called Zenobia) which had formerly been controlled by Zenobia of Palmyra and named for that queen. The fortress was in an apparently strategic position, because the hills on either side of the Euphrates allowed the river traffic to be controlled from this spot. Justinian's historian Procopius has left us a thorough catalogue of the Emperor's really remarkable building projects, of which the work at Halebiye/Zenobia was characteristic. "The Emperor Justinian," Procopius wrote, "rebuilt Zenobia completely and filled it quite full of inhabitants, and he stationed there a commander of select troops and a thoroughly adequate garrison, and made it a bulwark of the Roman Empire and a frontier barrier against the Persians."[13] I couldn't help thinking that Justinian must have been a busy boy: all these building and fortification projects, including Hagia Sophia (Procopius devotes an entire volume to the Emperor's building projects alone), waging all those wars, writing his law codes, putting down the Nike Rebellion, not to mention dealing with his redoubtable wife—the former circus dancer and insatiable lover, Theodora!

Zenobia/Halebiye is spectacular—"one of the greatest of all Byzantine fortifications outside the walls of Constantinople itself," according to historian Warwick Ball[14]—and it is horrifying to learn that its existence is currently threatened by a possible dam project (fig. 31). If you feel strong you can hike up along the gigantic walls, which proceed from lookout tower to lookout tower straight up the precipitous hillside. Catherine declined the exercise, so I went along with two giggling Indian ladies, mother and daughter, who carried umbrellas to protect their complexions—although the mild November sun couldn't really have done much harm. The green Euphrates flowed along in its unhurried manner below, birds of prey circled above, and aside from their cries, and the polite conversation of the Indian ladies, I was in pure, utter silence. It is the kind of place that reminds one—if there is any need of reminding—of the insanity of war. I thought of Auden's poem "Roman Wall Blues," about a Roman soldier on Hadrian's Wall who suffers from a headcold in the unaccustomed damp of the English climate and worries about his girlfriend back home. What were these Roman soldiers up to at Zenobia, out in the middle of nowhere? What was achieved? Was not Augustus's policy of live and let live vis-à-vis the Persians a wiser course than the belligerent policies of Trajan and Justinian, each of whom ultimately failed in their quest to conquer the Persians on their own turf? And why didn't they take a lesson from the fate of their predecessor Crassus (now primarily famous as a member of the First Triumvirate along with Caesar and Pompey), who met his death in an ill-advised raid across the Euphrates into Parthia? Crassus had been given the entire province of Syria as his own to govern, in 55 B.C. One would have thought this to have been ample, but he coveted Parthia, too. He met his end at the Battle of Carrhae, and according to Plutarch his severed head was brought to a nearby theater where the Parthian king was watching a performance of Euripides's *The Bacchae*; some wag then replaced the prop head of Pentheus on stage with Crassus's real one, dripping all over with gore. It was the end of the expansionist fantasy. The Romans were never to succeed in taming the land across the Euphrates. Reflections on modern geopolitics were inevitable, if unwelcome.

Justinian did not limit his improvements to military installations, but also built churches, public baths, and other municipal delights. Houses of worship were always made convenient to military barracks, and this juxtaposition is even more evident and imposing at nearby Resafa, or Sergiopolis as it was known in ancient times. This city, once a major religious and military center and now, though ruined, still one of the most impressive spectacles in Syria, was named for Sergius, a Christian soldier in the Roman army who along with his friend and fellow-officer (and lover, according to some accounts), Bacchus, was arrested for being a Christian and refusing to sacrifice to the pagan gods. As punishment the two were allegedly forced into women's clothing and paraded around the streets. Both were then horrifically tortured. Sergius was forced to run miles with nails driven into his shoes, then beheaded.

A shrine was built to Sergius's memory at Resafa, though for some reason Bacchus was left out of the deal (though a monastery in Maaloula, near Damascus, honors both saints). A few years later, when the Emperor Constantine declared Christianity a tolerated religion, the city was renamed Sergiopolis and became a popular pilgrimage center. Deserted though Sergiopolis/Resafa now is, Sergius has hardly been forgotten. In fact he and Bacchus have become gay icons for a new generation of Christians—though whether or not they were actually gay is a mystery that will probably never be solved.

A basilical cathedral was built over the original shrine, and Justinian launched a major overhaul of the place in the sixth century. According to Procopius, the church, "through its acquisition of treasures, came to be powerful and celebrated. And the Emperor Justinian, upon considering this situation, at once gave it careful attention, and he surrounded the church with a most remarkable wall, and he stored up a great quantity of water and thus provided the inhabitants with a bountiful supply. Furthermore, he added to the place houses and stoas and the other buildings which are wont to be the adornments of a city."[15]

This is no joke, especially about the water, for the monstrous cisterns built by Justinian are still intact, three underground caverns literally the size, and the shape, of cathedral interiors. It gives an idea of the amount of life this barren place must have supported, and so do the gigantic city walls and the three large churches (fig. 32). There is a phantasmagoric look to the spot, especially as you approach it across the desert: the brown ruins, made of a local gypseous stone, have settled and sagged and leaned into the earth over the centuries, and even those still standing have the look of unsuccessfully baked cakes. The Indian ladies with their umbrellas reappeared, and we climbed the ramparts together for a view over the endless desert expanse.

Syria contains so many significant ruins that Ugarit doesn't even make the cut in most guided tours of the country. Yet in some ways this ruined city, high on a bluff over the Mediterranean, provides the greatest historical thrill of all, for it was here, with settlement dating back to the eighth millennium B.C., that the alphabet originated—the one and only alphabet, from which all the world's alphabets derive. Experts have deemed Ugarit to have been possibly the first great international port in history (though the silting up of the harbor has meant that the former port is now three hundred feet from the sea). Ugarit has also proved enormously important as a well-preserved example of the biblical and pre-biblical Canaanite scene: this is the world from which the Israelites of the Old Testament were later to emerge.

The significance of the alphabet can hardly be overestimated, for before its invention there existed only pictographic writing like Egyptian hieroglyphs or modern Chinese. Tablets found here, now in the Damascus Museum, show a system of thirty symbols or "letters," each associated with one phoneme—the first example we have of the alphabetic principle. This Ugaritic alphabet was the inspiration for the Phoenician system of writing; this in turn gave birth to the Greek alphabet, which spread throughout the Mediterranean world and led to the development of the Latin and Arabic alphabets, among many others.

Walking around the ruins of Ugarit is an entirely different experience from what one gets at Mari, principally because the Ugarites built in stone rather than mud brick. Hence significant remains of palace, temples, tombs, and even ordinary houses survive to be visited, and you can get an actual idea of the city's layout and what life lived in it must have been like. Even now it's obvious that it was a rich culture, and archaeologists have found correspondences with contemporary buildings in Minoan Crete. The palace contains some ninety rooms, including a still-recognizable banquet hall, elaborate gardens, and an underground necropolis. There are also subsidiary palaces for minor royals, perhaps something like the grace-and-favor dwellings that distant relations of the Windsors enjoy in England today. There are impressive temples to Baal and Dagon—these would be the "idols" whose worship so offended the ancient Israelites. Sacked by the Sea People in about 1200 B.C., the city went into decline and eventually disappeared back into the earth, not to be rediscovered until 1928, when a peasant's plow struck part of a long-buried mausoleum.

It was a spot of singular beauty on the spring day we visited, as green as Ireland, carpeted with anemones and poppies, the Mediterranean sparkling beneath, the wind singing softly in our ears. We had the place to ourselves apart from a party of tiny schoolchildren, who at their teacher's behest greeted us politely in English. Why do so few tourists make it to Ugarit? Maybe because its nearest jumping-off point, the coastal city of Latakia, is so nasty. Latakia has an ancient and dignified history in its own right, having begun life as a village attached to the Ugaritic kingdom, then been turned into a major Hellenistic city under Seleucus I Nikator and renamed for his mother, Laodicea. But there are few traces of its former glory and no reason, so far as I could see, to visit the place (though we spent a pleasant enough evening in a waterside café full of gregarious locals). Even two hundred years ago, Lady Hester Stanhope was noting with displeasure that "Latakia is a dirty town."[16] It has certainly not improved, though as a home base for coastal sightseeing it may be unavoidable.

Bosra, on the Hauran plateau to the south of Damascus, in many ways summed up what I was coming to see as a peculiarly Syrian style of historical accretion, for in it there are essentially four cities built next to and on top of each other. There is the Nabatean city, which flourished in the century before and the century after the birth of Christ. There is the Roman, built after the area was conquered by Trajan in 106 A.D. and Bosra became the capital of the Roman province of Arabia. There is the Byzantine, when it became the seat of a bishopric and then an archbishopric, and its church (dedicated to SS. Sergius and Bacchus) became one of the greatest cathedrals of the East, as large in its day as Hagia Sophia and somewhat earlier in date. And finally there is the Arab city postdating the Muslim conquest, when Bosra was an important stop on the pilgrimage route to Mecca. All built in the brooding, rough, black basalt that crops up throughout the Hauran and forms the raw material of its houses and monuments and statues, these different historical layers are interwoven and superimposed (fig. 33). Here, next to a medieval mosque, you see what appears to be nothing but a dark pit in the ground; you step into it, and find yourself in a tiny, perfect, and elegant little Roman temple. Coming out, you espy a ruined Christian church around a corner.

Zakaria, our guide at Bosra—another overeducated and underemployed young man—filled us in on the background as we ate lunch in a garden restaurant opposite the old city, seated under a spreading fig tree. The food was superlative: a lamb and potato dish with rice and tomatoes, curried baby courgettes, eggplant stewed with peppers, and green beans—all with the best olive oil I have ever tasted. Zakaria, a trained archaeologist who works on digs at Bosra during the season, reckoned that ninety percent of Bosra had yet to be uncovered. Only the Byzantine and Islamic layers of the city were visible until the twentieth century, when archaeologists began digging there. Considerable progress has been made; they have dug down to the Roman level; but the question now, of course, is how to get down to the Nabatean level without destroying the Roman layer on top of it. As it is, we see only glimpses of the Nabatean material. The Roman works are extensive and in good shape. There

Figure 31. Halebiye.

Figure 32. Resafa.

Figure 33. A pillar at Bosra.

Figure 34. The theater at Bosra.

is a sizeable reservoir, about a third as large as the one in Central Park, with a perfectly good aqueduct that still serves the town after eighteen hundred years. There is a large suite of Roman baths, including a set of latrines that could accommodate 130 people at a time—a disturbing image. A spectacular second-century theater, also in harsh black basalt (fig. 34), can accommodate an audience of nine thousand and is used today as the venue for the biannual Bosra Festival of music and theater.

The Byzantine remains are similarly huge and imposing, with the centerpiece of course being the cathedral. Attention is also paid to the basilican church associated with the sixth-century Nestorian monk Bahira. This prescient monk is said to have met the young Muhammed there when the future Prophet traveled to Bosra with his merchant father. Bahira is supposed to have noticed the mark of prophecy on the boy's shoulder and seen clouds gathering over him to shield him from the sun, and these signs prompted him to predict his future as a prophet. Historians find the legend dubious, but many Muslims believe it and regularly visit the church to pay their respects to the monk's memory.

Then, up the street, there is the gorgeous black and white Mosque of Umar, dating to the eighth century though much rebuilt in the twelfth and thirteenth. It is still very much in use, and the day we were there we saw a group of tiny girls learning their lessons from a young lady who would be instantly recognizable as a kindergarten teacher anywhere in the world. Near the mosque is the so-called "modern city"—not modern, and certainly not a city—a village-sized community in which the houses have been built from ancient basalt blocks among the ruins—picturesque yet utterly casual and unselfconscious.

In compact form Bosra, like the larger Damascus, illustrates a fundamental difference between this very old world and the newer worlds of the West. Certainly in the Americas since the Conquest our instinct has been to tear down buildings and replace them with our own. At the beginning of the sixteenth century, Tenochtitlán, in Mexico, was possibly the greatest city in the world, rivaling Constantinople, Venice, and Paris, which

Europeans generally agreed to be the world's biggest metropolises. Today, few traces of the Aztecs' architecture remain in Mexico City, which grew up over Tenochtitlán; the Conquistadors and their heirs did their best to obliterate everything. The same is true at Native American sites in North America. Even in England, France, and Spain, more historically minded than America, there are few visible remains that predate the Middle Ages; one sees minimal traces of Saxon England or Merovingian France, for instance. Syria is totally different. There seems to have been no particular impetus for new settlers, or conquerors, to obliterate the traces of the vanquished. The custom the invading Muslim armies had of building a mosque *next to* a Christian church rather than destroying the church is symptomatic of what appears to be a widespread local tendency to leave older architecture alone, even if it seems worthless and defunct. A building might be converted into some new use; occasionally its parts might be plundered for recycling, as the Roman columns at Palmyra were used to build up the medieval fortifications; but Syria's conquerors seem to have felt no particular reason to raze something to the ground from ideological motives. An image that has been indelibly burned on Western eyes, that of Taliban members blowing up ancient Buddhist statues in Afghanistan, has led many Westerners to see the Muslim world as ruthlessly iconoclastic, determined to destroy any gods that are not their own. Here, the opposite is clearly the case, with pre-Muslim religious structures carefully conserved all over the country. The result is as rich a stew of stylistic and historical variety as I have ever encountered.

Finally, now, back to our own special ruin in Damascus, the Orient Palace Hotel.

It's another monument to faded pre-war glamour. Built by the French in the 1920s as part of an art deco ensemble of buildings facing the Hijaz Station—its opposite number across the street is now the Air Egypt building—it looks hardly touched since the 1950s or so. Its Gallic antecedents are still evident from the elevator buttons marked with SS (*sous-sol*) and RD (*rez-de-chaussée*), and from the tea-cups monogrammed "ORIENT PALACE DAMAS." When we inquired at the desk, we were told candidly that the hotel was "shabby but clean." The price was sixty dollars a night for a cavernous double room with a large bathroom. Long, wide, echoing institutional corridors with brown linoleum floors; exposed wiring; fluorescent lights. Because we were there in the cool weather, we were spared having to wrestle with the antiquated air conditioners, thank God. It was quite chilly in fact, and we had to request extra blankets.

But there was the beautiful breakfast of cheese, olives, eggs, and fresh bread laid out every morning; tea was brought to our rooms whenever we wanted it; there was the invariably cheerful service, the scrupulous settling of bills down to the last cent, the helpfulness over every little difficulty, and the undeniable truth that even faded grandeur is still grandeur of a sort, and still more appealing than jerry-built contemporary architecture or spurious glitz.

4 ✤ *Faith*

Damascus's Christian quarter, the week before Easter. This is *not* how I imagined Syria.

Pictures, icons, and statues of Jesus and his mother are everywhere; religious tableaux set up in front of every church vie with each other in garishness. Each house of worship in the quarter is mounting an extravagant Easter pageant, and the neighborhood buzzes with preparation and rehearsal. Every evening at dusk a teenage marching band assembles in a little square next to our hotel to practice the music they will play in the Easter Sunday procession—a noisy, giggling troupe with little control over the earsplitting squeals and squawks that emerge from their instruments. They resemble a painfully amateur version of the minor-key harmonies one hears at Sicilian street festivals, but loud, *loud*. On Easter Sunday itself, the whole neighborhood turns out *en fête*; tiny chicks are displayed for sale on the tops of the broken Roman columns along Straight Street (fig. 35).

William Dalrymple, who traveled throughout the Middle East—the birthplace of Christianity—visiting Christian communities, says that Syria is easily the best place in the region to be a Christian, and remarks also on the confidence of the Syrian Christians—a trait that must be evident to every visitor. As the Syrian Orthodox Metropolitan of Aleppo informed Dalrymple, "'If Syria were not here, we would be finished. Really. It is a place of sanctuary, a haven for all Christians: for the Nestorians and Chaldeans driven out of Iraq, the Syrian Orthodox and the Armenians driven out of Turkey, even some Palestinian Christians driven out of the Holy Land by the Israelis.'"[1]

Here is a contrast to the Easter scene:

The Great Synagogue of Aleppo, boarded up and deserted. This has a pedigree antedating the early Christian churches, venerable though they are. Around 1000 B.C. when King David's general Joab conquered Aleppo—Aram Soba, according to the Hebrew Bible—he is said to have laid the foundations of this house of prayer. Whether or not Aram Soba was actually Aleppo or some town further south is uncertain, but there is no doubt that the synagogue has very ancient foundations. The building probably dates from Byzantine times; it was destroyed by Tamerlane's armies in 1400, but quickly rebuilt by the faithful. It was burned again in 1947 during the anti-Zionist riots protesting the imminent creation of the State of Israel. After this trauma Aleppo's ancient Jewish community began to disperse, many of its members fleeing the country in 1948, the rest leaving over the course of the next twenty years or so. The synagogue was restored in the early 1990s, mostly from funds provided by Syrian Jews abroad. Today it stands empty, unused except for Jewish pilgrims who make occasional visits to the site.

How did these two religious communities, both so deeply entrenched in Syrian soil, arrive at such different fates? It is principally a question of historical accident rather than the European-style anti-Semitism we have come to expect from our own bitter experience, an accident that makes up just one of the countless strands of the region's exceedingly complex religious history.

Modern Syria is a secular country, with no official religion. This fact comes as a surprise to most Westerners, though secularism is in keeping with the socialist ethos espoused by the ruling Ba'ath Party.

The country is roughly seventy-five percent Sunni Muslim, ten percent Shi'a Muslim, ten percent Christian, and five percent other minorities. (Jews now comprise only a tiny handful.) Religion here is supposed to be a private matter, and so is one's style of dress: whether or not to wear the headscarf, for instance, is officially considered a personal decision, though of course most people conform to the expectations of their families and communities, as people do everywhere. Sharia law has a limited role in the Syrian legal system. The judicial system is principally based on the French model, introduced during the period of the Mandate, but sharia law is applied on personal issues like marriage, divorce, and inheritance. Non-Muslims are not compelled to adhere to these laws, and Christian churches maintain their own courts.

The tradition of toleration goes back to the Koran. According to that text, Christians and Jews were "people of the book," *dhimmi*, who like Muslims worshiped the God of Abraham and were therefore automatically to be accorded respect. "Dispute not with the people of the book," Muhammed ordered, "save in the fairer manner, except for those of them that do wrong; and say, 'We believe in what has been sent down to us, and what has been sent down to you; our God and your God is One, and to Him we have surrendered.'" The Muslims saw Islam less as a new religion than as the fruition of Christianity, and, further back, of Judaism. Jesus, like Abraham and Moses, is a prophet and a holy man in Islam; he is expected to return to earth at the Last Judgment, via the Jesus Minaret at the southeastern corner of Damascus's Umayyad Mosque.

So the earliest Arab conquerors of the Levant took the area from the Christian Byzantine Empire with a minimum of bloodshed and left churches and other religious structures standing. They were not the religious fanatics of the popular Western imagination, and the idea of religious pluralism was perfectly natural to them: the Middle East had after all been pluralistic for many centuries. The Byzantines and the Persian Zoroastrians had failed miserably in their efforts to impose religious unity, and the Arabs took a lesson from their lack of success. When the

Caliph Umar conquered Jerusalem in the year 637 he refused to render prayers to Allah in any Christian church. "If I do," he said, "some future Muslim will use it as an excuse to take the building and turn it into a mosque." This example set the pattern for the Arab conquests throughout the region.

Obviously the wisest course from the Arabs' point of view was to refrain from applying pressure on the conquered masses. Christians and Jews were not compelled to convert. Indeed, they were encouraged not to convert, for their new Arab overlords in Damascus saw Islam as a privilege to be enjoyed by themselves alone. Besides, the dhimmi were subject to a special tax, the *jizya*, in exchange for exemption from military service, and the Muslim administration would have hated to give up that source of revenue. The majority of Syria's population therefore continued to be Christian for centuries after the conquest.

Not, of course, that they were exactly the *equals* of Muslims. In the seventh-century Pact of Umar, the peace treaty offered by the Caliph Umar—submitted to by the Syrian Christians and later extended to include the Jews—non-Muslims were compelled to accept various constraints on their lives and ways of doing business:

> We shall not manifest our religion publicly nor convert anyone to it. We shall not prevent any of our kin from entering Islam if they wish it. We shall show respect toward the Muslims, and we shall rise from our seats when they wish to sit. We shall not seek to resemble the Muslims by imitating any of their garments, the qalansuwa, the turban, footwear, or the parting of the hair . . . We shall not mount on saddles, nor shall we gird swords nor bear any kind of arms nor carry them on our persons . . . We shall not sell fermented drinks . . . We shall not display our crosses or our books in the roads or markets of the Muslims. We shall use only clappers in our churches very softly. We shall not raise our voices when following our dead . . . We shall not bury our dead near the Muslims.[2]

A little harsh, but not by the standards of the time, nor even perhaps of our own. Christians were not threatened; Christian churches were not damaged; new churches continued to be built. In some ways the new Arab masters were actually more popular than the old Byzantine ones, for they tolerated the Monophysite doctrine the Byzantines had tried to suppress—the belief, that is, that Christ had only one nature, the divine, as opposed to the Chalcedonian doctrine ascribed to by the Byzantines, which said that Christ had two natures, human and divine. (The early Christians devoted an inordinate amount of time and energy to debating the type and number of Christ's natures.)

The career of an Arab Christian named Mansur, who has gone down in history as the church father John of Damascus, illustrates the unexpected ways in which Muslims and dhimmi could interact. John came from a long line of high-level civil servants who had served the Byzantine administration in Syria. Upon the Muslim conquest of Damascus in 635, John's father, Sergius, entered the employ of the city's new masters. So in turn did John himself, though he eventually left the Umayyads to enter the monastery of St. Saba and devote the rest of his life to prayer and polemic. John believed that Islam was a false religion and mocked Muhammed in his *Dialogue between a Saracen and a Christian* and *Heresies*, yet he deliberately chose to stay in Muslim employ rather than offering his services to the Byzantine Emperor in Constantinople, because he disapproved of the latter's enforcement of iconoclasm, the systematic destruction of religious images. He might not have approved of Islam, but he clearly accepted the Umayyad caliphs as successors to the Roman emperors.

Firmly in the ascendant, as they were for more than a thousand years in Syria, both under Arab and Turkish suzerainty, the Muslims could afford to be generous to their minorities. To paraphrase George Orwell, all Syrians were equal but some Syrians—the Muslims—were more equal than others. It was only in the nineteenth century, when the revolutions in Europe began the spread of liberal new ideas throughout the world, that Muslim rulers were pushed into a defensive position and began to react violently to what they saw as the diminishment of their special status.

The decrepit Ottoman Empire was crumbling, just as the European colonial powers were flexing their muscles and starting to pick up momentum in their epic struggle to gobble up Asia, Africa, and as much as they could of the rest of the world that still fell outside of their "spheres of influence." How was the Sublime Porte to regroup? Only by trying to keep pace with the Europeans, and if that meant adopting European social mores, then so be it. Under the liberal Sultan Abdul Mejid, the *vezir* Mustafa Reshid Pasha instigated a program of reforms collectively known as the Tanzimat, or reorganization of the Ottoman domains. He inaugurated it in 1839 with the Gülhane Decree, "in effect a charter of legal, social, and political rights, a Magna Carta for the subjects of the Empire,"[3] designed in accordance with Western notions of political and legal equality. Henceforth, Syrians and all other subjects of the Ottoman Empire were to be equal in fact as well as in theory. Education was to be the same for all faiths; military service was now required of everyone; army and civil service positions were open to all. Separate law courts for non-Muslims were now also prohibited.

All this was revolutionary not only by Ottoman standards but by any standards of that era. It should be remembered that in Britain the Roman Catholics were not emancipated until 1829, and Jews could not attain a seat in Parliament until 1858. From our historical perspective the Gülhane Decree seems a great leap forward, but at the time there was considerable displeasure, even from members of the religious minorities who were not at all happy about the prospect of losing some of their ancient privileges—especially the exemption from military service and their own special educational institutions. They also suspected that the Muslim backlash would be fierce, as indeed it turned out to be. The Muslims had always tolerated the dhimmi, but they had tolerated them as inferiors rather than as equals. This new decree struck at the very foundation of their worldview, in which Islam was absolutely superior to all other faiths.

In Syria the result was inter-religious strife such as the country had never experienced. In 1840, only months after the Gülhane Decree, the so-called Damascus Affair demonstrated what we can see in retrospect to have been the first example of European-type anti-Semitism in the region. An Italian priest and his servant disappeared mysteriously one day, and though there was good reason to suspect a local Turk who had recently been threatening him, a posse of Christians built up suspicions against the city's Jews, whom they accused of having ritually murdered the priest so as to use his blood in their religious ceremonies. This was a classic "blood libel" of the sort that had been practiced by hysterical mobs against Jews in Europe since the Middle Ages; it was the first example of such an event in Syria. The local Muslim authorities, eager to curry favor with imperialist France, which had already began applying pressure in the Levant, cravenly allowed the charges to be prosecuted.

The Muslims' relations with the Christians became far more troubled than with the Jews. The Tanzimat Reforms' social and political emancipation of the Christians was provocative enough; now, because the Christians were the beneficiaries of special protection by the European powers, they turned out to have a uniquely privileged position within the empire, above and beyond the Muslims. In hindsight, Syria's interfaith harmony up until that time really looks rather remarkable, considering its proliferation of sects. In the words of one historian:

> the Moslems were split into four orthodox schools, to say nothing of the schismatics—Shiahs, Dervishes, Sufis, Persians, and Bedouins. There were Sephardim and Ashkenazim Jews, the latter broken up into Parushim, Khasidim and Khabad sects. The Christians were divided into Maronite Catholic, Greek Catholic, Greek Schismatic, Armenian Catholic, Armenian Schismatic, Syrian Catholic, Jacobite, Latin Catholic, Copt, Abyssinian, Chaldean Catholic, and Chaldean Schismatic, as well as various Protestants. The esoteric Druses lived in the nearby mountains.[4]

What a hodgepodge! The delicate balance had held for a long time, but the resentments stirred up by the liberal reforms tipped it. Civil war broke out in the mountains of Lebanon between the Druzes and the Christian Maronites, and Christian refugees began pouring into Damascus. On July 9, 1860, a neighborhood riot lit the dry tinder, and Muslim hotheads embarked on a massacre that lasted eight days and killed some two thousand Christians—perhaps twenty percent of Damascus's Christian population. Curiously enough, the Jewish community was spared, showing that the rioters' onus was specifically directed against Christians and not against all dhimmi indiscriminately. An eyewitness account from a British army officer, Colonel Charles Churchill, sets the scene:

> The awful cry was caught up from mouth to mouth, a terrific commotion spread about like lightning from street to street. All business was abandoned, the shops were closed; and in less than a quarter of an hour an infuriated mob brandishing guns, swords, axes and every description of weapon was in full career to the Christian quarter.
>
> From all directions was seen and heard the rush of men armed to the teeth; and from unarmed women and boys, shouts, imprecations on the infidels, the *giaours*, and cries of "Kill them! Butcher them! Plunder! Burn! Leave not one alive, not a house, anything!"[5]

This terrible incident was a blow to Christian-Muslim relations, though the Christians eventually recovered their strong position in Syrian society. But what of the Jews, who for many centuries had enjoyed more cordial relations with the Muslim population than had the Christians? For the most part, Jews had enjoyed an easier time in the Middle East, where their rights and property were respected, than they had in Christian lands. After the crusading armies conquered Jerusalem in 1099, for instance, and slaughtered the city's Jews indiscriminately, it was to Damascus that the survivors repaired for asylum. Pogroms and blood libels by Muslims against Jews, long the disgrace of Europe, were unknown in Syria. (The Damascus Affair after all was instigated by Christians.) In the Middle Ages the Jewish rabbi Benjamin of Tudela, visiting Damascus from Spain, pondered the question of why Jews seemed to do so well in Muslim lands:

> I suppose it's in the national character of the three peoples that there's greater affinity between Jews and Muslims than between Jews and Christians. The reason would seem to lie largely in the religious practices and prescriptions, but history has played its part too. Once the Moslems came to dominate the lands around the Great Sea [the Mediterranean], it was Jews and Moslems, not Christians, who traded in the many Moslem kingdoms . . . Likewise it was Jews and Moslems who developed interests in the sciences. Moslems, like Jews, gave high priority to scholarship, and it's traditional for Muslim students, like Jewish, to travel from one place to another with a particular *sheikh*, or master. In contrast, any scholarship, even any literacy, among Western Christians is to be found in monasteries and scarcely affects the life of the ordinary Christian family man . . .
>
> The dispersal of learning among Moslems and Jews reflects the way they organize their religious communities. As the locus of Jewish scholarly life is the synagogue, so the locus of Islamic scholarly life is the mosque . . . which all men are obliged to attend. Both faiths give great importance to law, and study of the law is incumbent upon every Moslem and Jewish man. The *ulema* (learned men) are community leaders and interpreters of law, whose recognition and influence depend on their personal attainments; the *imam* who leads the congregation in prayer is appointed to do so for a short period for a small stipend—in the aggregate of their functions they are similar to rabbis and very unlike Christian priests, whose ordination imbues them with a mystique as intermediary between man and God and who live apart from the other members of their faith . . .

When we see the three faiths at worship, the most obvious dichotomy concerns art. Christians adorn their churches with paintings and sculptures of their holy personages, which practice to Jews and Moslems seems idolatrous: Moslems, like Jews, build and decorate their houses of worship without representing the human form. Also, while Jews and Mohammedans often make merry with music, both groups prohibit instrumental music in their houses of worship.

Even in naming themselves, the Christians are 'odd men out,' for they frequently identify a man by a personal characteristic, such as Long John or Baltazar the Bold, whereas Moslem and Jewish nomenclature usually identify a man by patronymic, e.g., the physician-philosophers Abu Ali ibn-Sina (Latin: Avicenna) and Moses ben Maimon (Greek: Maimonides).

These are ideas that have come to me in thinking about why it is that the Jews generally live better in Moslem kingdoms than in Christian.[6]

The Jewish community in Syria was diverse, having arrived in several waves. They had lived there since the reign of King David, a millenium before the birth of Christ, and by Roman times they made up a significant portion of the population, with some 10,000 residing in Damascus alone. After the Jews were expelled from Spain in 1492, many Sephardim moved to join their co-religionists in Damascus and Aleppo; others first went to Italy, and then immigrated to Syria in the seventeenth, eighteenth, and nineteenth centuries. These later arrivals were known as *Señores Francos*, and held themselves somewhat above the rest—a little like the German Jews among Ashkenazim in the United States today.

The Syrian Jews were a successful merchant class, and many did very well indeed. In the early part of the twentieth century, though, as Aleppo and Damascus declined as business and trading centers, a number of them left Syria for greener pastures—America, England, Egypt. Simultaneously, the rise of

Arab nationalism changed ethnic relations in Syria, with Zionist aspirations raising the hackles of the local Arabs. The Jews of Syria, traditionally well regarded, were now being identified as the Zionist enemy, whether in fact they happened to be Zionists or not. As one historian of the Aleppan Jews has written, "The parallel development of Zionism and Arab nationalism and the consequent struggle for Palestine, viewed by many Syrian Muslims and Christians as an integral part of Syria, isolated Syrian Jewry . . . This was especially true during the period of the Second World War and its aftermath, when the French Vichy regime implemented anti-Semitic policies and the heat of the Arab-Jewish struggle for Palestine became more intense."[7] Everything came to a head in December of 1947, when the United Nations General Assembly passed its resolution enabling the creation of a Jewish state in Palestine. Rioting broke out in Aleppo; synagogues were burned down and priceless Torahs and other sacred items destroyed.

My friend Renée Sassoon (née Renée Silvera) was eighteen years old at the time. "All hell broke loose," she says. "I'll never forget that day. I had to walk home ten blocks from school—it was terrifying, all the rioting, looting, burning. When I made it home we closed all the shutters but peeped out through the cracks. We could see the Silvera synagogue, which my grandfather had built, going up in flames. They were throwing the Torahs out the window. They didn't harm any people, but it was a bad time."

After this, most of the Syrian Jews departed to Lebanon, but Renée's parents stayed. Her father was a successful businessman who had built up a considerable fortune, and he feared that if he fled the country he would have to leave everything behind. Then the borders were closed to them; the Syrian government—believing that emigrating Jews would make their way to Israel, which Syria wouldn't recognize—refused to let Jewish citizens leave the country. They were welcome to stay, continue their lives, do business, but they could not emigrate. These restrictions remained in effect until 1992.

In 1949 Renée's parents sent her over the border into Lebanon, saying they would join her there a few days later. But it was ten years before they left the country, and as her father had feared, they had to leave their holdings behind. Other Jews got out when and as they could, so that now very few remain in the country.

Renée married another Aleppan Jew nearly twenty years older than herself who had left Syria to set up business in Japan in 1936; they moved on to the United States in the 1960s, where Rahmo Sassoon died in 2009. "My husband had only good memories of Syria," Renée says. "He left before all the troubles. He had friends in every sector of society, lots of Muslim friends, good relations with everyone he knew. For the rest of his life he missed Syria and thought kindly of it. I witnessed all the troubles, so I don't want to go back again, even though it's possible now. My brother is going, though."

So: Syria has had its share of inter-religious violence. Still, by regional standards it must be considered a success. Its current secularism has been hard-won, enforced with an iron fist by Hafiz al-Asad during his thirty-year presidency. His draconian tactics cost him his popularity among conservative Muslims, but he had little choice in the matter if he wished to protect the legitimacy of his regime, for he himself was a member of a religious minority, the Alawis—or Nusayris, as they were previously known.

This sect is centered in the northern Syrian mountains and the nearby city of Latakia, the Asad family's native region. Alawi rites and beliefs are so idiosyncratic that many have claimed, not without some justification, that the Alawis are not Muslims at all, and for years they were harassed by the majority Sunnis. Alawis are usually defined as an offshoot of Shi'a Islam, though their theology contains elements of pagan, Phoenician, Zoroastrian, Gnostic, and Christian dogma, and their rites have traditionally been celebrated in extreme secrecy. They celebrate Christmas, Epiphany, Pentecost, and the Persian Nowruz (New Year); they enact something like a mass (*Quddass*) with bread and wine, and like Christians they believe in a trinity, which tenet has caused them to be castigated as "polytheists" by more orthodox Muslims. The strange Alawi trinity consists of Ali (the son-in-law and nephew of Muhammed, worshiped by all Shi'a) at the apex and Muhammed and Salman a-Farisi, a Persian companion of Muhammed's, below him. Muhammed is supposed somehow to have emanated from the light of Ali's essence, Salman to have emanated from Muhammed.

It is not surprising that these eccentrics were deemed infidels by the more conventional faithful. The Alawis lived as an exploited underclass under the Ottomans, heavily taxed and often constrained to eke out meager livings as tenant farmers for oppressive Sunni landlords. It was not until the French Mandate of the 1920s that they began to emerge from their ancient isolation. The new French overlords, bitterly resented by the Sunni majority, cast around for allies among Syria's minorities and began to cultivate the Christian Maronites, the Druze, and the Nusayris, whom they renamed Alawis. They carved an Alawi "state" of some 300,000 people out of northern Syria and promoted Alawi interests, improving education for young Alawis and giving them special entrée into the military, a career path traditionally shunned by Syria's leading families. After the departure of the French in 1946, the new government in Damascus attempted to suppress these once-favored minorities, but the doors that had been opened could not be closed again. Young Alawis like Hafiz al-Asad, a poor boy who had received an excellent, French-sponsored education and would eventually attend the Air Force academy, had no intention of going back to their villages.

When Asad took over the government in 1970 (subsequently giving his bloodless coup a creepily Maoist-sounding title, "The Correction Movement"), he faced an unprecedented situation. Power in Syria had been in the hands of Sunni Muslims, after all, for thirteen hundred years. The situation called for considerable courage, not to say audacity, on Asad's part. The leader he had overthrown, another Alawi named Salah Jadid, had contented himself with exercising power behind an official Sunni front man, and initially it looked as if Asad would do the same thing: he took the job of prime minister and installed a figure-head Sunni as head of state. Only a few months later, though, he dropped this pretense and assumed full presidential powers. As for the question of making Islam the official state religion, which a vociferous opposition demanded, he refused. Islam, he said, should be "far removed from the detestable face of fanaticism . . . Islam is a religion of love, of progress and social justice, of equality for all, a religion which protects both the small and the great, the weak and the strong, a religion in tune with the spirit of the age."[8] In 1973 his constitution, officially upholding Syria's legal status as a secular state, was endorsed and passed.

Fundamentalist Muslims had always disliked the secular, socialist Ba'ath Party, and opposition to the Asad regime continued to grow within various Islamic groups including the Muslim Brotherhood, a movement of religio-political resistance aimed initially against the British in Egypt, which was founded in 1928 and subsequently spread throughout the Arab world. During the first decade of Asad's rule the Muslim Brothers carried out terrorist acts from their bases in the back streets of Aleppo and Hama, a campaign of violence that grew increasingly troublesome toward the end of the 1970s. The success of the 1979 Islamic Revolution in Iran strengthened their resolve, although the new Iranian leader, the Ayatollah Khomeini, declared the Alawi faith—and hence Asad—to be within the pale of Islam, something the Sunnis had always contested. Between 1979 and 1981 the Muslim Brothers were responsible for three hundred deaths in Aleppo; in revenge, some two thousand of their numbers were killed and hundreds more thrown into jail and tortured. A 1980 assassination attempt against Asad stirred him to vengeance, the more so since a year later his counterpart Anwar Sadat was murdered in Egypt.

The government backlash went into full effect, with Asad's dynamic, ambitious brother Rif'at, head of Syria's security forces, acting as hammerhead. A division of 10,000 soldiers and 250 armored vehicles was sent to Aleppo and remained there an entire year. Membership in the Muslim Brotherhood became a capital crime. The prison at Palmyra, in which members of the group were being held, was raided and about five hundred prisoners killed point blank. The conservative Muslim city of Hama, seething with Muslim Brotherhood cells, was a special problem, and on the night of February 2–3, 1982, Rif'at's forces there stumbled into an ambush led by the terrorist Abu Bakr. The call to *jihad* against the Ba'ath was sounded from the mosques, and the city went into all-out rebellion. But the fight was unequal. Government forces bombed Hama until whole neighborhoods were destroyed; at a conservative estimate, 10,000 citizens were killed. Rif'at's methods were brutal, and included the random execution of innocent civilians in reprisal for terrorist attacks. Old Hama was destroyed and a new city built in its place, rather in the manner of Haussmann's Paris, with the narrow streets of the neighborhood that had once sheltered insurgents being razed and modern boulevards cut through in their place.

Hafiz al-Asad, with his brother's help, had followed Machiavelli's famous advice: It is much safer for a prince to be feared than loved, if he is to fail in one of the two." Now Asad was feared, sure enough, and the Syrian branch of the Muslim Brotherhood, its leaders dead or in exile, seemed to have lost its claws. Interestingly enough, though, since Bashar's succession to the presidency in 2000, the Brotherhood has reappeared on the scene as a legitimate political party, eschewing violent resistance and sharia law and propounding democracy and free elections.

Today Hama is a nice enough town, almost sleepy: it shows few traces of its violent recent history. The pace of life seems radically different from the Levantine buzz of nearby Aleppo. To my untutored eyes the town looked no more conservative than any other in Syria; few women were heavily veiled, and Catherine, Arthur, and I attracted nothing but smiles and courtesy. The old part of town along the banks of the Orontes appears untouched by Rif'at's bombs and tanks, with the *norias*, huge and ancient waterwheels that are Hama's major claim to fame, still turning creakily in the breeze. There are now seventeen of these surprisingly large structures; it's hard to imagine what Hama must have looked like a few centuries ago, when there were a hundred of them in what was then a much smaller town. Archaeologists in nearby Apamea have unearthed a fifth-century mosaic illustrating one of these norias, so we know they have been in use along the Orontes for many centuries. Windmill and waterwheel technology was taken by the Crusaders back to Europe, where local methods were improved by Eastern innovations, and at Bayreuth in Germany one can still see the same type of noria that exists in Hama. Here in this recently chaotic town the norias' gentle croaks and moans add a note of rusticity to the atmosphere, bringing to mind the medieval poet Zuhayr:

> The water-wheels go round and round,
> The song-birds trill with merry sound,
> The hour is one of perfect joy,
> Bright and pure without alloy.[9]

In Hama we ate what was probably our best meal in Syria, at a totally unremarkable little lunch-counter-type joint with only one item on the menu—chicken. Half a chicken for each of us, free-range and impeccably grilled, fluffy rice with saffron and cardamom, and more than the usual assortment of side dishes: fresh peppers, mint, onions, pickled turnips, yogurt. The bill came to about three dollars apiece.

Hama's souq had a more leisurely feel to it than those of the bigger cities; we appeared to be the only foreigners at large that evening, and no one bothered to hawk anything to us. Families were out together, eating ice creams and stopping to buy pistachios and sweets at little corner sweet shops (fig. 36). We did the same, and were ushered hospitably to the one and only table—a plastic affair with two chairs—at the back of the room, where the proprietor came and served us coffee from one cup, in the traditional Arab manner:

> Pass the cup round to the right
> Don't pass it to the left.

> Pour first for him, and then for him,
>> You of the silver lute.[10]

The table was his, and not normally for customers; he was making a personal invitation to us and refused to let us pay for our snack, placing his hand on his heart in the gracious gesture characteristic of this part of the world. Back in the souq the people-watching continued to be good, and we spotted some excellent signage: "GINK SHOES onlygirls fifi fof," "DINTIST," "Dermatologist Venereologist," and a particularly mystifying one, "Smody Tex."

Hama got through its traumatic moment, then, and appears to be under control. But is this only a surface impression? Has the Ba'ath government really succeeded in imposing its secular vision on the country? Can overheated religious passions be subdued in the interests of national cohesion? The answer would seem to be a guarded *maybe*. The perception of the impact and number of religious fundamentalists is probably about the same as in the United States: lots of them or only a few, depending on your point of view.

But it was not always thus; in antiquity and beyond, Syrian religion was a byword for violent enthusiasm, weird sects, and every sort of unsavory religious excess.

We stand in Damascus's National Museum, Hall of Mari. Here are intact artifacts, four thousand years old: evidence of a complete civilization and a complete religion, with an individual and immediately identifiable style. Most striking are the alabaster sculptures of priests or worshipers, men and women alike, clad in the typically Mesopotamian long skirts called *kaunakes*—supposed to be of wool but looking much more like banana leaves or palm fronds—holding themselves in a characteristic "worshiping" posture, hands folded in front of the chest, one foot in front of the other. The written guide to the museum stresses, correctly I think, the figures' "aspect of gentleness, solemnity, smile and the look of contemplation and religious meditation." To this I would add humor, for the characters have a lively, charming look.

The religious cults of such city-states along the Euphrates were already complex in the Bronze Age, with statues of the gods filling in for the gods themselves and being put through their everyday motions by priests. These priests' function was to care for the images of the gods as though they were giant Barbie dolls, washing them, changing their clothes, feeding them, and daubing them with perfume as though they lived a physical life. The clergy was sizeable and hierarchical; already we see signs of the kinkiness and excess for which Syrian religion was to become notorious during the next millennia, for there is no doubt, as Assyriologist Georges Roux writes:

> that the temples of Ishtar, the goddess of carnal love, were the sites of a licentious cult with songs, dances and pantomimes performed by women and transvestites, as well as sexual orgies. In these rites, which may be found shocking but were sacred for the Babylonians, men called *assinu*, *kulu'u* or *kurgarru*—all passive homosexuals and some of them perhaps castrates—participated together with women who are too often referred to as 'prostitutes.'[11]

In the north of Syria we went to a pre-Christian holy high place infused with the desolate aura and the odor of ancient, even atavistic sanctity that we were to notice again and again on our journey through religious Syria. The mound of Ain Dara in the Afrin River gorge is a neo-Hittite site dating from about the tenth century B.C., with the remains of a temple—possibly dedicated to Ishtar—atop the promontory that looks out on the surrounding hills and olive groves, bleak in the gathering autumn and resembling, oddly enough, some recent David Hockney landscapes of the painter's native Yorkshire. As though to match the look of the place, there was an almost English chill in the air.

Ain Dara is distinctly weird. "It's like something out of an Ursula Le Guin novel," Catherine said. "Or even Star Trek." Indeed, for carved into the paving stones of the entranceway are huge bare footprints, each one three feet long, designed perhaps to intimidate the visitor, perhaps to indicate the gigantism often attributed to ancient gods and holy men (fig. 37). (Genesis, for instance, refers to the "nephilim" or giants who lived on the earth in the earliest times.) The prints certainly had the desired startling effect on us. On top of this, a ten-foot high black basalt lion guards the entrance, again something outsized, deliberately imposing and even threatening—but stylish of course, like all the sculpture of its period. Two more guardian lions flank an inner staircase, and along the inner walls there are the remains of eighty relief panels, carved with sphinxes and more lions (fig. 38).

Lions are specifically identified with Ishtar, but by the time we reached Ain Dara, a couple of weeks into our trip, we had started to understand that the image of the lion in this part of the world has always been intimately allied with divinity and power. This is true here throughout the millennia, no matter what dynasty or empire or religious system is holding sway at any given time, from Bronze Age Mesopotamia to the outposts of the Hittite Empire and even into the modern era. Curiously enough the name "Asad" means lion in Arabic, making the president's handle one of those that is almost too good to be true, like "De Gaulle." Unlike the name Atatürk, "Father of the Turks," which was assumed by the army officer Mustafa Kemal when he founded the modern Republic of Turkey, Hafiz al-Asad inherited his name ready-made: it had been bestowed as an honorific on his grandfather, a village power-broker and strong man. But it must certainly have come in handy for him, considering the ancient association hereabouts of the lion with divine powers, and throughout his thirty-year reign he rejoiced in the title "The Lion of Damascus." This has been harder for the milder

Bashar al-Asad to pull off, though some people, including his American biographer, have transferred the name to him. After you begin to notice the lions, you start seeing them everywhere. To walk through the extensive museums of Damascus and Aleppo and the wonderful provincial ones of Deir ez-Zor, Palmyra, Suweida, and Hama is to recognize the role the lion has played in the local imagination for eons. From the fourth millennium B.C. we see lions carved onto cylinder seals. At Deir ez-Zor on the Euphrates there is an extraordinary gold pendant of crossed lions, dating from third-millennium B.C. Mesopotamia. At the Hama Museum there is an eight-foot lion in black basalt, not unlike Ain Dara's, and from ancient Ebla there are also carved guardian lions, circa 1900 B.C. From Palmyra there is the great lion of al-Kath, now towering in the garden of the Damascus Museum, holding a horned oryx gently between its paws; there are also manifold Palmyrene representations of lions accompanying the gods Baal Shamin and Aphlad. The Temple of Azzanathkon at Dura Europos, third century A.D., shows the goddess seated between two lions. The mosaic museum at Maarat al-Numan houses an extraordinarily beautiful sixth-century mosaic, covering an entire wall, that shows a lion leaping through the air to devour a fleeing antelope. And the convention continues into the Muslim era: in the Damascus Museum, the tombs of two companions of the Prophet, Abu ad-Darda and Um ad-Darda, show the deceased accompanied by a lion. The inner doorway of the citadel of Aleppo, refortified in the Middle Ages, is guarded by two handsome, soulful-looking lions remarkably similar to those found at Ebla, carved three thousand years earlier. The cultural continuity, through millennia of often violent conquest and change, is astonishing (fig. 39).

The theme of the royal hunt comes up in the art of this region, just as it does in that of Western Europe; the monarch symbolically takes on the qualities of the majestic predator, and all the various religions of the area, whether Hittite, Assyrian, or even Christian and Muslim, make use of the iconography. At neo-Hittite Ain Dara you can see echoes of the fearsome stone lions who guard the gates at Hattusa, the Hittite capital in what is now Turkey.

Tell Halaf is another neo-Hittite site with a weird, syncretic religion and artistic style. A north Syrian settlement along the present Turkish border, it was originally excavated by a German engineer, Baron Max von Oppenheim, who began the work in 1911 and continued on and off until 1929. Many of his findings are now in the Aleppo Museum and were soon among our favorite works of Syrian art, gigantic and oddly cartoonish sculpted figures of dark basalt with bright white inlaid eyes; highly eccentric in their own context, they would look perfectly at home in the studio of a Picasso or a Henry Moore or even, I think, of a Fernando Botero or a Jeff Koons (fig. 40). Ross Burns, whose *Monuments of Syria* had been our alpha and omega throughout the trip, seemed to us obtuse in this instance, calling the sculptures "somewhat grotesque,"[12] the art of the neo-Hittites in general "a clumsy attempt to rival the monumentality of their Assyrian adversaries to the east."[13] This seemed to us deeply unfair. We found it easy to love the Tell Halaf figures, and it appears that their discoverer, von Oppenheim, felt the same, for there are several photographs showing him with his arm wrapped affectionately around one or other of these fantastic creatures.

Here is a cautionary tale for those who think works of art from Third World or "developing" countries should be moved to Europe for safekeeping. Von Oppenheim's findings were divided between the Aleppo Museum and Berlin, where a special Tell Halaf Museum was established to house them. Only a few years later the building was hit by an Allied bomb during the Second World War, and many of the Tell Halaf sculptures were blown to smithereens. It might be true that conditions in the Aleppo Museum are not ideal and that art is not displayed there to its best advantage, but the vagaries of history are hard to predict, and works of art might turn out to be just as safe here as anywhere.

"The cultus of the Syrian gods was often an appanage of the Syrian brothel," wrote nineteenth-century historian Theodor

Mommsen in a tone of high Victorian disapproval.[14] He might well have been thinking of Manbij, now a dusty, cheap-modern, utterly unappealing town in northern Syria. Most ancient cities have managed to hang on to at least a few traces of their dramatic past, but not Manbij. Odd, for during Hellenistic and Roman times, under the name of Hierapolis, it was perhaps the chief religious center in Syria, and it continued to be an important town right through the Christian era and the first centuries of Muslim rule. In antiquity Manbij/Hierapolis hosted the so-called cult of the Syrian Goddess—the ritualized worship of the deity Atargatis (elsewhere known as Ishtar, Ashtoreth, or Astarte), which was famous throughout the Roman Empire and made infamous in the second century B.C. by the satirical writer Lucian of Samosata, who published an X-rated account of the ecstatic goings-on at the sacred lake at Hierapolis.

Lucian was a Syrian whose native language was Aramaic, but like all educated Syrians of his time he wrote in Greek. His *De Dea Syria* is a risqué work, and classicists over the years have not known quite what to do with it; it was too important to be left out of the canon, but no one wanted to draw attention to it. It was conspicuously missing from the large 1905 edition of Lucian's collected works, and though it made it into the 1927 Loeb Classical Library, its translator chose to render it in Chaucerian Middle English, of all things—making it just difficult enough to be opaque to the modern reader but not so difficult as to make it impenetrable to the merely prurient. The translator defended his choice by pointing out that Lucian had himself composed it in an archaic form of Greek, that of Herodotus, who lived several centuries before him. Still, this reeks of self-justification.

Lucian (who refers to the Syrian Goddess familiarly as Hera, further emphasizing her one-size-fits-all nature) gives due weight to the general belief that the God Dionysus had visited Hierapolis and perhaps even founded its temple:

> There are in the temple many tokens that Dionysus was its actual founder: for instance, barbaric raiment, Indian pre-

cious stones, and elephants' tusks brought by Dionysus from the Aethiopians. Further, a pair of phalli of great size are seen standing in the vestibule, bearing the inscription, "I, Dionysus, dedicated these phalli to Hera my stepmother." This proof satisfies me. And I will describe another curiosity to be found in this temple, a sacred symbol of Dionysus. The Greeks erect phalli in honor of Dionysus, and on these they carry, singular to say, manikins made of wood, with enormous pudenda; they call these puppets. There is this further curiosity in the temple: as you enter, on the right hand, a small brazen statue meets your eye of a man in a sitting posture, with parts of monstrous size.[15]

Lucian then describes the bizarre rituals of the cult. These involved long stints of standing upright on the giant phalluses, in which practice might possibly be found one source of inspiration for the ascetic Christian stylites who flourished a few centuries later. What is it about these pillars, phallic or otherwise, that is supposed to enhance holiness? Is it another manifestation of the apparently universal human inclination, especially visible here in the Near East, to attach spiritual import to high places?

The place whereon the temple is placed is a hill: it lies nearly in the center of the city, and is surrounded by a double wall . . . The entrance to the temple faces the north; its size is about a hundred fathoms. In this entrance those phalli stand which Dionysus erected: they stand thirty fathoms high. Into one of these a man mounts twice every year, and he abides on the summit of the phallus for the space of seven days . . .[16]

The worshiper climbs up the phallus, says Lucian, by the same technique as those who climb palm-trees in Egypt or Arabia, and during the week he spends there is visited by various supplicants:

Many visitors bring him gold and silver, and some bring brass; then those who have brought these offerings leave them and depart, and each visitor gives his name. A bystander shouts the name up; and he on hearing the name utters a prayer for each donor; between the prayers he raises a sound on a brazen instrument which, on being shaken, gives forth a loud and grating noise. He never sleeps; for if at any time sleep surprises him, a scorpion creeps up and wakes him, and stings him severely; this is the penalty for wrongfully sleeping. This story about the scorpion is a sacred one, and one of the mysteries of religion; whether it is true I cannot say, but, as it seems to me, his wakefulness is in no small degree due to his fear of falling.[17]

Lucian goes on to describe the castration ceremonies whose gruesomeness resounds through the centuries:

During these days they are made Galli [eunuch priests]. As the Galli sing and celebrate their orgies, frenzy falls on many of them and many who had come as mere spectators afterwards are found to have committed the great act. I will narrate what they do. Any young man who has resolved on this action, strips off his clothes, and with a loud shout bursts into the midst of the crowd, and picks up a sword from a number of swords which I suppose have been kept ready for many years for this purpose. He takes it and castrates himself and then runs wild through the city, bearing in his hands what he has cut off. He casts it into any house at will and from this house he receives women's raiment and ornaments. Thus they act during their ceremonies of castration.[18]

Animals were ritually sacrificed, and sometimes humans as well:

There is also another method of sacrifice, as follows: They adorn live victims with ribbons and throw them headlong down from the temple's entrance, and these naturally die after their fall. Some actually throw their own children down, not as they do the cattle, but they sew them into a sack and toss them down, visiting them with curses and declaring that they are not their children, but are cows.[19]

A perusal of all this will show that by this time (the second century A.D.) the religious syncretism of the Greco-Roman world, which had for so long been its strength, had begun to get impossibly complex. The Syrian Goddess of whom Lucian writes has been variously identified with Athena, Aphrodite, Selene, Rhea, Ishtar, Artemis, Nemesis, and Hera. The rites were becoming ever more extreme, the manifestations of the deities more interwoven and confusing.

The Roman Empire was always religiously inclusive, picking up local gods and adapting them to their own purposes throughout their colonies. Syria, at the crossroads of so many trade routes, was particularly syncretic, sometimes wildly so. First there were the ancient Babylonian gods; then the Semitic Arab gods; the Phoenician gods; the Anatolian gods penetrating Syria from the north; the Parthian gods from the east. In the wonderful museum at Suweida in southern Syria (practically empty, like all provincial Syrian museums), we found a Roman-era door lintel of local manufacture with Aphrodite and Eros on one side, Athena on the other, and in the middle none other than the Semitic deity Baal Shamin! In the Palmyra museum, too, we witnessed countless signs of this syncretism, a weird combination of Greco-Roman style and Eastern subject matter. Limestone panels of clearly classical style show camels kneeling, laden with goods and covered in rugs. The famous tomb sculptures that depict entire families look Roman, and even Etruscan, but the figures' clothes and boots are in the Parthian style and their expressions as they look off into eternity anticipate the blank gaze of the Byzantine.

The Syrian city of Homs was the center of another strange cult in antiquity. For centuries an important stop on the caravan route to Palmyra, Homs today is a backwater; even Muhammed

Four, who had by now taken measure of our incurable sightseeing bug, told us not to bother with it. Of course we did anyway, for we couldn't pass up the site of the sun cult of Emesa, Homs's name in Roman times.

The sun deity who presided at Emesa was Elagabal, and his emblem, a mysterious black stone, was worshiped of course at a high place—the promontory in the middle of the old town where the remains of the medieval citadel now stand. (Such black stones, worshiped throughout the Levant, are known as *baetyls* and are believed to be metaphoric "homes of God." The most famous of them is the Kaaba at Mecca.)

The priests of Elagabal were important citizens in ancient Syria, so much so that the daughter of one of their number was considered a very acceptable match for the rising military genius Septimius Severus, who would become Roman emperor several years later. Julia Domna was widely admired and is still a local heroine in Syria today, both for having given birth to a Syrian line of Roman emperors and because of her considerable personal qualities, famously celebrated by Gibbon in the eighteenth century. "She possessed," he wrote, "even in an advanced age, the attractions of beauty, and united to a lively imagination, a firmness of mind, and strength of judgment, seldom bestowed on her sex . . . She was the patroness of every art, and the friend of every man of genius." But Gibbon seldom gave himself over to unbarbed praise, and he went on to say that "The grateful flattery of the learned has celebrated her virtue; but, if we may credit the scandal of ancient history, chastity was very far from being the most conspicuous virtue of the empress Julia."[20]

Julia Domna's two sons, Caracalla and Geta, were named joint emperors after the death of Septimius Severus, but such divisions of power are seldom successful. Caracalla soon had his brother murdered and assumed sole rule. When he himself was assassinated in an army coup, Julia Domna's sister intrigued to have her own son, at that time priest of the Emesan cult, proclaimed emperor in turn; he took the name Marcus Aurelius Antoninus Augustus, but was generally known as Elagabalus because of his priestly origins. He had the sacred black stone of Emesa carried to Rome, and he replaced Jupiter as chief god of the Roman pantheon with the Syrian Elagabalus, compelling the Romans to submit to the new cult. According to the authors of the *Historiae Augustae*, he established worship of the Sun God "on the Palatine Hill close to the imperial palace; and he built him a temple, to which he desired to transfer the emblem of the Great Mother, the fire of Vesta, the Palladium, the shields of the Salii, and all that the Romans held sacred, proposing that no god might be worshiped at Rome save only Elagabalus. He declared, furthermore, that the religions of the Jews and the Samaritans and the rites of the Christians must also be transferred to this place, in order that the priesthood of Elagabalus might include the mysteries of every form of worship."[21]

The excesses of this young emperor combined deviant sex, religion, and profligacy mingled in what was coming to be seen as a typically Syrian mélange. Amazing tales circulated about his ability to come up with new and outlandish ways of throwing away the riches of the Roman treasury, and sexual as well as financial extravagances would come to be associated with this devotee of the Sun God:

> A long train of concubines, and a rapid succession of wives, among whom was a vestal virgin, ravished by force from her sacred asylum, were insufficient to satisfy the impotence of his passions. The master of the Roman world affected to copy the dress and manners of the female sex, preferred the distaff to the scepter, and dishonoured the principal dignities of the empire by distributing them among his numerous lovers; one of whom was publicly invested with the title and authority of the emperor's, or, as he more properly styled himself, of the empress's husband.[22]

Elagabalus was inevitably deposed in his turn, after a mere four years in power, and the black stone of Emesa was returned to Syria where it continued to be visited and worshiped until the end of the fifth century, the height of the Christian era in Syria. Today there are no traces of the cult left to visit, and even the medieval citadel that replaced the temple of Elagabalus has disappeared except for the remains of a few stone walls. The large, bare mound rising from the center of the modern town was clearly an important place in its day, one of the traditional sacred high places where deities were known to make their homes; today, the only notable structure on it is a cell phone tower.

Such tales of theological excess and confusion go far toward explaining the spiritual revolution that overtook the Roman Empire, including Syria, in the second and third centuries. Paganism, which for a thousand years had provided a comprehensible world-view based on specific rites and duties, no longer satisfied the spiritually hungry citizens of late antiquity. There was a general turning inward, to the cultivation of the individual soul's relation to eternity rather than to traditional, publicly expressed religious activities.

The systems of thought that arose to meet this new need all made their own contributions to the rich spiritual fruitcake of Syria. Stoicism had long been part of the mix; in fact Posidonius, from the school of Apamea in Syria, taught its tenets to Cicero in Rome. Neo-Platonism, a key stepping-stone between paganism and Christianity, also flourished at Apamea (fig. 41). The philosopher Aemelius founded a Neo-Platonic school there, and Numenius, who taught there, is believed by many to be the real founder of Neo-Platonism rather than Plotinus, who is usually credited with that distinction. Other notable Syrian Neo-Platonists included Iamblichus, also from Apamea, and Longinus, a disciple of Plotinus and Queen Zenobia's court philosopher at Palmyra. (I can still remember plowing my way through Longinus's deadly treatise "On the Sublime" in graduate school, though there is now some uncertainty as to whether or not he actually wrote it.)

To all serious men of late antiquity, Bertrand Russell has told us, "the world of practical affairs seemed to offer no hope, and only the Other World seemed worthy of allegiance. To the Christian, the Other World was the Kingdom of Heaven, to be enjoyed after death; to the Platonist, it was the eternal world of ideas, the real world as opposed to that of illusory appearance. Christian theologians combined these points of view"[23]—so that Neo-Platonist thought came to imbue the Christian faith. The world, according to its tenets, is even presided over by a trinity, anticipating that of the Christian church: the One, Spirit, and Soul. Neo-Platonism marks the beginning (in the West) of the spiritual practice of looking inward rather than outward, a shift in thinking that marked the change from the classical to the Christian temper and was certainly not an unmixed blessing: some have dated the decline of science and the spirit of inquiry that took place during the early Christian period to this cultural moment.

Syria was a center of Christianity from the very beginning, was even, if you are referring to "greater Syria," its birthplace. Three of Jesus' disciples came from the Golan Heights; the Gospel of Matthew is supposed to have Syrian origins; Tatian's *Diatesseron*, the combined version of the gospels used until the fifth century, was Syrian; and it was at Antioch, at that time Syria's major city, that Paul and other early missionaries established their base of operations. After the destruction of Jerusalem by the Romans in 70 A.D., Antioch became the world capital of Christianity.

For many years the cult of Jesus was considered just one more strange Oriental sect. Lucian treated the Christians as pitiful simpletons, a bit of a joke really:

> They still reverence that great one, the man who was crucified in Palestine because he brought this new mystery into the world. The poor creatures have persuaded themselves that they will be altogether immortal and live for ever; wherefore they despise death and in many cases give themselves to it voluntarily. Then their first Law-giver [Jesus] persuaded them that they were all brethren, when they should have taken the step of renouncing all the Hellenic gods, and worshiping that crucified one, their soph-

ist, and living after his laws. So they despise all things alike, and hold their goods in common: though they have received such traditions without any certain warrant. If then an artful imposter comes among them, an adroit man of the world, he very soon enriches himself by making these simple folk his dupes.[24]

Plus ça change! Televangelists take note! But the faith continued to spread; by the third century it was a force to be reckoned with, though still regarded with suspicion and a measure of revulsion by educated pagans. In the second century, the city of Dura Europos, as we have seen, contained a church that was an actual public building and not simply a room in somebody's house. By the early fourth century, when the Emperor Constantine declared Christianity to be a tolerated religion within the empire and began promoting it through his own conversion and his ambitious program of church-building and ecclesiastical patronage, Syria was thoroughly Christian. Throughout the Byzantine era and up until the Arab invasion of the seventh century, it was perhaps the heart of the Christian faith. This was a thoroughly ecclesiastical age:

> From the fourth to the sixth centuries monks, priests, bishops, nuns, anchorites, flourished as never before and never after. Church buildings, chapels, basilicas, monasteries, all with a new style of architecture involving domes, bell towers and prominent crucifixes, dotted the land. Hermit caves were enlarged or created. Pillars were erected on which stylites curiously enough lived and died. Pilgrimage boomed. Vows and prayers at tombs of saints were considered more efficacious than visits to physicians. Byzantine architectural remains and religious relics are today more numerous than those of all other ages together.[25]

This is true: the limestone massifs of northern Syria are sprinkled with their remains. As many as seven hundred "Dead Cities," or more properly, ruined Byzantine provincial towns, can still be visited. Northern Syria, as Lawrence wrote in amazement, is *"packed with ruins*, Xian, of the Vth and VIth cent. mostly: massive basilicas and pandocheions and lauras: private houses a few: tombs in abundance: inscriptions were all in Greek: in parts of my journey I seem to have been the first European visitor."[26] There are more Byzantine architectural remains in this region, it turns out, than in Istanbul/Constantinople itself. What is more, nothing has been touched, disturbed, reworked. Visiting one of these forgotten, windswept spots, one gets a glimpse of what provincial life must have been like during the late Roman Empire (fig. 42).

At Serjilla, one of the largest and best preserved of these Dead Cities, we were taken in hand by a diminutive teenager, son of the local schoolmaster, who was bursting with enthusiasm to show us around and thrilled when he heard we were American. "I like very much America," he bubbled. "I like very much Rambo, Sylvester Stallone, James Bond."

Wishing to take full credit for this *embarras de richesses culturelles* I did not disabuse him about James Bond's national origin. The boy dragged us at a quick pace over the ruins, pointing out the well-preserved shells of church, travelers' inn, and bathhouse, with particular attention to the sophisticated plumbing techniques and materials. Limestone seems to have been the only building material; blocks of it lie everywhere, as though hurled down by giant children. Having seen several other Dead Cities, we were struck by a certain regional uniformity to the architecture, as though the builders had followed standard patterns. The configuration of the blocks even suggested giant Lego bricks, fitted together in conventional, repeated motifs. Early versions of Sears houses, perhaps (fig. 43).

Ecclesiastical buildings—churches, monasteries, pilgrimage centers—make up a significant proportion of such ruins. The craze for pilgrimage began as early as the reign of Constantine, when his mother—later beatified as St. Helena—struck out for Jerusalem in search of the True Cross. She found it, too, as well as the nails used to impale Christ. (One of them she had made into a bit for Constantine's horse.) Soon pilgrimage was not only fashionable but big business, as was monasticism, an invention of the Egyptian St. Antony, whose example inspired the world—whether for good or ill has never quite been agreed on. After Antony's death in 356 there was a veritable stampede to the desert in search of spiritual highs.

Egyptian monks tended to be cenobites—members of a religious community—while Syrian monasticism was of the solitary variety, stressing celibacy, physical endurance, and extreme asceticism. The rationalist Edward Gibbon—no surprise!—found the craze thoroughly repulsive:

> It was the practice of the monks either to cut or shave their hair; they wrapped their heads in a cowl, to escape the sight of profane objects; their legs and feet were naked, except in the extreme cold of winter; and their slow and feeble steps were supported with a long staff. The aspect of a genuine anachoret was horrid and disgusting; every sensation that is offensive to man was thought acceptable to God; and the angelic rule of Tabenne condemned the salutary custom of bathing the limbs in water and of anointing them with oil. The austere monks slept on the ground, on a hard mat or a rough blanket; and the same bundle of palm-leaves served them as a seat in the day and a pillow in the night.[27]

Inevitably this sort of asceticism assumed histrionic forms and became something of a competitive sport, each anchorite vying with the next to see who could outdo the other. In fact they were often referred to by themselves and others as "athletes," and God was "the umpire":

> The most devout, or the most ambitious, of the spiritual brethren renounced the convent, as they had renounced the world. The fervent monasteries of Egypt, Palestine, and Syria were surrounded by a *Laura*, a distant circle of soli-

tary cells; and the extravagant penance of the Hermits was stimulated by applause and emulation. They sank under the painful weight of crosses and chains; and their emaciated limbs were confined by collars, bracelets, gauntlets and greaves of massy and rigid iron. All superfluous incumbrance of dress they contemptuously cast away; and some savage saints of both sexes have been admired, whose naked bodies were only covered by their long hair ... The most perfect Hermits are supposed to have passed many days without food, many nights without sleep, and many years without speaking; and glorious was the *man* (I abuse that name) who contrived any cell, or seat, or a peculiar construction, which might expose him, in the most inconvenient posture, to the inclemency of the season.[28]

Gibbon's shudder of distaste, the characteristic reaction of the Enlightenment intellectual to religious zeal of any sort, would have been shared by the educated pagans of the monks' own time, who looked on the excesses of the anchorites with fastidious horror. That the monks were often illiterate and brutish didn't make them any more attractive. As Paul Johnson has pointed out, "Monasticism attracted misfits, bankrupts, criminals, homosexuals, fugitives, as well as the pious; it was also a career for raw peasant youths who could be drilled into well-disciplined monkish regiments to be deployed as an unscrupulous bishop might think fit."[29] A cultivated Neo-Platonist or Stoic could only be appalled.

Where did all this take place? Catherine and I were curious to see Cyrrhus (formerly Hagiopolis), the resting place of SS. Cosmas and Damian and a major center of monasticism in the fourth and fifth centuries, but now a peaceful, romantically desolate rural hamlet not too far from Aleppo. We started on a gray morning in mid-November, the first really chilly day of our visit; when we came down to breakfast at the Baron, Mr. Walid had lit both the oil lamp and the woodstove and placed our table strategically between the two. The drive from Aleppo—

with Muhammed Three, Mr. Walid's son—was pretty, once we escaped the shoddy suburbs with their cement villas set off by weirdly oversized, framed gates—the kind of bombastic structures I once heard an American developer refer to, unironically, as "entrance statements." But about half an hour out of town, it all petered out and we were in agricultural country. Big commercial olive groves with cherry trees were planted at intervals, orange-hued in the autumn. Then came the little individual gardens: figs, walnuts, pistachios, roses, vegetable patches.

We soon turned off onto a dirt road that took us fifteen or twenty miles further, passing through hills that folded over and over on each other and through a series of ever-tinier villages: al-Muhabbabeh, Karkeen, 'Atiyeh, Dorakly, Saeer, Seem. The smell of wood smoke permeated everything. We stopped at Saeer to buy some biscuits and juice at the tiny general store; the shopkeeper, his wife, and three little children gaped at me as though I had just touched down from Mars. Leaving Saeer, the road continued over a couple of Roman bridges—two thousand years old, never constructed with motor traffic in mind, and still, miraculously, in use. Here as everywhere in the former empire, the works of the Roman legions have survived better than any other feats of engineering: Roman roads, bridges, and walls continue to function, usually without any noticeable sign of decrepitude.

Then on to Cyrrhus. Everywhere more olive trees, with colorfully dressed, red-cheeked Kurdish families gathering branches from atop ladders, or sitting on blankets on the ground, plucking olives from the cut boughs and arranging them in bright piles. From time to time shepherds would appear, driving their flocks along unhurriedly. Deep in the green heart of the olive grove, there rose a hexagonal Roman tomb tower, once the resting place of a Roman soldier, now the tomb and pilgrimage site of a Muslim saint.

When I had heard about the anchorites' "flight to the desert," this was hardly what had come to mind. Far from being dry and sterile, it was probably the most fertile and inviting landscape I had yet encountered in Syria. Maybe these monks didn't do themselves quite as badly as they pretended. I had to assume that "desert" was more a figurative than a literal term, meaning a place deserted of people. But how deserted could it have been, with all these holy men and their followers thronging the streets of the little city of Cyrrhus?

We know much about the doings of these prodigies, thanks to the writings of Theodoret, Bishop of Cyrrhus from 423 to 450, who wrote a history of the Syrian monks and was an eyewitness to much of what he described. There was Acepsimas, for instance, who stayed sixty years in a cell without speaking or being seen. "He received the food that was brought to him by stretching his hand through a small hole. To prevent his being exposed to those who wished to see him the hole was not dug straight through the thickness of the wall, but obliquely, being made in the shape of a curve. (The food brought him was lentils soaked in water.)"[30] Ugh! Then there was Abraham:

> . . . bread was for him superfluous, water superfluous, a bed useless, and use of fire superfluous. At night he chanted forty psalms antiphonally, doubling the length of the prayers that occur in between; the rest of the night he sat on a chair, allowing a brief rest to his eyelids . . . [T]his wonderful man throughout the time of his episcopacy took neither bread nor pulses nor greens cooked by fire and not even water, which is considered by those reputed clever about these things to be the first of the elements in utility; but it was lettuce, chicory, celery, and all plants of the kind that he made his food and drink, rendering superfluous the skills of baking and cooking.[31]

Some of the anchorites exercised great imagination in devising new and ever more baroque hardships with which to torment themselves. Some grazed in the fields like sheep, subsisting on grass; others took up their abodes in the dens of animals. But the king of all these, certainly the one whose fame has spread the widest and lasted the longest, was St. Simeon Stylites, the pillar-stander.

Simeon was the son of a shepherd near what is now the Turkish border who came in the year 412 to the monastery at Telanissos. A true athlete of God, he scorned the run-of-the-mill monastic penances as insufficiently arduous, seeking to outdo all his rivals in self-denial. At the monastery "he had eighty fellow contestants," Theodoret tells us, "and outshot all of them; while the others took food every other day, he would last the whole week without nourishment." Afraid that monks endowed with a less robust constitution than Simeon's might really harm or even kill themselves in their efforts to compete with him, his superiors asked him to leave the monastery, whereupon he took up residence in a dry cistern; there he stayed, until forcibly removed by the other monks. Eventually he embarked on a life as a solitary, and rumors of his ascetic practices were so extreme and outlandish that he became a famous holy man and object of pilgrimage. Soon, however, he got fed up with all these pilgrims and their attempts to acquire sanctity through proximity, touching and mauling him, and so he devised the clever expedient of standing on a pillar to get away from them all. This pillar was not tall enough; he procured another, about fifty feet high. A railing was built around the top so he would not fall off while sleeping and food was brought once a week by disciples who climbed up to him on a ladder. It is said that pieces of his excrement, dropped off the pillar and collected in baskets, were prized as holy relics. But let Gibbon set the scene:

In this last and lofty station, the Syrian Anachoret resisted the heat of thirty summers, and the cold of as many winters. Habit and exercise instructed him to maintain his dangerous situation without fear or giddiness, and successively to assume the different postures of devotion. He sometimes prayed in an erect attitude, with his outstretched arms in the figure of a cross; but his most familiar practice was that of bending his meager skeleton from the forehead to the feet; and a curious spectator, after numbering twelve hundred and forty-four repetitions, at length desisted from the endless account. The progress of an ulcer in his thigh might shorten, but it could not disturb, this *celestial* life; and the patient Hermit expired without descending from his column.[32]

Gibbon's out-of-hand dismissal of the monastic phenomenon seems a little harsh:

> A prince, who should capriciously inflict such tortures, would be deemed a tyrant; but it would surpass the power of a tyrant to impose a long and miserable existence on the reluctant victims of his cruelty. This voluntary martyrdom must have gradually destroyed the sensibility both of the mind and body; nor can it be presumed that the fanatics who torment themselves are susceptible of any lively affection for the rest of mankind. A cruel, unfeeling temper has distinguished the monks of every age and country; their stern indifference, which is seldom mollified by personal friendship, is inflamed by religious hatred; and their merciless zeal has strenuously administered the holy office of the Inquisition.[33]

Is this really fair? The monks of *every* age and country? Certainly not; but these extremists are certainly a little creepy. Simeon was heard to say that the only pleasure he still indulged in was the persecution of Jews. Theodoret, who knew him personally, remarked that "he does not neglect care of the holy churches—now fighting pagan impiety, now defeating the insolence of the Jews, at other times scattering the bands of the heretics, sometimes sending instructions on these matters to the emperor, sometimes rousing the governors to divine zeal, at other times charging the very shepherds of the churches to take still greater care of their flocks."[34] These activities reveal a surprising worldliness in a man who made a career out of appearing to be unworldly.

Plate 1. Men at the mosque.

Plate 2. Mosaic wall at the Umayyad mosque.

Plate 3 (ABOVE).
The hakawati in action.

Plate 4 (LEFT).
The Azem Pasha Khan.

Plate 5 (LEFT). *An ajami ceiling in Aleppo.*

Plate 6 (BELOW). *The church at Mar Musa.*

Plate 7 (LEFT). *Krak des Chevaliers.*

Plate 8 (BELOW). *The Aaron family in Damascus.*

Was Simeon a genuine mystic? A fraud? We're still not sure, though he has had any number of passionate supporters and equally vociferous detractors. Gibbon's rationalistic attitude was still current a century later, when William Lecky claimed that "there is perhaps no phase in the moral history of mankind of a deeper or more painful interest than this ascetic epidemic. A hideous, distorted and emaciated maniac, without knowledge, without patriotism, without natural affection, spending his life in a long routine of useless and atrocious self-torture, and quailing before the ghastly phantoms of his delirious brain, had become the ideal of the nations which had known the writings of Plato and Cicero and the lives of Socrates and Cato."[35]

But Lecky's contemporary Lord Tennyson, in his long monologue poem about the Stylite, demonstrates the new sympathy toward religious enthusiasm that characterized the evangelical Victorian age. Tennyson's poem is a sophisticated imagining of the ascetic's inner life as a cauldron of conflicting emotions: vanity, fear, genuine religious fervor, inchoate passion. This was rehabilitation of a sort, but poor old Simeon was to suffer true ridicule in the godless 1960s with the appearance of Luis Buñuel's devastating movie *Simon of the Desert*. Buñuel, a communist and passionate anti-cleric, found ample evidence for human idiocy in Simeon and his motley parade of fans and clients. His Simeon is not so much a charlatan as a naïf, whose long, mournful face reflects the joyless self-importance of his creed. At one point he is petitioned by a man whose hands have been cut off by priests as a punishment for theft: Simeon actually heals him, and after giving the saint peremptory thanks the man goes off, cursing his wife and slapping his child with his miraculously restored hands. Satan, in the form of Mexican actress Silvia Pinal, comes several times to tempt him and appears to have succeeded by the end, for in the final scene we see Simeon (accompanied by the alluringly feminine Satan) suffering in a noisy modern European disco—perhaps his vision of hell. *Simon of the Desert*, made during Buñuel's political exile in Mexico, was filmed on a shoestring budget, but the director still managed to give us an image of what the circus around Simeon's pillar must have looked like when (as described by Theodoret):

> everyone hastened to him, not only the people of the neighborhood but also people many days' journey distant, some bringing the paralysed in body, others requesting help for the sick, others asking to become fathers; and they begged to receive from him what they could not receive from nature ... So with everyone arriving from every side and every road resembling a river, one can behold a sea of men standing together in that place, receiving rivers from every side. Not only do the inhabitants of our part of the world flock together, but also Ishmaelites, Persians, Armenians subject to them, Iberians, Homerites, and men even more distant than these; and there came many inhabitabts of the extreme West, Spaniards, Britons, and the Gauls who live between them. Of Italy it is superfluous to speak.[36]

Simeon's fame had spread so far that when he died in 459 an enormous monastic complex, complete with pilgrimage city, was erected to house the celebrated pillar and handle the crowds of pious sightseers. Completed late in the fifth century, the church of St. Simeon with the pillar enshrined inside was the largest church in the world until the construction of Hagia Sophia. In Europe there would be nothing comparable to it until the late Middle Ages.

Catherine and I started from the ruins of Deir Samaan, the pilgrimage city. The day was one of intense color, the deep green of grass broken up by the clear gray of the rocks that peppered the countryside and the walls of the crumbling Byzantine structures, clouds swirling through the chill sky, and the piercing reds and yellows of wildflowers. Deir Samaan, which started as the humble village of Telanissos, is another of the northern Syrian Dead Cities and perhaps the most magnificent of them.

The tranquil silence at Deir Samaan now must be entirely different from the uproar that seems to have prevailed during the Stylite's lifetime and for several centuries thereafter. For even after the complex's erection it had a vivid history, being damaged by earthquakes during the sixth century; fortified as a military site by the Byzantine armies when they reclaimed the area from the Arabs in the tenth century; sacked a few years later by the Arabs; at peace under the Hamdanid dynasty of neighboring Aleppo; and sacked again twenty years down the road by Egyptian forces. A place of bustle, fervor, and contention for hundreds of years, and then, for the next thousand, a backwater, a spot only for prayer and solitary contemplation.

Heading through the complex we passed two *pandocheions*, or inns for pilgrims, in surprisingly good shape after having been abandoned for a millennium. (The Greek *pandocheion*, curiously enough, turns out to be the word from which the modern Arabic *funduq*, hotel, is derived.) Thence we stepped onto a sacred way, the Via Sacra of about half a mile long that goes steeply up the hill toward the great church at its summit. Peasant families were harvesting the olives on either side of the path. With each step upward the broad panorama of the outspread Afrin Valley beyond us expanded even further.

While the architecture of the ensemble is Byzantine, the decoration still has classical elements, with florid Corinthian capitals strewn about on the ground and quite a number of them still atop their columns. They are executed with a certain freedom, often diverging from the standard arrangement of acanthus leaves in straight rows to show the same leaves moving sideways, as though being blown by a stiff breeze—a variation devised perhaps by some rebellious or bored local workman. Another idiosyncratic Syrian variation on classical norms (fig. 44).

Even in its ruined state the great church of St. Simeon retains its imposing aura; like the Umayyad Mosque, it is the work of a confident faith. The complex, built at a turning point in architectural history between the Roman and post-classical Byzantine periods, achieves a stylistic harmony, with a strong foretaste of the Gothic that was later to dominate ecclesiastical architecture (fig. 45). The church was conceived on a mammoth scale, composed not of one but of *four* basilicas, each large enough to be a sizeable church in its own right; they are arranged in the shape of a cross around an octagonal courtyard in which the famous pillar is given central pride of place. That idol itself has lost most of its glamour over the centuries, for so many pilgrims and tourists have chipped off hunks of it as souvenirs that it is a stubby little affair now, a mere six or seven feet tall (fig. 46).

We repaired down the hill to the café, where tables were spread out under sheltering evergreens and the proprietor was squeezing pomegranates in his big brass juicer. We settled down to glasses of juice, mint tea, and Drekish water, then sampled our host's homemade pomegranate paste, which he was selling in recycled plastic water bottles. He assured us it was an essential ingredient in local cuisine, but I was not sure I could find a use for it at home and declined to buy any, a decision I regretted when stirring up an eggplant dish a couple of months later. The proprietor's two little children were having a pretend tea party at a nearby table and came over to offer us a biscuit.

At length we got up and went back for a final look at Simeon's shrunken, unprepossessing old pillar. A glorious marmalade cat was lying atop it, dozing in the fading rays of the afternoon sun.

After the Islamic takeover in the Middle East, the Christian churches there were often referred to as "captive." This is a misleading term, for a great many of these churches continued to flourish under the Muslims, who interfered in their rites and liturgy considerably less than the Byzantine authorities had done. Even today a number of churches of astonishing antiquity are still in use.

Right across the valley from the great crusader fortress Krak des Chevaliers is the Monastery of St. George, for instance, where you first step from the modern quadrangle into the so-called "New Church"—nineteenth century, that is—then to the "Old Church," fourteenth century, and thence down a narrow stair into the sixth-century stone cells of the early monks. Going even further back there was a Greek temple on the spot, and St.

George is supposed to have appeared to the Emperor Justinian in a vision, urging him to build the place. We noticed there the sometimes poignant contrivances by which ancient objects are made to meet contemporary needs when funds are scarce: ornamental chandeliers that were clearly designed to have oil lamps appended have been rigged out for electricity and now sport curly low-energy light bulbs; the stone baptismal font, very ancient, has been fitted with a tin basin and a modern chrome faucet.

In Damascus I took to attending church services when the opportunity presented itself. At the Greek Orthodox patriarchate my first Sunday, the pews were about half full. I know nothing whatever about Greek Orthodox protocol but felt little compunction about attending as I was sure that, as with mainline Protestant churches in the United States and Anglican ones in England, they need all the bodies they can get—"bums on seats," as the English say. There was some very nice chanting. The Armenian Apostolic Orthodox Church down the street was a pretty little place with lots of incense and organ music. At one point someone came along each aisle, air-kissed each of us in turn, and said—in English to me—"Jesus Christ be with you." "And also with you," I replied awkwardly, being a sometime Episcopalian and not having any other responses ready to hand. There were some interesting types among the other congregants, including a few fashion-forward young girls in tight jeans, skimpy tops, and piled-up hair, sporting spike heels that would have done a drag queen proud.

The area immediately to the north of Damascus is rich in Christian sites and active Christian communities. In the town of Maaloula there are actually people who still speak Aramaic: the resistance to the Arabic language was so strong here that their Syriac version of Aramaic—the language spoken by Jesus—has never quite died out. It seems that Maaloula is the last place on earth where this is still a living language. The monastery of St. Sergius, perched atop Mount Maaloula, is one of the oldest in Syria, a Byzantine structure built on the site of a pagan temple. Descending from here through a deep, dramatic gorge, you can walk to the Greek Orthodox convent of St. Thecla. This lady was an early follower of St. Paul who heard his sermons on chastity and decided to preserve her own against her family's wishes. While she fled her intended bridegroom, it is said, the earth opened to make a path for her; this is the origin of the impressive ravine (fig. 47).

At nearby Seidnaya, the Convent of Our Lady of Seidnaya—a sixth-century edifice looming high on an outcropping over the town—houses an image of the Virgin said to be a very early copy of the one painted by St. Luke. Like many other Christian sites in Syria this is a pilgrimage spot for Muslims as well; the roots of the two faiths are so long and tangled, and they have so many saints, prophets, and holy men and women in common, that one eventually just gives up trying to keep it all straight. Seidnaya has ecclesiastical buildings even older than the Convent of Our Lady: there are the Chapel of St. Peter, converted from a Roman tomb, and the third-century Cherubim Monastery. Not far from town there is a cave that is supposed to have sheltered the prophet Elijah, with a chapel built alongside it.

Then there is Deir Mar Musa, a monastery high on a mountainside in the desert northeast of Damascus (fig. 48). The road becomes too steep for cars so you have to do the last mile on foot; suitcases and big backpacks are hauled up on a device something like a primitive ski lift. There are quite a few bags, too, because the place has become a popular stop on what remains of the Hippie Trail. The monastery, founded in the seventh century, rebuilt in the Middle Ages, and abandoned in the nineteenth century, was brought back to life in the 1980s by an Italian priest, Paolo dall'Oglio, and is now a contemplative community open to anyone willing to pitch in and help with cooking, cleaning, and other tasks. Peter and I were there with our daughters; a cloud of Armenian teenagers instantly descended on them and bore them off, peppering them with questions and pressing email addresses upon them. The walls of the tiny church are covered with marvelous medieval frescoes in a singular style, more Egyptian Coptic than Byzantine (plate 6).

At the Church of the Virgin's Belt—the al-Zunnar—in Homs, we were taken in hand by a chatty young man who related the strange history of the belt. The Virgin died in 56 A.D., he said, and three days later her body was carried to heaven by angels. This was witnessed by St. Thomas, though he happened to be in India at the time. St. Thomas asked her for a sign so he could prove to the other apostles what he had seen, and she passed down her belt. After St. Thomas's death the belt stayed in India until 394 A.D., when it was taken to Urfa (formerly Edessa) in modern Turkey, with the saint's relics, and a century later to St. Mary's Church in Homs. In due course, when "security began to get bad" (I took it that by this he meant the Arab conquest) the people of Homs buried the belt under the altar. Here it stayed until renovation work in 1852 when it was rediscovered—to great fanfare and rejoicing, according to our guide. For some reason it was then reburied and forgotten about all over again until 1953 when, as the church's pamphlet says, "God again willed that this valuable treasure be available for believers to receive its blessing," and it was unearthed by the local Patriarch. "The news of this discovery spread throughout the city of Homs, and people from all the Christian denominations flocked to the church to receive the blessing of the holy belt."

Finally, Ezraa. For the price of about a dollar I rode in a cramped minibus to this little town, about fifty miles south of Damascus in the Hauran. Here there are two sixth-century churches still in active use, and I headed up the hill for the half-mile walk from the bus stop to the old town. Everyone I passed said hello, and a beautiful little girl of eleven or twelve ran after me to ask my name.

I went first to the church that seems to get more press, the Greek Orthodox Church of St. George, called in Arabic Mar Jirjis. This, if you care to believe it, is the actual burial place of Mar Jirjis, whose tomb is displayed inside the building. He is a holy man to the Arabs as well as the Christians, supposed to have been a Palestinian soldier in the Roman army who tore up a copy of Diocletian's decree forbidding Christianity. How this political activist became the dragon-slayer of legend is still a mystery—unless perhaps the dragon is supposed to symbolize the Roman army. The great man's resting place is tucked with the usual Syrian casualness into a corner of what appears to be a storeroom.

Mar Jirjis is probably the oldest church in continual use in Syria; it was built in 515 on the site of a pagan temple, as can be deduced from the Greek inscription over the west door: "What was once an abode of demons has become a house of God; where once sacrifices were made to idols, there are now chairs of angels; where God was provoked to wrath, now he is propitiated." Architecturally Mar Jirjis is significant as one of the earliest examples of the centralized church, which is typically a square building topped with a circular dome (though Mar Jirjis is octagonal rather than square); along with the cathedral at Bosra, it pre-dates the better-known examples of the style in Constantinople, Hagia Sophia and the Church of SS. Sergius and Bacchus, and possibly helped to inspire them. What I found particularly charming about the place that early winter day was the fact that its pure and venerable profile was marred by a big, shiny, plastic Christmas tree that someone had affixed to the roof (fig. 49). These churches may be national monuments and historical wonders, but they are still very much working churches.

The priest, a plump and cynical fellow, showed up to give me a cursory tour, the collection box obviously at the top of his agenda. I moved on to the Greek Catholic Church of St. Elias, in use since 542. This was locked, but a friendly, one-armed man who spoke no English ran to get the *khoury*, the priest—Father Elias, a tall, distinguished-looking man in his fifties with shaky English but excellent French. He took me round the simple but perfectly conceived church, built in the black Hauran basalt like its neighbor Mar Jirjis. In his twenty years' service at the church, he had made a number of restorations and improvements such as removing much of the plaster and cement that had long obscured the original walls, and he talked about his plans for the future, which included turning a very ancient outbuilding into a library and hostel. As it was, he could not even afford a tourist pamphlet with photographs. It was another case of something I saw over and over again in Syria—staggering cultural riches but no capital for repair, enhancement, publicity, or tourist development.

We left the church, waving at the one-armed man who was now taking tea with a lady friend on a nearby rooftop; they lifted their glasses to us as we went by. Father Elias took me to his home for lunch, where I shared the midday meal with his wife and their three children: smiling eighteen-year-old Myra, studying for her *baccalaureate*, and two little fellows who looked like cartoon caricatures of naughty boys, one plump and one thin. Myra conversed with me in halting schoolgirl English, but the boys spoke broad American—"Because of computer games," said their mother. The plump one kept catching my eye and laughing conspiratorially. We consumed a large meal, every bite of which had come from the family garden, and when I left, Father Elias said to me, "Now you have a home every time you are in Syria. This is your home."

Most Westerners are under the impression that Syrians are fanatically Muslim, for this is the image our media seems determined to put across, but extreme religious enthusiasm was clearly more characteristic of pre-Muslim Syria: who could outdo the ascetic monks or the acolytes of the Syrian Goddess? The more extreme Islamic practices, such as requiring women to be heavily veiled, were not practiced during the early years of Islam. The impetus that caused Islam to turn in a more puritanical, "fundamentalist" direction was contact with fundamentalist Christendom in the form of the Frankish Crusaders—the *Franj*, as they became known throughout the Muslim world. When the European crusaders first arrived in the Muslim East at the very end of the eleventh century, the Syrian lands were ruled by a disorganized collection of Turkic princes, the Seljuks. In 1071 the Seljuk Turks had conquered Anatolia (modern Turkey) from the Byzantines at the Battle of Manzikert—an event that sent shock tremors through the Christian world—and in the next few years they had moved southward into Syria, taking Damascus and Jerusalem. By the time the Crusaders arrived a couple of decades later, the Seljuks were firmly installed, but the individual principalities were not unified and there was no sense of cohesion: as the Crusaders created city-states of their own (Antioch, Edessa, Jerusalem), the remaining Seljuk rulers—of Damascus, for instance, and Aleppo—were just as likely to form alliances with the Franj leaders against their fellow Muslims as vice-versa. They did not, in other words, share the Christians' view of the Crusades as a Holy War, and as long as they treated battles as skirmishes for land or plunder rather than as a religious challenge they were unable to hold back the Franj armies.

The Muslim leader who turned the tide was an Arabized Turk named Nur al-Din, the prince of Aleppo, son of the famous warrior prince Zengi. He gained success by finally uniting all the Muslim leadership under the concept of *jihad*. While Zengi had been a hard-living, hard-drinking character, Nur al-Din was pious and even puritanical, with the political astuteness to understand that only a common spiritual struggle could unify the disparate petty monarchs, each intent on his own interests. He promoted Sunni Islam with the touch of a skilled propagandist, providing in his own person the role model of the virtuous prince. Nur al-Din

> understood the invaluable role of psychological mobilization, and he therefore built a genuine propaganda apparatus. Several hundred men of letters, religious figures for the most part, were entrusted with the mission of winning the active sympathy of the people and of thereby forcing the leaders of the Arab world to flock to his banner . . .
>
> Nur al-Din supervised his corps of propagandists personally. He would commission poems, letters, and books, and always took care that they were released at the time when they would produce the desired effect. The princi-

ples he preached were simple: a single religion, Sunni Islam, which meant a determined struggle against all the various "heresies" . . . a single objective, *jihad*, to reconquer the occupied territories and above all to liberate Jerusalem.[37]

Nur al-Din brought military and political aspirations together under the banner of Sunni Islam. Until then, the region's holy men had been more concerned with fighting heresies within Islam than with waging jihad against the infidel; now their efforts were turned toward pushing back the Franj. Nur al-Din took Damascus from its Seljuk leader in 1154, and for the first time since the ninth century the two great cities of Damascus and Aleppo were united under one rule. Damascus had always remained a center of Sunni orthodoxy (as opposed to Aleppo, which veered toward Shi'ism), and Nur al-Din made it the capital of his jihad; Damascus now resumed its status as a great Sunni capital, a title it had lost upon the defeat of the Umayyads in 750 and the removal of the caliphate to Baghdad. Nur al-Din set out to promote a pure, ascetic vision of Sunni Islam, banning wine and even music in his military camps. The Shi'a and other heretics within Islam were marginalized and pressured to toe the line. In Damascus, the Christians and Jews were pushed into the eastern area of the city that they have occupied ever since.

The reigns of Nur al-Din, his famous successor Saladin, and Saladin's Ayyubid dynasty of rulers constituted a golden age for architecture in both Aleppo and Damascus, and a walk through either of those cities still gives a flavor of what things must have looked like in their heyday: it was Nur al-Din's achievement to merge the individual styles of the two cities into the distinctive Arab medieval style that still adorns them. The adoption of the *muqarnas* or honeycomb dome would prove one of the most lasting architectural features of the age, a style, originally Mesopotamian, that would come to grace not only Syrian structures but later monuments in Egypt and, perhaps most famously, the Alhambra in Spain. Its first appearance in Syria is over Nur al-Din's tomb in his Damascus madrasa. Another innovation of the period is the distinctively Syrian *ablaq* technique, the use of contrasting colors in alternating stripes—an obvious use to be made of the local proliferation, in equal quantities, of golden limestone and black basalt. This Damascene invention would prove an important element of later Mamluk and Ottoman design, and it eventually made its way not only to Spain, whose Muslim rulers adopted the technique in local style, but also to Christian Italy, where its characteristic gay stripes can still be seen on the cathedrals of Siena and Orvieto.

The creation of madrasas was central to the Sunni political-theological program of Nur al-Din and his successors: eleven of these religious schools were built in Damascus alone under Nur al-Din's aegis, and new ones continued to spring up throughout the Ayyubid and Mamluk periods. The madrasa served as a combination school and mosque where students could live and imbibe the principles of Islamic law taught by learned clerics. They were generally endowed by leading citizens or rulers as a *waqf*, or foundation, and the founder would be given the privilege, after his death, of occupying a tomb in a prime spot within. Nur al-Din's own madrasa-mausoleum complex, the Madrasa Nuriye al-Kubra in Damascus, set the pattern for what followed throughout Syria and Egypt and can still be visited today, though the structure of the madrasa itself has been somewhat diminished. In a note of typically Syrian eclecticism, two Byzantine columns, complete with acanthus-leaf capitals, appear inside the austere Muslim tomb chamber.

I found something both comical and endearing about the Madrasa Adiliye, which was begun in Nur al-Din's time and finished in time to house the tomb of al-Adil "the Just," Saladin's brother and successor. Al-Adil is famous in Crusading history not only through the reflected glamour of his brother but as a sympathetic, chivalric figure in his own right: his brother's deputy at the Muslim reconquest of Jerusalem in 1187, he was famously merciful to the Christian prisoners. He was also a shrewd statesman and a judicious diplomat who exchanged chivalrous courtesies with his titular foe, Richard the Lionheart, and even entertained Richard's idea that al-Adil should marry Richard's sister so that the couple could rule Jerusalem jointly— a Saracen-Franj merger designed to bring peace to the region. (This quixotic plot came to nothing, as the lady was *not* amused at the prospect of marrying an infidel.) Tourists are welcome to wander into the madrasa, which is still in use, and see al-Adil's tomb. Both Catherine and I are bibliophiles and accustomed to living in an awkward clutter of books, but the mess in the Adil-iye library was something to behold: disorganized sheaves of paper, books popping out of shelves and onto the floor, some of them arranged in piles right up to the edge of the great man's tomb, which was nearly obscured in all the mess (fig. 50). The friendly guardian gave us tea and chatted away in incomprehensible Arabic. Here al-Adil the Just was remembered and honored, but he seemed to have become more a part of the madrasa's furniture than an object of veneration. Not a bad posterity.

Nur al-Din and his successors also built hospitals, or *maristans*. The hospital as we know it today is actually an Islamic invention, in keeping with the idea of Islam as a comprehensive social system and way of life in which care for the sick and unfortunate is a moral imperative of the community. Like the madrasa, the maristan was funded by a *waqf*, and admission to the hospital was free of charge and open to all. Charity, after all, is one of the five pillars of Islam: not a moral obligation, as in Christianity, but a direct command. Many of the practices still followed in Western hospitals today were Arab innovations, including the division between inpatients and outpatients, the dispensing pharmacy, the separation of different diseases into different wards, and the use of patients to teach medical students.

The Muslim idea of health care for all as society's obligation has also, I think, indelibly colored Western thinking, making us—yes, even in America—not quite comfortable with the principles of capitalism when they are applied to medicine. While we were in Syria the debate was raging back home over President Obama's proposed health-care bill, a process followed with horrified fascination by Syrians. My young friend Saeed almost wailed: "Why would anyone *want* a health care system that lets people die if they don't have any money?" The answer, I ventured, is that no one really does, not even ideologically pure American capitalists, which is why the issue is so troubled and apparently insoluble within our financial system. Americans who cannot understand the sympathy Hezbollah has inspired in Lebanon and Syria should look beyond its terrorist activities. Hezbollah, Arabic for "God's party," has from its beginnings committed itself to providing essential health and social services: in Lebanon, where it now holds a significant number of seats in Parliament, it sponsors schools and hospitals, helps farmers, provides clean drinking water, and organizes garbage removal, all in places that have received few such services from the national government.

The beautiful Maristan Nur al-Din in Damascus, founded by that monarch in 1154, still stands (though substantially rebuilt in later centuries) and functioned as a working hospital until the nineteenth century; medieval Arab medical ideas, very forward-thinking for their time, are incorporated in the architecture both here and in the fourteenth-century Bimaristan Arghun in Aleppo, which is open as a museum of science and medicine and whose architectural features incorporate the ideals of the humane treatment of the mentally ill that prevailed in the Arab world at that time. The sounds of water and music were deemed beneficial for soothing the patients' shattered nerves, and in the Bimaristan Arghun a cooling fountain flowed in the courtyard into a pool of fish; patients would sit in the *iwan* enjoying the flowing water and the music played on the oud, a stringed instrument that anticipated the lute and guitar and is still popular in Muslim countries—lots of Syria's nicer restaurants feature an oud player at dinner. Music was traditionally thought to have healing properties, and each string of the oud was associated with a metaphysical concept or temper, the sound of each string thought to stir a different emotion. When all the strings were plucked in the correct manner, a curative process was supposed to be effected.

The image of the lunatics enjoying music and flowing water is a pretty one, but medical practice degenerated after the glory days of the medieval caliphate. By the time Gertrude Bell visited Syria in 1911, she was greeted with a horrific scene at the Bimaristan al-Malik ez-Zahir in Aleppo, a hospital for the criminally insane: "Through narrow window slits, feeble shafts of light fall into the dank well beneath and shiver through the iron bars that close the cells of the lunatics. They sit more like beasts than men, loaded with chains in their dark cages, and glower at each other through the bars; and one was sick and moaned upon his wisp of straw, and one rattled his chains and clawed at the bars as though he would cry for mercy, but he had forgotten human speech."[38]

Nur al-Din meant to be inclusive in his Sunni revival. As well as providing care for the sick and indigent he drew the mystic Sufis into the fold and built monasteries, *khanqahs*, for them: the remains of his Khanqah Abu al-Bayan can still be seen in Bab Touma Street in Damascus. Sufism is a spiritual practice that ideally enables the practitioner to attain a more direct contact with the deity than is achieved through formal religious practices. It developed in the early ninth century and was much influenced by the asceticism and celibacy of Christian monks: the name Sufi even derives from the word for wool (*suf*) which the mystics wore in imitation of these forebears. The Sufis eventually developed an organization vaguely approaching monasticism and the monastic orders, and this organization began in Syria.

The whirling of the Sufi dervishes is a well-known image across the world, and it was one thing I had *no* particular desire to see: it has always seemed to me intrusive and voyeuristic to witness someone's religious ecstasy performed as a kind of showbiz stunt, and I hate watching anything that smacks of "native dances." But so many people recommended the experience that I finally gave in and was not sorry to have done so, for the rhythmic athleticism of the dance is spectacular. There is clearly no religious onus attached to performing the dance in public. The performer at our restaurant was a portly middle-aged man of tremendous dignity, who seemed enveloped in an aura of spiritual well-being. The spinning was mesmeric even to the uninitiated; the dance, and *sama*, the art of spiritual listening, are supposed to lift the watcher into the same trance that the dancer experiences, and I must say it came close. I was interested to note that the spectators were not by any means all tourists. In fact there was a great-looking couple at the next table, fleshy bon vivants—the man with a huge belly, his wife bursting out of a clinging, low-cut, bright dress. Rather than experiencing *sama* these two seemed to be simply enjoying a festive night out, occasionally shouting their approval of the dervish and sucking on an outsized hookah.

This sort of mysticism is the very antithesis of the religious fanaticism that terrifies the secular. In fact fanaticism among educated Syrians—as among educated Americans and Europeans—seems to be perceived as somehow *infra dig*, in Islam the province of puritanical Wahhabist Saudis (Bedouin rubes with oil money and a smattering of first-generation sophistication) or of the Shi'a who definitely stand out in mostly Sunni Syria, personifying the kind of overheated fervor once associated with the stylites and other histrionic early Christians. Ten kilometers south of Damascus center, the Sayyida Zeinab Mosque presents the same circus-sideshow atmosphere that must once have prevailed at Cyrrhus and St. Simeon. All the guidebooks sneer a bit at the garish architecture and décor of this king-size modern mosque, built with Iranian funds. It *is* a bit glitzy, dome and walls decked out in real gold and glittery mirrored ceilings that look as though disco balls might drop down from them at any moment. But a country that has given the world Las Vegas, Graceland, and Trump Tower has no room to scoff at other nations' lapses in taste.

I was not sorry to don one of the cloaks that are available to visitors, for that morning I had committed the unspeakable fashion "don't" of wearing a bright orange bra under a translucent green shirt, and had attracted some bemused glances. Wandering into the mosque I stumbled inadvertently into the inner sanctum where none but the faithful are allowed. This is the space from which women (the men have a different spot) have access to what is supposed to be the tomb of Zeinab, sister of the Shi'a hero Husayn and granddaughter of Muhammed (though a shrine in Cairo claims the same distinction).

Here, at long last, I found the kind of extreme religious enthusiasm that Westerners associate with the Muslim world. Women sobbed and wept, kissed the door as they entered, kissed the grille in front of the tomb, kissed the walls. They later wiped off the spittle with little green cloths provided especially for the purpose, but it still seemed a remarkably unsanitary procedure considering the hysteria over swine flu that was at that moment sweeping the world. I was fascinated to see that they seemed able to turn the tears on and off at will, like a water tap; they would weep visibly—real tears—while going through their ritual prostrations and kissing whatever there was to be kissed, then immediately revert to their normal behavior with business-like briskness. One mother with a little girl of about four or five I found especially interesting. Both of them were weeping, the child looking to her mother for affirmation as though wanting to make sure she was getting it right, in the way that children do; they prayed together, performed their prostrations, and then turned away, cheerful once more.

As with all ecstatic sects, one wonders how much of the emotion is genuine and how much is mere convention—and what do we mean by "genuine," anyway? Two images that have always horrified skeptics are the Shi'a penitents ceremonially flogging themselves at Ashura parades commemorating the death of Husayn at Karbala, and the Catholic penitents at Seville's Holy Week procession, togged out in robes bearing an unsettling resemblance to Klan regalia. Something about the kind of emotional excess on show at Sayyida Zeinab pushes the same buttons. Is the contrast with the restrained dignity of the Sunnis indicative of some fundamental difference in the two sects' approach to spirituality? Can it be compared with the traditionally striking contrast between Protestant and Catholic modes of display? Or, nowadays, with the difference between mainline American Protestantism and charismatic evangelical Christianity?

In any case there are plenty of Shi'a holy sites in Syria. An archaeologist acquaintance of mine who has worked on digs near several Shi'a sites explained it rather bluntly: "The Shi'ite pilgrims follow all the places Husayn's head touched down on its way to the Caliph at Damascus after Kerbala. The head of Husayn was supposedly exhibited in the Great Mosque and *supposedly* buried there. They probably just threw it out, I guess.

"Then all these relatives schlepped along on the way to Damascus, some died along the way, and they set up shrines. There's even a shrine called *Mashhad al Tilh*—the Shrine of the Miscarriage! That's where one lady had a miscarriage and bled on the ground. Now the country is full of these little shrines for all these members of the house of the Prophet."

I had certainly noticed groups of Shi'a pilgrims, usually ancient yokels from the countryside under the care of tall, turbaned clerics, who look exactly like the Iranian mullahs of American nightmare but herded their wards about in a motherly fashion. These old people gaped and gawped at the big city sights; at the underpass near the Damascus Citadel, we saw two old men, nervous at the prospect of mounting an escalator, hold hands and venture onto it, giggling.

The archaeologist also had some thoughts on the nature of Shi'ism, which he likened to American values in some respects. "The Shi'ite concept of heroism is similar to the American," he said. "In most cultures, a hero is someone who kills a lot of people. The Shi'ites think a hero is someone who has been murdered, who has been martyred. The Americans are the same. When they talk about a hero it is usually someone who has been killed."

I was struck by this thought, and by a certain exhibitionism shared by Shi'a Islam and American evangelical Protestantism, in both of which systems the public aspect of faith seems to have trumped the private. Sunni attitudes to Shi'a theatricality were personified in Muhammed Four, who would purse his lips in disapproval every time he witnessed such displays. One particularly bizarre shrine in the Barada Valley earned his special displeasure: the tomb of Abel—yes, that Abel!—high on a bare windswept peak of the Anti-Lebanon mountains.

One might have thought that such a spot would be of interest to all monotheists, but for some reason it seemed to be frequented exclusively by Shi'a Muslims: the parking lot was jammed with tour buses from Iraq, Iran, and even Russia. Vendors nearby were doing a land-office business in bolts of fabric, of all things, with black-veiled ladies eagerly fingering cloth in various shades of—what else?—black. Muhammed Four told us to watch our purses. This was the first and last time he ever gave us this warning, so we felt it might have had something to do with his feelings for the Shi'a. Inside the shrine, the weeping Shi'a circled an immense marble casket containing the bones of the patriarch. This was at least fifteen feet long. (Muhammed Four reminded me that according to the Old Testament, Adam and his family were giants, *nephilim*.) Could this be serious? When was this tomb discovered, anyway? What made people think it was Abel? When was the last time someone had opened it to have a look inside?

Muhammed Four told us a joke:

"Two thieves stole a large amount of money and wondered where to hide it. Eventually they buried it in the ground and put a gravestone on top of it, and told everyone it was the grave of a holy man they invented, named al-Azzaz.

"Everything was fine for a while, but soon a lot of people started visiting the grave and praying to al-Azzaz, the great saint and healer. Before they know it the place had become a pilgrimage center for miles around.

"Eventually, one of the thieves decided to check on the buried money, so one night he dug under the grave. There was no money! It was gone! So he went to his friend, the second thief.

"'Our money is gone! What could have happened to it?'

"'I don't know, I don't know!' shouted the second thief, seemingly distraught. 'No one in the world knew about it except for you and me, and I swear it wasn't me—by the bones of al-Azzaz!'"

Extremist sects exist even among the already extreme Shi'a, and of these perhaps the most fascinating to outsiders has been that of the Assassins. They were an offshoot of the Isma'ilis, who themselves had split off from the mainstream of Shi'a Islam in the ninth century. The Isma'ilis were extremely powerful for a time, founding the city of Cairo and establishing the Fatimid caliphate that ruled North Africa, the Eastern Mediterranean, Sicily, and the western part of the Arabian peninsula until Saladin crushed the remnants of Fatimid power in the twelfth century.

The Assassins were the first modern terrorists, and their ability to spread fear has never been equalled, not even by the I.R.A. or al-Qaeda. The sect was founded in 1090 by Hasn Ibn al-Sabbah, a Persian Shi'a who sought to purify the lands newly conquered by the Sunni Seljuk Turks. His methods, honed in Persia and later exported to Syria, still raise a shudder. His minions would disguise themselves as merchants and snoop around the city or town where their intended victim lived, getting a feeling for his comings and goings. Then they would strike— usually in a mosque or other public place, for as with modern terror attacks, the more witnesses there were, the greater the desired effect tended to be. The Assassin himself, like the modern suicide bomber, usually died in the process. Therefore the training given these men had to be very strict. Horror stories of the Assassins' iron discipline were legion. The crusading prince Henri de Champagne was once invited by the Assassin leader, Rashid al-Din Sinan, for a visit at his mountain castle. Showing off to his distinguished guest, the Old Man of the Mountain (as he was called) shouted out a command and two of his followers instantly leapt out of the window to their deaths. The Old Man politely inquired whether Henry would like the performance to be repeated, an offer the prince hastily declined.

The Assassins carried out some spectacular hit jobs, one of the most successful being the murder of the Franj prince Conrad of Montferrat, Lord of Tyre, during the Third Crusade. Far more often, however, they colluded with the Franj and struck instead against their fellow-Muslims: in the early twelfth century, while Syria was struggling against the Franj invaders, the Assassins bumped off the emirs of Damascus and Aleppo and, most destructively to the Muslim cause, Ibn al-Khashshab, the inspirational *qadi* of Aleppo, who was attempting to unite the Syrian Muslims against the invading Crusaders. They even made an attempt on the life of Saladin during the great general's siege of Aleppo, with four Assassins mugging him in his tent and managing to slice his cheek with a knife before he got away.

Fear spread throughout Saladin's army, and he decided to end the situation for good by laying siege to Masyaf, the Assassins' Syrian stronghold—but then, mysteriously, he lifted the siege after only a few days. The most popular explanation of this change of heart was terror: he woke one night in his tent to find on his pillow a poisoned dagger and some hot cakes. Just why hot cakes should be threatening I couldn't quite figure out—in fact I tasted a lot of delicious ones that were being sold all over the place during Eid—but evidently this was a threat that made sense to Saladin, for from then on he avoided the Assassins. It was left to the ruthless Mamluk Sultan Baybars, the man who booted the last of the Crusaders out of Syria, to finally destroy the Assassins' network, and that was not until nearly a century after Saladin's attempt.

How do we get the word "assassin"? No one really knows. The Crusaders claimed that it derived from "hashish," the Arabic word for "grass," because the Old Man's minions were high on some kind of weed when they committed their terrible deeds. Most people now consider this dubious. In any case, wouldn't the choreographed style of the assassinations observed by the Crusaders require that the killers be at a *heightened* state of alertness rather than the reverse? Nevertheless, the word "assassin," meaning a political murderer rather than a Muslim heretic, passed into the European languages.

It's possible that this was the first appearance of the Mad Mullah in the world's consciousness. No one, I think, is more terrifying to the average human than people who are really *not afraid to die*, especially when it is in a cause we don't understand or sympathize with. The definition of "fanaticism," I imagine, must be passionate commitment to a cause not one's own; take the average American's horror of Japanese kamikazes during World War II as compared with their admiration for the leaders of doomed commando operations on the Allied side. The Isma'ili Assassin made an impression Christendom has never forgotten; he is surely the first example, and the prototype, for the Muslim suicide bomber who haunts the popular imagination of the West today.

Modern Isma'ilis are respectable citizens who make up about ten percent of Muslims worldwide and whose leader, the Aga Khan, is a paragon of good works. One of his special projects, the Aga Khan Trust for Culture, is bringing significant amounts of money and expertise to historic sites in the Middle East where the need for responsible stewardship is huge and funds are usually very limited. In Syria the trust has undertaken the conservation and revitalization of the Aleppo Citadel, the Castle of Saladin (the Crusaders' Château de Saône), and Masyaf, the Assassin stronghold.

Masyaf today is almost impossible to reconcile with its history as the redoubt of the fearsome Assassins. It is small by Syrian standards, cozier and more domestic than the Crusader castles—I'm even tempted to say *cute*. Can these really be the windows from which Rashid al-Din Sinan's fanatic followers jumped to their deaths? The castle would not look out of place in Belgium or Luxembourg, with its golden stones, many recycled from an earlier Byzantine site, slumbering in the sunshine. The wealth of the Aga Khan Trust is evident from the excellent condition of everything here, the tourist-friendly layout, and even clean bathrooms—with toilet paper, *mirabile dictu*. The trust has not only done vital engineering work on the castle but has also created a visitor center and a guidebook and has trained its personnel to a high level of professionalism. After all, the Isma'ilis have a rich cultural, philosophical, architectural, and artistic heritage, which includes far more than the bizarre Assassins, and they are proud of it.

Toward the end of our stay in Syria, Muhammed Four offered to take us on a final tour of sights in the outskirts of Damascus. One place in particular he wished us to see. "Last time I went there, I swore I would never go back," he said, "but for you I will do so."

"Are you sure *we* want to do it?" I asked. "What's wrong with it?"

"You will see."

It was quite a trip. First through Malki, the posh diplomatic neighborhood. Interesting boutiques with names like Gosh Cosmetics and Just a Women. The various embassies were lodged in nice-looking villas—all except the American, which was set off by itself, swathed in barbed wire and bristling with guards. Its only near neighbor was Iraq—"safe here under the American wing," Muhammed Four commented dryly. We wanted to photograph it, but he warned us that one of the U.S. Embassy guards might take that amiss.

Then through the smart resort area of Yafour. Like many neighborhoods here that are expensive and considered desirable, it looked a grim place, with forbidding gated communities and bombastic entrance statements. But soon these thinned out and we were in real country, with an occasional little roach coach by the side of the road serving tea and cakes, or more permanent structures selling local specialties: pickles, apricots, peppers, grape paste, pomegranate syrup, honey, dried yogurt. Then we were in the Wadi Barada—the Barada river gorge—with the mouths of ancient Roman tombs dotting the hillside above us. Much to Muhammed Four's discomfiture I climbed the steep precipice into these little caves to get some pictures (fig. 51); he stood unhappily watching my progress through field glasses until I was safely back on level ground. Then upward onto the

Jebel Qassioun, the mountain above Damascus from which you can see the city spread below around the remains of the oasis that originally gave it birth. Some claim that Abraham himself, the founding prophet of all three of the great monotheistic religions, was born on this mountain.

We were now in a neighborhood built on what appeared to be the steepest part of the slope, with streets heading directly upward toward the mountaintop. Muhammed Four's Peugeot would go no further; he parked it, and we sought out a driver whose job it was to shuttle passengers up and down the narrow streets in a miniature pickup truck. We clambered into the back with some effort and went on a real Mr. Toad's Wild Ride, zipping up the narrow passageways at a terrifying pace and all but pinning the pedestrians to the wall as we went. School had just let out, and there were crowds of little boys heading home for lunch, carrying loaves of fresh bread to their families. As so often, I wondered at the adaptability of human beings and their willingness to live in the most unlikely spots, for this was even more inconvenient than Telegraph Hill in San Francisco and without that neighborhood's compensations. How do you get groceries, bags, furniture up these inclines? What do old people do—never leave the house?

Then suddenly the road became too narrow even for this supercharged little vehicle, and we continued on foot. Now I understood Muhammed Four's aversion to the spot, for it was a long, long slog: first up through narrow streets that were more like staircases than thoroughfares, then onto the bare mountainside, where steps had been cleft into the rock (fig. 52). Up and up and up. My thrice-weekly sessions at the gym were paying off, but Catherine and Muhammed Four, sedentary people, huffed and puffed and groaned. Now we were emerging onto a rocky summit that was as close to the heavens as you could get around here, surely the ultimate high place of all the holy high places we had seen.

This was the Cave of Forty Men, the Arbaeen—the very spot, so it is thought, where Cain killed Abel, or where Qabil killed Habil to give them their Arabic names. Some of the tales in the Muslim Hadiths are extremely close to the Genesis version; here is their telling of the first murder:

> Recite to them the truth of the story of the two sons of Adam. Behold! they each presented a sacrifice [to Allah]: It was accepted from one, but not from the other. Said the latter: "Be sure I will slay thee." "Surely," said the former, "Allah doth accept the sacrifice of those who are righteous.
>
> "If thou dost stretch thy hand against me, to slay me, it is not for me to stretch my hand against thee to slay thee: for I do fear Allah, the cherisher of the worlds.
>
> "For me, I intend to let thee draw on thyself my sin as well as thine, for thou wilt be among the companions of the fire, and that is the reward of those who do wrong."
>
> The selfish soul of the other led him to the murder of his brother: he murdered him, and became himself one of the lost ones.
>
> Then Allah sent a raven, who scratched the ground, to show him how to hide the shame of his brother. "Woe is me!" said he; "Was I not even able to be as this raven, and to hide the shame of my brother?" Then he became full of regrets.

A little mosque has been built next to the cave, and the Imam, who must lead a quiet life in this solitary place, showed us in. The cave had an air of great antiquity; it seemed that people had been worshiping here a long, long time. The Imam told us that after Abel's murder the mountain itself shook in outrage for seven days until the wall of the cave opened, mouthlike, to scream. And sure enough there is a gap in the wall, very much like a mouth with a tongue protruding. Something resembling a handprint is on the ceiling nearby; this is where the Angel Gabriel, or Jabriel in Arabic, lifted his hand to hold up the roof of the cave. It has been smoothed over the centuries by generations of sightseers and pilgrims who have placed their own hands on the holy spot.

Qabil took Habil's body to the Anti-Lebanon mountains and, following a raven's example, buried him; that was the place where we had seen the giant tomb and the Shi'a shrine. But the cave itself remained a holy place, perhaps the oldest known holy place in this very old land. Legends have accrued to it, usually in a spirit of ecumenicism. Abraham is said to have prayed in the cave. So have Jacob, Moses, Jesus, and even St. George, lest any Christians feel excluded. Pilgrims of all three faiths still come to pray here. Muhammed Four performed his ritual genuflections before the altar; Catherine and I, though not believers, were nevertheless impressed by the place's aura of ancient sanctity, and by its smiling Imam. We sat there in the falling afternoon shadows, savoring the utter silence broken only by the cawing of a circling bird—a descendent perhaps of Qabil's raven? The tomb of our Imam's predecessor lay nearby; his cat stretched, eyes narrowed, along the stone wall. This, we thought, might be the very birthplace of monotheism. Considering all the trouble it has caused in the world, it seems a peaceful spot.

Figure 35. Easter in Damascus.

Figure 36. Sweet shop.

Figure 37. Footprints at Ain Dara.

Figure 38. Lion at Ain Dara.

Figure 39. A lion at Damascus Museum.

Figure 40. Catherine with a Tell Halaf man.

Figure 41. Catherine and Arthur at Apamea.

Figure 42. Arthur at Serjilla.

Figure 43. Serjilla.

Figure 44. Acanthus leaves at Qalaat Simaan.

Figure 45. Qalaat Simaan.

Figure 46. Simeon's pillar.

Figure 47. St. Thecla's gorge.

Figure 48. Mar Musa.

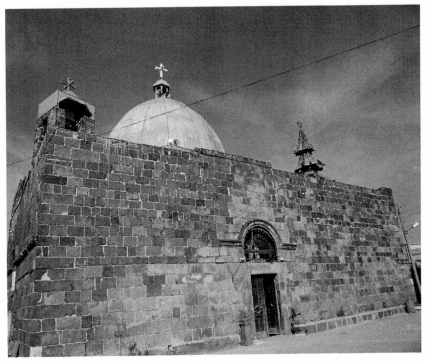

Figure 49. Mar Jirjis with a Christmas tree.

Figure 50. Library at Madrasa Adiliye.

Figure 51. A Roman tomb at Wadi Barada.

Figure 52. Steps leading up Mt. Qassioun to cave of the Arbaeen.

5 ❖ *Fighting*

Syria has been fought over for millennia. Strange, considering how much of the land is rocky and barren. There are traces of these past wars everywhere. We were astounded, for instance, while driving on the highway from Homs to Damascus, to see a sign for Qadesh, the site of one of the most famous battles of antiquity—in fact the largest chariot battle ever fought, a titanic clash between Egyptians and Hittites more than three thousand years ago. Ramses II's famous relief panels and inscriptions at Abu Simbel, Karnak, and Luxor have spread the fame of this battle, which he grandiloquently claimed as a great victory. And it was accepted as such until the twentieth century, when new evidence indicated that it was more of a tie and might even have been a modest win for the Hittite army. Like countless successful leaders throughout history, Ramses knew that making people believe you won is almost as good as actually winning, and he also knew that great artists create great propaganda: the reliefs are beautiful works of art that have created an indelible picture of Ramses triumphing over his groveling, cringing enemies.

Hafiz al-Asad took up this lesson, but his artistic choices were not as felicitous as Ramses'. The Tishreen Panorama outside of Damascus was perhaps the weirdest and in its way the most exotic sight I was to see in Syria. It seemed to embody modern Syria's identity crisis, demonstrating all the contradictions that bedevil the country's efforts to find its place in the world. There is the need to be seen as militarily strong; the wish to be loved and to be perceived as a peacemaker; the desperate desire to prove to the world that Israel, not Syria, is the aggressor in the region and that Syrians caught up in the Arab-Israeli struggle are—well not *victims*, exactly, because that wouldn't fit the desired image, but definitely more sinned against than sinning.

Outside the building is displayed plenty of booty from the '73 war: captured Israeli jeeps, tanks, missiles; wrecked helicopters; pulverized aircraft. (One horrifically twisted hunk of metal is labeled "crash of fantom war plane: America made.") There's also a Czech-made MIG-21 and the space capsule used by Syria's first astronaut, Muhammed Faris, when he embarked on a Soviet-Syrian space venture in 1987. A giant bronze statue of Hafiz al-Asad, fist raised in triumph, looms in front of the building's entrance (fig. 53).

There is something very un-Syrian-looking about this structure, which is more reminiscent of a California mega-church or funeral parlor than a Middle Eastern museum. It made more sense to me when my guide Muthanna said it was designed by a North Korean team, the same group responsible for the Victorious Fatherland Liberation War Museum in Pyongyang. Hence the never-never-land air of clean sterility, the international totalitarian kitsch style, and the truly weird paintings, one in particular—rather in the style of 1950s Maoist propaganda art—called "Patriotic Union Portrait," an aesthetically improved Hafiz al-Asad flanked by Syrians of every ethnic group and sector of society.

Even more sinister were the hundreds of oaths of fealty various underlings had signed to Hafiz al-Asad—*in blood*. The florid red signatures jumped from the page with rude violence. Did Asad have any idea how medieval this would look to the rest of the world? What is the purpose of displaying them—to instill fear in the populace? I doubt it, because the current president, Bashar al-Asad, cultivates a pacific, modern image totally at odds with such ancient barbarism. Is the purpose simply to show how devoted everyone was to the defunct president? Who can say?

In contrast to all these notes of belligerence and triumphalism are the paintings (also North Korean kitsch) of various key moments in Syrian history—all chosen, it seems, to emphasize Syria's role as a peacemaker. There is the King of Ebla making a peace treaty with the King of the North in the third millennium B.C., possibly the first peace treaty in human history. There are Zenobia and Wahballath in the Roman theater at Palmyra, announcing the city's freedom to the assembled Senate. There is Saladin accepting homage from the defeated Frankish leaders after the Battle of Hattin: both the Dome of the Rock and the Church of the Holy Sepulchre are visible in the background, indicating, as Muthanna told me, Saladin's inclusivity and clemency to all faiths.

The panorama itself is surprisingly effective, a 360-degree-perspective sound and light show re-enacting the 1973 battle in which the Syrians, storming the Golan Heights, took back the town of Quneitra, which the Israelis had seized in 1967. Seeing the whole thing in 3-D made sense of the battle, and of the geography of the place. I could finally understand that recapturing this small area, which is all that the Syrians achieved from the war, was more than a symbolic victory. For the spit of land is a strategic spot surrounded on three sides by Syrian territory, and the watchtower there provided Israel with a perfect position from which to spy on nearby Damascus. The panorama purposely emphasizes Israeli atrocities: in the town of Quneitra schools, hospitals, mosques, and Christian churches were all destroyed, and the creators of the panorama make much of this. For similar purposes Damascus has decided that the actual town of Quneitra should be left in ruins, just as it looked after the 1973 ceasefire, when the Israelis, expelled, went about destroying the town and taking away anything that might conceivably be of value. The Syrians have kept Quneitra, now in a UN-monitored demilitarized zone, as a sort of museum of Israeli aggression, quite an effective propaganda tool.

Syria is covered with the scars of past battles, to the point where a trip around the country amounts to a lesson in the history of defensive building. Justinian's massive fortifications we have seen. The castle-builders of the Middle Ages took it all a step further. A tour around the great Syrian castles, Crusader and otherwise, demonstrates that competitive castle-building escalated at that time into something of an arms race, with the largest of these—the Aleppo Citadel, Krak des Chevaliers, and other strongholds in Palestine and Jordan—becoming all but impregnable. "The development of castle architecture must be seen as the result of a continuing dialectic between attack and defense which gave the advantages sometimes to one, sometimes to the other," says Hugh Kennedy, a historian of Crusader castle-building.[1] Franks and Muslims learned from one another; as soon as an innovation was seen to be effective, it was eagerly adopted by the other side, then improved upon. And of course the Franks had special needs, special requirements for defensive building. Short on manpower, they had to have castles that were particularly strong and easy to defend and which were at the same time large enough to function as independent towns that could live without having to count on the cooperation of the surrounding countryside.

The usual technique of siege warfare was to blockade a castle and starve out the defenders. As a result the castles grew bigger and bigger, so that a large defending army could hold out for months. Krak des Chevaliers is the granddaddy of all these castles, larger and more massive in style than anything in Europe, dominating the Homs Gap in the Jebel Ansariyya mountain range that leads to the Mediterranean coast—entirely outsize and out-of-scale. It is almost impossible to convey one's first impression of it, driving over the hill to see it in the distance, spread across its wide spur of mountain (fig. 54, plate 7). "As the Parthenon is to Greek temples and Chartres to Gothic cathedrals," gushed architectural historian T. S. R. Boase, "so is the

Krak des Chevaliers to medieval castles, the supreme example, one of the great buildings of all time."[2]

Originally built by an emir of Homs, it was taken over by the Franj after the First Crusade and eventually given to the Knights Hospitaller, a secular order pledged to aid and support the Crusading presence in the Middle East. They rebuilt and expanded it until it could keep a garrison of 2000 soldiers going for months, with nine cisterns inside for water as well as a windmill, enormous ovens, and a very deep well. The cobbled, stone-vaulted passageways are wide and high enough to take heavy horse traffic (fig. 55). As the decades after the First Crusade passed and the Franj presence in Outremer ("overseas," the French word for the Crusader states) began to look as though it might be permanent, "The size of castles tended to increase, particularly when the Military Orders built castles for themselves or took over castles from the lay nobility," wrote Sir Steven Runciman, the historian of the Crusades. "In the castles of the Orders there were no ladies to be accommodated; and though high officials might be provided with elegant quarters, every resident was there for a military purpose. The larger fortresses, such as Krak or Athlit, were military towns capable of housing several thousand fighting men and the servants necessary for such a community . . ."[3]

What's so surprising when you visit Krak is how *Western* the place looks, how incredibly French—so French, indeed, that when the *Service des antiquités* set about restoring the castle under the Mandate they actually declared the place a "monument of France." For by the time of Krak's thirteenth-century renovation by the Hospitallers, a new style had swept Outremer, brought from Europe by the French King Louis IX when he came East on his disastrous crusade. Krak's beautiful chapel shows the transition from Romanesque to Gothic; the loggia with its ogival vaulting and the great hall are purely Gothic (fig. 56). We found it somehow touching that the Gothic love of ornament had made its mark even on this grimly functional place. One room was incongruously decorated with a band of rosettes: it looked like someone's fantasy of Rapunzel's bower. Outside, the five defensive towers rise high into the sky, joined by the smooth curtain walls designed to provide no possible toehold for an invader.

It was hard to see how this fortress ever could have been taken. Nur al-Din was defeated in his attempt to storm it in 1163; Saladin wisely bypassed it on his rampage up the coastal area after Hattin. It was only in 1271, its defending forces reduced to a mere 200, that Baybers succeeded in forcing its surrender.

We stayed at the Hotel Baybers nearby, looking out from our room on what I suppose was the most outrageously dramatic view I have ever had in a hotel. The castle in all its massive glory was right in our face, only a few hundred feet away across a ravine. Steep hillsides with undulating terracing rose all around (fig. 57). It was a funny little hotel, so inexpensive that I felt sad the owners hadn't capitalized on the incomparable view. They sold a few cheap tchotchkes and had a stash of used European books they offered for free. Arthur even managed to find one in English, a tattered old Charlie Chan paperback Catherine and I practically tore to shreds in our eagerness to get first dibs. The owner sold beer, and in the bar a jolly English backpacking family caroused far into the night. The three of us tested several of the local restaurants while we were there, all good but unpretentious to put it mildly, with their bare floors and fluorescent lighting. One, run by what appeared to be a pair of male lovers, was like all gay-run businesses, just *that* little bit better than the rest. They served a lovely lunch on the terrace overlooking the valley, with an array of delicate vegetables and the best "bolo"—at least that's what it sounded like—I had on the trip: a sort of lemonade mixed up in the blender with fresh mint, looking like pesto sauce but refreshing and delicious. As we ate we were surrounded by cats who climbed onto our laps and wreathed round our feet. When our elegantly made-up host came out, I was afraid he might get angry at us for feeding them, but all he did was toss a big chicken leg to the largest feline, apparently his special pet. Beneath us, in the little garden full of fruit trees, two kittens chased a butterfly.

Homosexuality is officially a crime in Syria, but I saw plenty of men on my travels who appeared to be openly gay. There is conflicting testimony about levels of toleration. The website globalgayz.com says that the law against homosexuality or acts "against nature" (Article 520 of the 1949 penal code) are "de facto suspended" and "instances of persecution are limited to nonexistent." An anonymous British blogger visiting Syria was surprised to find that "as it turns out, there is actually a fairly lively gay scene in Damascus. And in that secular Arab way, it appears to be tolerated, as long as one sticks to one's assigned part to play." He was particularly struck by Damascus's al-Jadid Hammam: "Now, I've spent enough time in the Middle East to surmise that this was probably a 'sauna with covert action' as such places are sometimes described. Well, I was wrong. It turned out to be a scene with very OVERT action." He observed heavy cruising and wild action, and "even the behavior of the guys was typical . . . There were macho guys, quiet types, and screaming queens whose lilting voices bounced off the tiles in all directions. If only I could understand Arabic, I thought."

Others, though, complain that the authorities can and do use knowledge about citizens' sexuality to blackmail them, discourage them from political dissent, and otherwise keep them in line, and that law enforcement officers have low tolerance for people they consider sexual deviants. Still it was easy even for me, a visitor with little command of the language, to see that there is a strong gay scene here, active if discreet. The Internet of course has been a hugely liberating factor as it is under all repressive social systems. Bashar al-Asad has officially promoted Internet use in Syria while simultaneously banning the use of Facebook, but young people seem to have no problem getting around such restrictions: everyone I talked to said it was easy to "get a proxy," whatever that might mean. The Internet has made it all but impossible for the authorities to mold opinion and behavior the way they did under Hafiz al-Asad.

In any case, our boys at the restaurant near Krak seemed to feel no pressure to tone down their personal style. One of their friends took us walking around the castle. Until the *Service des antiquités* cleaned the place out in 1934 and started restoration work, he said, a settlement had grown up inside the crumbling castle, eventually expanding into a community of several thousand people. His grandparents had been among the villagers who were removed and resettled by the French authorities in the nearby village of al-Husn. The family had been in the region, he said, eight hundred years—since the time of the Hospitallers themselves.

Qalaat Saladin, formerly Sahyun and known to the Crusaders as the Château de Saône, is very nearly as romantic a sight as Krak. In the words of an intoxicated Lawrence, who visited the place in 1909 while researching his dissertation on Crusader Castles: "Sahyun, perhaps the first castle I have seen in Syria: a splendid keep, of Semi-Norman style, perfect in all respects: towers galore: chapels, a bath (Arabian) and a Mosque: gates most original: and a rock-moat 50 feet across in one part, 90 feet in another, varying from 60 to 130 feet deep: there's a cutting for you! And in the center had been left a slender needle of rock, to carry the middle of a drawbridge: it was I think the most sensational thing in castle-building I have seen: the hugely solid keep upstanding on the edge of the gigantic fosse."[4]

First fortified by the ancient Phoenicians and much later by the Byzantines, it was taken by the Crusaders in the twelfth century and rebuilt in French style. Its first Franj lord was one Robert of Saône, who rejoiced in the nickname Robert the Leprous. Robert fell afoul of Tughtagin, the Seljuk ruler of Damascus. Refusing to renounce Christianity he was decapitated by Tughtagin, who then inlaid the corpse's skull with jewels and used it as a drinking cup—for centuries a popular method of recycling one's enemy.

Unlike Krak, which appears wholly impregnable, Qalaat Saladin looks as though it would be very difficult to defend. Situated on a high mountain ridge between two steep gorges leading down from the Jebel Ansariyye, it has very long defensive walls—extending fully seven hundred yards in one direction—enclosing a long, narrow area with the castle itself at one end. How could the available manpower, always limited in Outremer, have been able to patrol this large perimeter? The north side of the fortress is built on high cliffs so that not much fortification was necessary, but the southern end needed massive reinforcement. In the end, though, it was the north end that was to give way before the mangonels of al-Zahir Ghazi, Saladin's son and lieutenant, in 1187. The Château de Saône reverted to Muslim rule for good.

The romance of the situation, the Gallic elegance of the building, the great donjon with its groin vaulting, and the fantastic nature of the engineering have ensured the castle's lasting fame. Even academic commentators write of it in breathless tones. Its immense moat, says one team of scholars,

> nearly 450 feet long and over 60 wide, is one of the most impressive memorials the Latins left in the Holy Land. Its walls, the haunt of black and scarlet rock-creeper, rise sheer for 90 feet and the battlements tower above. No drawbridge could span such a channel in a single sweep, and the Crusaders therefore left a needle of solid stone to carry their bridge across. It stands like an obelisk and recalls those works of the Nile with which this labour of carving some hundred and seventy thousand tons of solid rock alone seems comparable.[5]

This needle of rock is indeed a miracle of engineering, and the task of digging out the ninety-foot gully by hand with only the rather basic tools that were available at that time appears scarcely conceivable (fig. 58).

But builders believed in "thinking big" in those days, no doubt about it. The ruined Qasr al-Hayr, for instance, an Umayyad hunting palace deep in the eastern desert, is so immense and grandiose—maybe two city blocks in size—that it invites comparison with giant edifices like Versailles, the Escorial, or perhaps Madison Square Garden (fig. 59). The Aleppo Citadel also seems weirdly out of scale—even now, when Aleppo has grown and spread to encompass a couple of million souls, it dominates the cityscape on its enormous mound, with its 150-foot walls perched atop a steep glacis, its entry bridge, and its monumental gateway (fig. 60). Ibn Jubayr's observations still hold good, though they were made in the twelfth century before the Citadel underwent substantial renovations by the Mamluks a few decades later: Aleppo's "fortress is renowned for its impregnability and, from far distance seen for its great height, is without like or match among castles. Because of its great strength, an assailant who wills it or feels he can seize it must turn aside. It is a massy pike, like a round table rising from the ground, with sides of hewn stone and erected with true and symmetrical proportions."[6] We lunched one day high on a rooftop restaurant on the outskirts of the town, and the sight of the Citadel thrusting up like a volcano through the center of the old city was still a dramatic one (fig. 61).

The Aleppo Citadel remained in Muslim hands from the Arab conquest on, never falling to the Crusaders—though it was substantially damaged by the Mongols, who invaded the strategically situated Aleppo over and over again. A contemporary chronicler describes Hulagu's terrifying first arrival, in 1259:

> Crossing the Euphrates, he surrounded Aleppo without warning. The inhabitants, trusting in the impregnability of their citadel, refused to surrender and continued to do battle.
>
> At the Jews' Gate was Uruqtu Noyan, at the Anatolia Gate was Ket Buqa Noyan, at the Damascus Gate was Su'unchaq, and Hulagu Khan was camped at the Antioch Gate.
>
> A *chaptar* [stockade] was assembled around the city, and catapults were installed. For a full week the battle was fought hard by both sides, but in the end, in Dhu'l Hijja 657 [November 19–December 17, 1259], it was taken from the Iraq Gate and a full week of massacre and pillage ensued, during which many people were killed. For forty days and

nights they battled against the defenders in the citadel, and catapult stones and arrows rained from both sides. Amir Qorchan, Achu Siikdrchi, and Sadun Gurji were wounded several times in the face, for which the padishah gave them large rewards, saying, "just as rouge is an adornment to women's faces, red blood is a cosmetic adornment to the faces and beards of men."[7]

The Syrian Mamluk forces actually succeeded in defeating the Mongols in 1260 at the historic Battle of Ain Jalut, which turned back the tide of Mongol aggression. But Aleppo was captured again in 1271, 1281, and 1299, and the Mongol threat did not finally disappear until twenty years after that.

What we see today is mostly the work of Saladin's Ayyubid heirs—al-Zahir Ghazi, for instance, was responsible for the dramatic glacis—and then the Mamluks, who refashioned the entryway and turned it into one of the masterpieces of medieval military architecture, as dramatic in its way as Edinburgh Castle or the Tower of London. Invaders would first have to brave a large entrance tower; then a drawbridge over the moat; then, if they were lucky enough not to be hit while crossing, they would have to make a sharp turn on the other side to get into the inner gateway, making it impossible to build up momentum for a run at the door with a battering ram. This principle has been observed throughout the extended entry, with progress impeded by a series of bends and zigzags designed to slow down intruders so that arrows could be shot at them and hot oil, stones, and excrement poured onto their heads from the machicolations above. (This pattern was repeated in the city's magnificent Qinnesrin Gate, also a Mamluk construction.) At the Citadel's entryway, a total of five doors must be breached before an invading army finally gets into the castle proper.

The day we visited the Citadel this circuitous entrance was jammed with clamoring school groups, the older children pushing through boldly, the younger ones shepherded by sweet-faced teachers. They were all singing, believe it or not, the "I Love

You, You Love Me" song from *Barney*. We shoved along in our turn, passing under the series of carved lions that were supposed to guard the fortress from its enemies. Once inside, we emerged from the passageways onto the summit of the mound, where there must have been a virtual city in the Middle Ages (fig. 62), including a forty-room Ayyubid Palace and a Mamluk hammam, now fitted out with startling wax figures in various stages of dress and undress. There is also an exquisite mosque and a nineteenth-century army barracks that has been turned into a café. Underneath it all are endless dark passages and dungeons: this is where the medieval rulers put their VIP Crusader prisoners, formidable enemies like Joscelin of Edessa and Reynald de Châtillon, of whom more below.

But though most of the Citadel's fabric is now medieval and reflects medieval technology and styles of warfare, the spot of course has much more ancient precedents. Here Julian the Apostate sacrificed to Zeus. Going further back, the Seleucids built a fortress here, whose traces are no longer visible. There is a Mosque of Abraham built on the foundations of what had once been a church dedicated to Abraham, for here the patriarch is supposed to have come to milk his cow (the Arabic word for Aleppo, Haleb, derives from the word for milk). Here, too, was another of the supposed resting places for John the Baptist's peripatetic head. Going even further back in time, there was a Temple to the Weather God, dating from about 1700 B.C., now in the process of excavation.

In any European city the houses that face onto a place as historic and spectacular as this would be prime real estate, owned and scrupulously maintained by the city's upper class and bristling with expensive tourist shops. There is nothing like that here: these are perfectly ordinary-looking, even shabby structures, some of them clearly proletarian, with laundry hanging out to dry and plastic bird cages on window sills. What shops exist are modest little hardware and general stores. Troupes of boys in school uniforms wander about in search of mischief, looking like urchins out of a Truffaut movie.

The Damascus Citadel is quite different from its counterpart in Aleppo. It is one of the very few citadels in this part of the world that is not on high ground. Instead of being on a hilltop well within the city, it was built along the banks of the Barada, right inside the city's northwestern walls. In front of it, facing the blaring traffic of the Sharia ath-Thawra, stands an equestrian statue of its most famous denizen, Saladin, looking a little like a lower-grade version of Richard the Lionheart at London's Houses of Parliament. Same period, same stance, same good looks, same general air of nobility. But the most interesting aspect of this statue is not the view from the front, featuring Saladin's handsome face, but the one from the back: for there, groveling in chains, are the Crusader leaders Guy de Lusignan, King of Jerusalem, and the infamous Reynald de Châtillon, Prince of Antioch and Lord of Transjordan—the most hated of all the unpopular Franj invaders.

Reynald seems to have been a true sadist. Among other atrocities, he had the Orthodox Patriarch of Antioch arrested for refusing to back his intended invasion of Cyprus, and had him beaten until his head was raw and bleeding. Reynald then spread honey on the wounds and left him all day chained on the roof of the Antioch citadel in the hot sun to be tormented by insects—as Monty Python's Terry Jones has said, "like a sort of human fly-paper."[8] Reynald then proceeded to ravage Cyprus, a friendly Orthodox Christian island that had aided the Crusaders when they first came east. The devastation inflicted by Reynald's armies was such that Cyprus never regained its former prosperity. It is still a poor island today.

After this adventure Reynald was arrested by Muslim armies during a raid and spent fifteen years languishing in the Aleppo Citadel. On his release he discovered that his wife was dead and he was no longer Prince of Antioch—it was through her that he had gained the title in the first place—and he hastily married another Frankish heiress, Stephanie, the ruler of Transjordan. Installed with her at the great castle of Kerak (in present-day Jordan), he was tantalized by the rich caravans passing by on their way to Mecca. Why not raid them and take all the loot for himself? He began raiding these caravans full of religious pilgrims and merchants, murdering and torturing the men and keeping the survivors prisoner at Kerak. Both Christians and Muslims were outraged, for it was the local tradition to respect pilgrimage routes. Reynald's contemporary Ibn Jubayr noted that "The Christians make the Muslims pay a tax, which is applied without abuses. The Christian merchants in turn pay duty on their merchandise when they pass through the territory of the Muslims. There is complete understanding between the two sides, and equity is respected. The men of war pursue their war, but the people remain at peace."[9]

Reynald had broken the truce, and now hostilities were renewed between Damascus and Jerusalem. At the Battle of Hattin in 1187, Saladin achieved an epochal victory and followed it up with a whirlwind campaign during which he took more than fifty Crusader positions and reduced the Crusader presence to a small, feeble state. Jerusalem was retaken after nearly a century of Christian rule; in contrast with the Crusaders' behavior—the warriors of the First Crusade had turned Jerusalem into a charnel house when they took it in 1099—Saladin displayed tremendous clemency.

But he made a couple of exceptions in this policy. The Templars and Hospitallers, those ideologically driven exponents of militant Christianity, were put to death. Saladin also turned his attention to his old enemies Guy and Reynald, and ordered them brought to his tent directly after the Battle of Hattin. Here is an eyewitness account by 'Imad al-Din al-Asfahani, one of Saladin's men:

> Salah al-Din [Saladin] invited the king [Guy] to sit beside him, and when Arnat [Reynald] entered in his turn, he seated him next to his king and reminded him of his misdeeds: "How many times have you sworn an oath and then violated it? How many times have you signed agreements that you have never respected?" Arnat answered through an

interpreter: "Kings have always acted thus. I did nothing more." During this time, Guy was gasping with thirst, his head dangling as though he were drunk, his face betraying great fright. Salah al-Din spoke reassuring words to him, had cold water brought, and offered it to him. The king drank, then handed what remained to Arnat, who slaked his thirst in turn. The sultan then said to Guy, "You did not ask my permission before giving him water. I am therefore not obliged to grant him mercy."

After pronouncing these words, the sultan smiled, mounted his horse, and rode off, leaving his captives in terror. He supervised the return of the troops, then came back to his tent. He ordered Arnat brought there, advanced toward him, sword in hand, and struck him between the neck and shoulder-blade. When Arnat fell, he cut off his head and dragged the body by its feet to the king, who began to tremble. Seeing him thus upset, the sultan said to him in a reassuring tone: "This man was killed only because of his maleficence and his perfidy."[10]

This, then, is how Reynald came to be depicted in such an undignified posture beneath Saladin's statue. It's tempting to see the Citadel itself as Saladin's castle, but in fact what we see today is largely the restored work of his brother al-Adil, who rebuilt it on a massive scale after succeeding Saladin. It had fallen into disrepair not because of Crusader attacks but because rivals within his own family, the Ayyubids, had made attacks attempting to unseat him; there had also been a devastating earthquake in 1201. Al-Adil considerably enlarged the earlier Seljuk construction and added an elaborate palace complex including mosques, a hammam, and even a souq. It is characteristically Ayubbid work, similar to European fortifications of the same period with its massive stone blocks and barrel-vaulted ceilings.

A huge job; but only decades later it was destroyed by the Mongols under Hulagu, who succeeded where the Crusaders had failed and laid waste to Damascus in a lightning campaign of unspeakable brutality. Sultan Baybars rebuilt most of it afterward, but in 1400 it was visited by a conqueror as terrible as Hulagu—Tamerlane, who pulled it down all over again. The great historian Ibn Khaldun actually met with that particular Scourge of God at the gates of Damascus in 1400 and gave an eyewitness account of the attack on the Citadel. Tamerlane, he wrote,

> pressed the siege of the Citadel in earnest; he erected against it catapults, naphtha guns, ballistas, and breachers, and within a few days sixty catapults and other similar engines were set up. The siege pressed ever harder upon those within the Citadel, and its structure was destroyed on all sides. Therefore the men [defending it], among them a number of those who had been in the service of the Sultan, and those whom he had left behind, asked for peace. Timur granted them amnesty, and after they were brought before him the Citadel was destroyed and its vestiges completely effaced.
>
> . . . Then he gave permission for the plunder of the houses of the people of the city, and they were despoiled of all their furniture and goods. The furnishings and utensils of no value which remained were set on fire, and the fire spread to the walls of the houses, which were supported on timbers. It continued to burn until it reached the Great Mosque; the flames mounted to its roof, melting the lead in it, and the ceiling and walls collapsed . . .[11]

Tamerlane was one of history's most terrible conquerors, an intelligent and educated man whose violent acts have fascinated people throughout history. It was his pleasure to pile up pyramids of the severed heads of enemy soldiers outside the gates of the cities he attacked, and he would kill captives by dropping them into tall towers one on top of another until the tower was full to the brim and the unhappy victims were crushed and suffocated. Christopher Marlowe's sixteenth-century drama *Tamburlaine the Great* illustrated the contradictions in the character of this military genius who had a fatal streak of barbarism. One of the great theatrical experiences I have ever had was seeing Albert Finney in the title role at the RSC when I was young. I wondered whether our friend Abed had ever produced it at the University of Aleppo, or whether the subject might still prove too emotional in this particular place. Edgar Allan Poe wrote "Tamerlane," a long monologue poem about the conqueror, again trying to understand the impulse not only to conquer but to terrorize:

> I wrapp'd myself in grandeur then,
> And donn'd a visionary crown—
>   Yet it was not that Fantasy
> Had thrown her marble over me—
> But that, among the rabble-men,
> Lion ambition is chained down—
> And crouches to a keeper's hand—
> Not so in deserts where the grand—
>   The wild—the terrible conspire
> With their own breath to fan his fire.

In spite of damage caused by an earthquake in the eighteenth century and a civil war in the nineteenth, the Damascus Citadel continued to be used as a prison, and sometimes even as a place of shelter. Christians took refuge there during the 1860 massacre. The writer Jean Genet claimed to have been imprisoned there by the French military authorities in the 1930s, but he probably invented this tale (in which case Damascus must be one of the few cities in the world where he *wasn't* put in jail). The Citadel was still a prison in the 1980s, and some prominent members of the opposition spent time there in Hafiz al-Asad's day. But in 1986 the government handed it back to the City of Damascus, and since 2000 it has been the subject of a large Franco-Syrian excavation and restoration project, with the goal of opening it to the public. Today, the place seems benign enough, despite its bloody history. In the shelter of its walls, where the Barada River runs alongside it, the Swiss have joined the Syrians in creating a lovely "Ecological and Botanical Garden": local workers have been hired to plant and cultivate a rich variety of local vegetation including fruit trees, ornamental plants, rock plants, and flowers. It has an educational purpose—to show Damascenes the biodiversity of the Barada basin—but it is also an irresistible oasis in the middle of the dusty city, with shade, sweet smells, flowers, and even a pretty café under the scented jasmine trees.

So often here, former scenes of carnage are now deceptively tranquil. The town of Ma'arat al-Numan, not far from Apamea, is nowadays a quiet, rather nice little town, its main attraction a spectacular mosaic museum, unobtrusively tucked into a sixteenth-century khan that now functions as a madrasa. All the mosaics here are Byzantine, fifth and sixth century, and all, it seems, were discovered by local farmers plowing their land. We were completely blown away by this place, for none of the guidebooks had featured it particularly and we never would have made the trip if Muhammed Four hadn't insisted. Room after room contained superb mosaics, many on a very large scale covering entire walls (fig. 63), quite complete and in good repair. Funds, though, were obviously limited, for the lighting was poor and several of the works were protected—held together, possibly—by plastic wrapping. Most of the images were secular rather than Christian, and many featured animals: a lion devouring a bull, comical ducks, peacocks sitting on an urn, a stunning image—about ten feet by eight—of a lion leaping, mouth open, at a fleeing gazelle against a patterned background of rosebuds. As Catherine remarked, here one could suddenly see and understand the transition from late antique to medieval art. If this collection of mosaics were lent *en masse* to the Metropolitan Museum in New York, we thought, they would be able to mount an entire blockbuster show, "Christian Masterpieces of the Middle East" or some such thing, and attract art lovers by the thousands. Here in Ma'arat, the works go practically unseen. It hardly needs saying that we were the only visitors that day.

It was only as we were leaving and I was writing down the name of the town that I realized that this was where the most infamous episode of the Crusades took place. In 1098, soldiers of the First Crusade launched a siege against Ma'arat after their conquest of Antioch and succeeded in breaching the walls after a couple of weeks' efforts. The nobles leading the Crusader army, Bohemond of Taranto and Raymond of Toulouse, promised safe conduct to the Saracen defenders if they surrendered, but when the defenders duly laid down their arms, they were massacred in cold blood, thousands of them. Some of the besiegers themselves were starving, for it was winter and there was little forage to be had. Even the Christian chroniclers were appalled at what came next:

> I shudder to say that many of our men, terribly tormented by the madness of starvation, cut pieces from the buttocks of Saracens lying there dead. These pieces they cooked and ate, savagely devouring the flesh while it was insufficiently roasted. —Fulcher of Chartres

> In Ma'arra our troops boiled pagan adults in cooking-pots; they impaled children on spits and devoured them grilled. —Radulph of Caen

> Not only did our troops not shrink from eating dead Turks and Saracens; they also ate dogs! —Albert of Aix

Cannibalism was not to become a habit of the Crusaders, but this one incident was enough to persuade the Muslims of Europeans' moral inferiority, and surely no single event of the Crusades was such a PR disaster for the Latin Christians as this one. As the Muslim chronicler Usamah Ibn Munqidh, a child in a nearby village at the time of the incident at Ma'arat, saw it, "All those who were well informed about the Franj saw them as beasts superior in courage and fighting ardor but in nothing else, just as animals are superior in strength and aggression."[12] It is due to such deeds that a number of historians, Western as well as Muslim, have come to see the Crusades not as the glorious project we used to be taught about in school but as the last of the barbarian invasions.

Or straightforward colonialism, perhaps? Religion, like the *mission civilisatrice*, has often served as a cloak for simple land hunger. In the West the myth of Crusades as something more exalted than a mere land grab was constructed around the exaltation of certain characters, such as Richard the Lionheart, who gave a heroic aspect to the project. T. E. Lawrence played a similar role in the scramble for the Middle East after World War I; the images he provided gave readers (and subsequently moviegoers) the impression that the war against the Ottomans was a holy cause rather than a struggle for territory and political advantage. Take his version of the entrance of the Allied troops into Damascus in 1918, for instance:

> Every man, woman and child in this city of a quarter-million souls seemed in the streets, waiting only the spark of our appearance to ignite their spirits. Damascus went mad with joy. The men tossed up their tarbushes to cheer, the women tore off their veils. Householders threw flowers, hangings, carpets, into the road before us: their wives leaned, screaming with laughter, through the lattices and splashed us with bath-dippers of scent.
>
> Poor dervishes made themselves our running footmen in front and behind, howling and cutting themselves with frenzy; and over the local cries and the shrilling of women came the measured roar of men's voices chanting, "Feisal, Nasir, Shukri, Urens," in waves which began here, rolled along the squares, through the market down long streets to East gate, round the wall, back up the Meidan; and grew to a wall of shouts around us by the citadel.[13]

The reality was rather different. Allenby and Lawrence didn't enter the city until two days after the Australian Light Horse Brigade, though Lawrence rather fudges this fact in his account.

Neither was the enthusiasm for Faisal universal: many Damascenes saw him and everyone else from the Hijaz as foreigners and feared (as did the French) that he would prove nothing more than a British puppet.

But it's amazing how much of what we know about this moment in history, or think we know, comes from the Lawrence account, especially as interpreted by David Lean's *Lawrence of Arabia*. As filmmaking goes this is a work of art; as history it is unreliable, though less egregiously mindless of reality than many historical films. Still it contains some seriously misleading scenes, the most destructive of which has probably been that in which the council of Arab leaders, finally faced with the chance of controlling their own fate for the first time after the defeat of the Turks, argue among themselves so childishly that the wise, experienced British have to step in. In reality the council elected Faisal king in an orderly manner, and he ran a national government perfectly competently until the French, determined to lay claim to Syria, enforced their U.N. Mandate with a full-scale military invasion of the country and sent Faisal and his government packing.

Lawrence's version of political events is seldom to be trusted. Here he describes the scene that led to his departure from Damascus after the 1918 liberation:

> . . . [W]e were told that Feisal's special train had just arrived from Deraa. A message was hurriedly sent him by Young's mouth, and we waited till he came, upon a tide of cheering which beat up against our window. It was fitting the two chiefs [Feisal and General Allenby] should meet for the first time in the heart of their victory; with myself still acting the interpreter between them.
>
> Allenby gave me a telegram from the Foreign Office, recognizing to the Arabs the status of belligerents; and told me to translate it to the Emir: but none of us knew what it meant in English, let alone in Arabic; and Feisal, smiling through the tears which the welcome of his people had

forced from him, put it aside to thank the Commander-in-Chief for the trust which had made him and his movement. They were a strange contrast: Feisal, large-eyed, colourless and worn, like a fine dagger; Allenby, gigantic and red and merry, fit representative of the Power which had thrown a girdle of humour and strong dealing round the world.

When Feisal had gone, I made to Allenby the last (and also I think the first) request I ever made him for myself—leave to go away. For a while he would not have it; but I reasoned, reminding him of his nine-year-old promise, and pointing out how much easier the New Law [i.e., Feisal's rule] would be if my spur were absent from the people. In the end he agreed; and then at once I knew how much I was sorry.[14]

This passage thoroughly bears out Kinglsey Amis's summing-up of *The Seven Pillars of Wisdom* as "a piece of pretentious bullshit." Even Lawrence himself, the great self-mythologizer, admitted that the Damascus chapter was full of half-truths. There were a great number of other interested parties, British, Arab, and French, at the actual meeting described above, and it was nothing whatever like the warm and fuzzy scene he cooked up for posterity. Here is Desmond Stewart's account of it in his biography of Lawrence:

Allenby then spelt out British policy. It was in full accord with the Sykes-Picot Agreement: Feisal was to administer inland Syria with French guidance and finance and, for the time being, a French liaison officer would work alongside Lawrence, who was to assist him in every respect.

Feisal, ivory with rage, protested that he knew nothing of France in the matter. He was prepared to accept British assistance; he had understood from the Adviser whom Allenby had sent him [i.e., Lawrence] that the Arabs were to have the whole of Syria, including Lebanon but excluding Palestine. A country without a port was useless to him. He declined to recognize French direction in any manner or to accept a French liaison officer.

Allenby, apparently surprised, turned to Lawrence.

"But surely you told him the French were to have a protectorate over Syria?"

"No, Sir, I did not."

Bowing to superior force Feisal withdrew from the conference. Lawrence then burst out that he could not possibly work with a French liaison officer. He was due for leave. He thought he had better take it at once and get off to England.

"Yes," said Allenby, "I think you had."

. . . Next day, the 4th, Lawrence left Damascus. Traveling in a Rolls Royce by way of Palestine, he was in Egypt four days later. His abrupt departure confirmed that his interest in the capture of Damascus had been essentially political, since, for the Arabs, weeks of fighting still lay ahead.[15]

This piece of history was made especially poignant for us one day on a drive through the Barada Valley, when we came across a sweet-smelling cypress grove with a memorial to Yusuf al-Azmah. In 1920 the thirty-six-year-old al-Azmah was Faisal's Minister of War and Chief of Staff. While Faisal had finally given in to French aggression and offered his unconditional surrender, al-Azmah determined to fight to the end, and gathering his meager forces at Khan Maysalun a few miles west of Damascus, he put up a suicidal resistance. There was no way he could have held out against the vastly superior French forces (mostly soldiers from France's colony of Senegal), and he must have known he would be killed. But he felt it was important to make it clear to the world that Syria had resisted and that France was there only by force. On July 24, 1920, al-Azmah died at Maysalun and his forces were wiped out. Faisal left the country three days later.

We have all heard the word "martyr" used a little too freely (by now I took the Shi'a variety about as seriously as my friend the archaeologist did), but when the word was used for al-Azmah I did not object; he seemed to me the real thing, and I found the tomb of this brave man a moving, peaceful place, totally lacking in militaristic bombast.

The French always justified their colonial project by vaunting their *mission civilisatrice*, but Syria was treated like conquered territory and punished for its resistance. General Henri Gouraud, visiting the tomb of Saladin, cried, "My presence here signifies the victory of the cross over the crescent!" It seemed that the French had finally won the Crusades, after nearly a thousand years! Gouraud, commander of the French Army of the Levant and in effect the colonial governor of the whole region, enforced his power viciously. The locals were treated as *sales Arabes*. Jean Genet, who served with the French forces there in the late 1920s and early 30s, recalled that the general "had transformed Damascus into a pile of ruins. He had fired cannons, and we had strict orders always to move around with a weapon and in groups of three, and we had to keep to the sidewalk. If any Arabs, or anyway any Syrians, women or old men, passed by or came towards us, they were the ones who had to step down off the sidewalk."[16]

Syrian politicians and notables who had in any way challenged the French presence were sentenced to death, imprisoned, exiled, even sent to distant French colonies. The press was strictly censored, and use of the French language was enforced in schools and courts. The French appeared to be trying to create another Algeria here, imposing their language and civilization by force of arms—*not* exactly in accordance with the terms or in the spirit of the League of Nations Mandate.

Not that it was all bad: The French vastly improved roads, railways, and public services; they also established the *Service des antiquités* that supervised so many important archaeological projects and created the country's impressive network of museums. (Interestingly, one of the civilian High Commissioners in the 1920s was Henry de Jouvenel, one-time husband of the novelist Colette.) But Mandatory rule was brutal, French cultural arrogance bitterly resented by the heirs to this ancient civilization. When Adham Khanjar tried to assassinate General Gouraud in 1921 and was put to death, he became a national hero.

Damascus still bears the traces of French bombs and bullets. Three rebellions were put down with overwhelming military force. During the major rebellion in 1925, French forces, based in the Citadel, bombed the city from airplanes and sent tanks through, creating widespread destruction. They also cut down a large portion of the Ghouta orchards. A year later revolt broke out again and was even more cruelly suppressed, with the French cutting off the water supply in the Maidan district as well as bombing the area and killing about one thousand people. The end of the Mandate was set for 1939, but when the time came, France refused to hand over power and dissolved Syria's nascent chamber of deputies. France's defeat by Germany the following year and her subsequent withdrawal from the League of Nations ended any legal justification for the Mandate, but still she hung on tightly. In 1945, with strikes and riots against French rule breaking out all over the country, Damascus was subjected to large-scale bombing and shelling yet again. At the end of the war the Syrians appealed to the brand new United Nations, which brokered the final French withdrawal. "Evacuation Day," 17 April 1946, is still a national holiday in Syria.

Over the ages Syria has provided asylum for refugees uprooted in wars and conflagrations all over the region. The Salihiye district on the slopes of Mount Qassioun, now one of Damascus's posher neighborhoods, was originally established to house Palestinian refugees from the massacre following the Crusaders' conquest of Jerusalem in 1099. Armenians flocked to Syria when the Seljuk Turks conquered their country; centuries later more waves of them poured in, fleeing the 1915 Armenian genocide in Turkey. All these people, staying on, came to form important strands of the country's fabric.

Now it's the Iraqis: but the numbers are so staggering it's hard to see how they can be incorporated without trauma to the larger society. At the time of my visit an estimated 1.5 million refugees had crossed from Iraq into Syria since the American invasion and the subsequent sectarian violence had made life there intolerable for so many. Considering that the total population of Syria is only 18 million, the impact this mass immigration has on the society can be imagined. First of all the cost of living has soared, especially in Damascus; the price of real estate, both sales and rentals, has skyrocketed. Then the labor market has become completely saturated. Unemployment was already a problem in Syria, and once the refugees arrived it rose to dire levels. The demands on the national economy and infrastructure have become almost intolerable. Medical care and basic education are free in Syria, free to Iraqi refugees as well as Syrian nationals, but the system was unprepared to deal with so many new clients, and the overcrowding in schools, hospitals, and clinics has made impossible demands on the government budget and capabilities. In Iraqi neighborhoods crime has risen, child labor abounds, and many desperate families have been pushed to the final expedient of sending their daughters into prostitution. The majority of Iraqis in Syria are unemployed. They wait, helpless, for the opportunity to go home, to emigrate to some country better prepared to meet their needs—in North America, perhaps, or Europe—or for their status in Syria to be normalized so that they can legally earn a living.

"WELCOME TO THE CAMP OF THE SAYYIDA ZEINAB," I read as I enter one of the new Iraqi neighborhoods that has popped up on the outskirts of Damascus. A sort of cross between a refugee camp and a shantytown, it is a little like the Brazilian *favelas* that are growing at lightning speed around Rio de Janeiro. There's a huge building effort going on all around me, an entire makeshift city rising from a sea of concrete blocks. As with the *favelas*, one can see that in fifty years, maybe even twenty, the district will have become an intrinsic part of the city, with roads, water and electricity supplies, and businesses pushing their way into it and linking it with other neighborhoods. After all, it's the way most cities have historically expanded, though the exclusive use of concrete will give this place a more drab look than is common in the older districts.

It's almost the first time I've felt uncomfortable being a Western woman alone, especially since I'm not very conservatively dressed, and the first time I've had any fear of crime. I do get some pointed looks, but no one challenges me, and some smile. I go into a pudding shop where the only other customers are an exotic family of Pakistani Shi'a on pilgrimage to the Sayyida Zeinab Mosque. The father is a kindly-looking man with a cottony white beard, in a nightcap-type troll hat, wearing a white robe with baggy trousers, the son his nine-year-old mini-me. The restaurateur refuses to accept our tips.

I think of Riverbend, a young computer programmer who blogged from Baghdad from the beginning of the American invasion. She managed to keep her identity a secret while sending devastating blogs to the outside world. We Americans get only the most lopsided news about Iraq and our role there, so her work would have had untold significance in the States—had enough people bothered to read it. She got more readers elsewhere though, and was awarded the French *Lettre Ulysses* Award for Literary Reportage.

In 2007 Riverbend and her family could take no more and immigrated to Syria. From Damascus, she marveled on the experience of crossing the border between the two countries:

> How is it that a border no one can see or touch stands between car bombs, militias, death squads and . . . peace, safety? It's difficult to believe—even now. I sit here and write this and wonder why I can't hear the explosions.
>
> I wonder at how the windows don't rattle as the planes pass overhead. I'm trying to rid myself of the expectations that armed people in black will break through the door and into our lives. I'm trying to let my eyes grow accustomed to streets free of road blocks, hummers and pictures of Muqtada and the rest . . .[17]

A few weeks later, she was getting accustomed to her new home—slowly:

Syria is a beautiful country—at least, I think it is. I say "I think" because while I perceive it to be beautiful, I sometimes wonder if I mistake safety, security and normalcy for "beauty." In so many ways, Damascus is like Baghdad before the war—bustling streets, occasional traffic jams, markets seemingly always full of shoppers . . . And in so many ways it is different . . .

The first weeks here were something of a cultural shock. It has taken me these last three months to work away certain habits I'd acquired in Iraq after the war. It's funny how you learn to act a certain way and don't even know you're doing strange things—like avoiding people's eyes in the street or crazily murmuring prayers to yourself when stuck in traffic. It took me at least three weeks to teach myself to walk properly again—with head lifted, not constantly looking behind me.[18]

Like countless other readers, I looked forward to Riverbend's next entry. But that was it. After four years of regular blogging Riverbend was suddenly silent. And as I write now, more than two years have passed since that last posting. It seems inconceivable to me that she would simply have lost interest and stopped writing without announcing the fact on her blog: she had many thousands of avid readers, after all, and she knew her contributions were valued. It's hard to avoid the thought that something must have happened to her. Something as simple as a traffic accident, or was her identity finally discovered? If so, could she have been silenced? Who had the most to fear from her outspokenness? The American occupiers, it would seem, or the unpopular Iraqi politicians they have raised to power.

Figure 53. The Tishreen Panorama Museum.

Figure 54. Krak des Chevaliers.

Figure 55. Halls inside Krak.

Figure 56. Gothic details at Krak.

Figure 57. Hillside terracing near Krak.

Figure 58. Sahyun (Château de Saône).

Figure 59. Qasr al-Hayr.

Figure 60. Aleppo Citadel.

Figure 61. Aleppo Citadel and the city from above.

Figure 62. Inside the Citadel.

Figure 63. Mosaic at Ma'arat.

Figure 64. Posters in Damascus.

Figure 65. Bashar al-Asad.

Figure 66. Smokers at a Damascus café.

Figure 67. The presidential palace outside of Damascus.

Figure 68. Saladin's tomb.

6 ❖ *Leaders*

It's the first thing you notice when you land in the country: the presidential portraits in every office, in every public space, looming on billboards over traffic intersections, pasted over walls and fences (fig. 64).

Most of the posters and portraits are of Bashar al-Asad, who has been president now for a decade. But there are still lots of Papa Hafiz, as well as Brother Basil (Hafiz's eldest son and heir apparent, who died unexpectedly in 1994). There are plenty of outsize statues of Hafiz, in squares, in front of public buildings, or by the side of the highway, and they usually depict him either in paternal mode—the Father of his Country—or in some triumphalist posture, a modern, business-suited Saladin. And there are still quite a few portrayals of Basil, officially deemed a "martyr" though he was in fact a Goodtime Charlie who partied hard and died not in military action, as one might deduce from the iconography and rhetoric, but while driving too fast along the airport highway. A sinister-looking fellow, Basil is invariably depicted with sunglasses and a three-day stubble. In the couple of years after Basil's death, paintings of this threesome—Hafiz, Basil, and Bashar—were labeled "the Leader, the Example, and the Hope."

Lisa Wedeen, a scholar who has written extensively about the Asad propaganda machine, describes how

> . . . Basil can be unequivocally glorified only after his death. Pictures of the son wearing military fatigues, making the pilgrimage to Mecca, or performing at equestrian matches began to grace the walls of public buildings, shops, and classrooms in January 1994 immediately following his fatal car crash. Cameos of Basil were printed on neckties and featured on some wrist watches at that time. Posters continue to proclaim him the "martyr," the "eternal knight," and Syria's "hope."[1]

And what of Qardaha, the Asad family's natal town near Lattakia, where their mausoleum can be visited by the public? Here the iconography is even more intense, the religious symbolism even more brazen. A painting of Hafiz al-Asad's mother, Na'isa, looks as though it really ought to be on black velvet: she is actually shown wearing a halo, while Hafiz avidly kisses her hand. Another painting shows Na'isa, with halo and *wings*, flanked by Hafiz and the thuggish Ri'fat—a most peculiar Holy Family.

The Asad personality cult was the brainchild of Ahmad Iskandar Ahmad, Hafiz al-Asad's Minister of Information during the 1970s and early 1980s. It was ratcheted up as an attempt at PR damage control after the massacre of the Muslim Brothers at Hama in 1982—and again a year later following Hafiz's massive heart attack, after which he seldom went out in public. Ahmad choreographed the multiplication of all these presidential images and encouraged the constant repetition of the president's name in the press and on the lips of administrators, governors, and Ba'ath Party functionaries—like a travesty of the traditional Muslim invocations of the Deity. This was the period, too, of the gruesome blood oaths, and of the *bay'a*, the individual or collective pledge of allegiance to the leader. (This practice, originally a purely religious one, had been adapted from the traditional Muslim bay'a to Islam and Muhammed, a secular appropriation of the holy that shocked pious Muslims.)

Ten years after the death of the father, though, the son is firmly in power and nowadays the public iconography is pretty much all about Bashar. The giant posters are disconcerting, Orwellian (fig. 65). And yet this is not a very threatening face. With its receding chin and wide brow it even looks mild, intellectual; in fact the whole personality cult seems utterly at odds with the enlightened and modern image Bashar tries to project to the world. Bashar al-Asad didn't set out to be a leader, after all; he was an up-and-coming London ophthalmologist until his brother's death propelled him into a position of power. Removed from his happy and successful career at the Western Eye Hospital in London, Bashar was rushed back to Damascus to assume the role of Syria's new "Hope."

Syria-watcher and blogger Joshua Landis has discussed the Asad family in terms of the traditional Arab leadership quality called *zaama*, which roughly translates to "aura of invincibility." "Zaama is crucial to leadership in Syria as it is in all patriarchal societies," Landis has commented. "But Syria is more patriarchal than most. Although tribalism in any kind of pristine form has disappeared from much of Syrian society, its forms and virtues remain very much alive."[2]

Does Bashar al-Asad possess zaama? To look at him one might doubt it; he exudes none of the hammer-headed authority of his father or the brute machismo of his brother. And one can hardly imagine him requiring blood oaths or bay'a. Indeed one wonders just how seriously his threats are taken. In October 2009 Bashar, as befits a former doctor, issued a presidential decree banning smoking inside Syria's cafés, restaurants, and all other public spaces. This seemed a daring and even provocative move given the amount of nargileh-puffing that goes on in every café in the country. After all, alcohol is not served in Muslim establishments; with smoking banned, too, what would happen to Syria's colorful café culture? As it turned out there was no cause for alarm: when I returned to the country a few weeks later, nothing at all seemed to have changed. The same dozy old men nodded over their hubble-bubbles (fig. 66); the same crowds of young people laughed and chattered and passed the pipe.

So what happened to the ban, with its threatened fine of 2000 Syrian pounds (about $46) that was supposed to punish transgressors? Everyone simply ignores it. According to an International Crisis Group report cited by Bashar's biographer, between 2000 and 2004 Bashar signed more than nineteen hundred decrees, laws, and orders, but very few of these were actually put into effect.[3] As Bashar himself grumbled, "We have lots of ideas, but we do not know how to implement them. We issue laws, but we do not implement them. I issue a decree and the government should implement it, but now I have to follow up on everything all the time."[4]

Yet Bashar has always displayed a pragmatic toughness that leads me to believe his perceived zaama is never far from his thoughts. His policy of firmness when dealing with the United States, his refusal to accept our "if you're not with us you're against us" ultimatum, has been crucial in this respect: Bashar knows that if he should ever look like Washington's lapdog in the eyes of his countrymen, his dynasty will be as doomed as that of the late Shah. "When our interests have matched, the Americans have been good to us," he has commented. "When the interests have differed, they wanted us to mold ourselves to them, which we refused."[5] The regime's friendship with Iran, he insists, is not designed as a provocation to America but is simply *Realpolitik*, an acknowledgment that both countries are major powers in the region and have important mutual interests. The Asads, father and son, have achieved popularity—and a good deal of their popularity is genuine—in part through not caving to pressure from greater powers. They have been well aware that a lasting peace in the Middle East cannot be brokered without their cooperation, and have held out boldly for their own national interests.

And when American officials have had the temerity to criticize Asad's record on civil liberties, he laughs right in their faces.

"Our laws are tough and strict and whether they are right or wrong that is an issue for Syria," he has insisted. "We don't allow anyone to make our internal issues a matter for relations. Europeans and Americans supported the occupation of Iraq. Talking about values has no credibility any more. And after what happened in Gaza they have no right [to criticize us] at all."[6]

When Bashar came to power in 2000, his initial moves toward political dissidents were placatory, and liberals in the country got quite excited over what they dubbed, a little prematurely as it turned out, a "Damascus Spring." Bashar's inaugural speech, promising significant political and economic reform, raised much hope. Six hundred political prisoners were released in November of that year, and Damascus's notorious Mezzeh prison was shut down. A hopeful crowd of intellectuals, artists, and media people formed the Committee for the Revival of Civil Society in Syria, calling for rule of law, an independent judiciary, and an end to the "state of emergency" that had been nominally in effect since 1963. Civil society activists released manifestoes, most significantly the "Statement of 99" in 2000 and the "Manifesto of the 1000" in January 2001, which actually demanded a multi-party system and the end of Ba'athist monopoly.

But the Damascus Spring was quickly followed by a Damascus Winter, when Bashar withdrew many of the carrots he had held out—whether on his own accord or under pressure from his father's "old guard," which still yielded much of the power in Syria, has never quite been determined by outsiders. Still, the level of fear and mutual suspicion has proved much lower under Bashar than it was under Hafiz. One political dissident who was imprisoned under both presidents has commented of his most recent incarceration, "I would like to describe the prison as a five-star jail compared to prisons during his father's time."[7]

Commentator Peter Beaumont has smartly summed up the enigma of Bashar al-Asad. "Who is the real Bashar?" he asks:

Is he the accessible and visible President with his pretty young wife, who goes to the theater, opera and cinema, in contrast with a father rarely seen outside of official events? Who dines in the restaurants of Damascus with his family and likes music and would like, as he once said, to improve his people's lives with 'the tool of democracy'? Or is he his father's son: a leader surrounded by a tiny circle of family advisers . . . who is ruthless and astute, a great dissimulator capable of playing, and winning, a long game?[8]

The jury is still out.

The personality cult inaugurated by Hafiz al-Asad, in which the physically absent leader was made present through a proliferation of images, might have grown from a conscious or unconscious acknowledgment of Arab tribal traditions, according to which the leader derives power and prestige from his accessibility to the public. Following Arab precedent, the leader must see and be seen; he must mete out justice and bestow benefits in person, and in full view of the community. These requirements are in accordance with the egalitarian principles of Islam and they were established at the very beginning of Islamic history, under the rule of the first four Caliphs, collectively known as the *Rashidun*, or rightly-guided ones: Abu Bakr, Umar, Uthman, and Ali.

These four men, each of whom was a close connection and follower of the Prophet, attempted to embody the Islamic social ideals in their own persons, and their example has been held up ever since as a model of enlightened rule. Stories have been passed down through the generations about these men's simplicity and humility. Uthman, known as "Ghani"—generous— slept on bare sand in the courtyard of the Great Mosque, and delivered food and supplies to the poor in person. Umar wore rough, patched clothes and labored alongside his men to clear the ground for the new Dome of the Rock at Jerusalem. During famines he would politely abstain from eating: "If I do not taste suffering," he said when his companions protested, "how can I know the suffering of others?" One story has it that when Umar rode from Medina to the newly-captured Jerusalem he and his attendant had only one camel between them and took turns riding it. As they approached Jerusalem it was the attendant's turn to ride, but he pressed Umar to mount, saying that it would look undignified for the Caliph to enter the holy city on foot while he rode. Umar declined, reminding him that all believers were equal in the eyes of Allah, and the attendant had as much right to ride as did he.

Islamic leaders from those days on seem to have had some trouble striking a balance between zaama and the sort of *noblesse oblige* personified by the Rashidun. Yasir Arafat operated like a tribal sheikh of the old school, highly accessible, dispensing favors and benefits to his inner circle with ostentatious generosity. Iraq's Saddam Hussein personified zaama, but forgot about the Rashidun and their egalitarian notions of leadership (as Arafat did not): Saddam's monstrous presidential palaces amounted to exactly the sort of excess the Rashidun were reacting against, exemplified in their day by the notorious pomp and luxury of the Persian and Byzantine courts. Hafiz al-Asad purposely aimed for a more subtle balance. His zaama was flaunted in the statues, the blood oaths, the mysterious disappearances of his political enemies—indeed his whole personality radiated zaama—but in the tradition of the Rashidun he lived in relative simplicity, bringing up his family on the third floor of an unremarkable middle-class apartment building, an apartment Bashar and his family still inhabit today. It's true that just out of town there is a gigantic "presidential palace," surprisingly reminiscent of Krak des Chevaliers in terms of size, shape, and imposing position (fig. 67), but that is only for official functions and visiting heads-of-state and diplomats; the president's day-to-day work is carried out in a modest building in the Rowda district of Damascus. Bashar and his wife, Asma, go out of their way to give the impression of being ordinary Syrians with an ordinary Syrian way of life.

So many of the issues that confront contemporary leaders in this region are the same that dogged former ones. It was in this part of the world, after all, especially in the city-states along the Euphrates, that early notions of monarchy were developed and worked out. By the early second millennium B.C., the concentration of authority in the person of the monarch and the development of a sizeable bureaucracy had greatly increased the king's importance; for the first time the focus of civic life shifted from the temple to the palace. Each king had to come to an individual solution to balance the various roles of monarchy: military, administrative, and spiritual. The question of zaama was crucial, as always. It can most amusingly be seen at work in an eighth-century B.C. treaty text between Assur Ninari and Mattuwali, the ruler of Arvad, inscribed on a basalt stone in the Damascus Museum. Assur Ninari invokes curses against the country of Arvad's monarch if he neglects his side of the treaty; here it is, in the Museum's quirky English translation:

> May his land be devastated, his sons and daughters . . . A spirit exploding like lime stone.
>   May Mattuwali and his sons desert their homeland forever.
>   May Sin of Harran wrap the with leprosy like garment?
>   May they run out of fuel (Animal Dropping)
>   May the Lord Haddad, afflict them with famine and poverty until the people of Arvad eat each other. May the rain stop and Assur change their houses into mounds of accumulated wastes.

This sounds very much like the saber-rattling that periodically emanates from some countries today. Had Assur Ninari heard of economic sanctions, he would surely have approved of the concept.

Political leaders can be divided into delegators and micromanagers. Cuneiform tablets from the second millennium B.C. court at Mari displayed at the Aleppo Museum show the great Zimri-Lim to have been of the latter school. Here he writes to his queen, Shiptu:

> I am now directing to you female weavers, among which there are priestesses. Select the priestesses and assign (the

rest) to weaving establishments. Choose from among these and previous weavers thirty—or as many as are worth selection—handsome ones, who have no blemishes from toe to head hair, and assign them to Warad-ilishu. Have Warad-ilishu teach them Subarean dances; but their figures are not to be changed. Be careful with their ration so that their looks won't change.

No matter, it seems, is too trivial! Here is another, in which he demonstrates a rather advanced understanding of the nature of infectious disease:

I have heard: "Nanna has an infection, and since she is often at the palace, it will infect the many women who are with her."

Now give strict orders: no one is to drink from the cup she uses, no one is to sit on the seat she takes, and no one is to lie on the bed she uses, lest it infect the many women who are with her. This is a very contagious disease!

And of course leaders, then as now, had their sycophants, toadies, and petitioners. Here is a letter addressed to Zimri-Lim by one of his provincial governors:

Ever since I reached Saggaratum five days ago, I have continually sent truffles to my lord. But my lord wrote me: "You have dispatched truffles that are not good." But my lord ought not to condemn me with regard to truffles. I have sent to my lord what they have brought me . . .

The most successful leaders, here as in every other country, have been those who have successfully combined zaama with some sort of spiritual authority. Even the leader of a nominally secular and socialist country cannot afford to neglect the spiritual role. Like other secular leaders before him, Hafiz al-Asad solved the problem by investing the idea of nationhood and national destiny with spiritual import and casting himself in a paternal role.

No Syrian leaders have ever been more successful than Nur al-Din and Saladin in combining zaama with an aura of spiritual enlightenment. Saladin was the one perfect knight, the leader whose aura was so powerful that rival potentates have felt obliged to make pilgrimages to his Damascus tomb, either in homage or vindictive triumph. General Gouraud, as we have seen, visited Saladin's tomb in the spirit of rubbing the Saracen's nose in the "final" French victory. In 1898, Kaiser Wilhelm II had paid a more respectful call, ordering a gilded bronze wreath for the tomb inscribed "Wilhelm II, German Emperor and King of Prussia, in memory of the hero Sultan Saladin." At the Damascus banquet held in his welcome, Wilhelm made a gracious speech in which he spoke of the privilege he felt at being "upon the spot where one of the most chivalrous rulers of all time once dwelt, the great Sultan Saladin, a knight *sans peur et sans reproche*, who often had to teach his adversaries the true nature of chivalry."[9] Twenty years later, upon the defeat of the same Kaiser and his Ottoman allies, Lawrence seized the bronze wreath and dispatched it to the Imperial War Museum in London with a note remarking that they might as well have it "since Saladin no longer required it."

Saladin's mausoleum in a small white building adjoining the Umayyad Mosque is a simple place, as befits the spiritual heir to the Rashidun and their spartan values. A sign in English marks it as "The True grave for vortuous body of conqueror al-Sultan Salah al-Din al-Ayoubi," and the body itself reposes in a wooden tomb of the Ayyubi period; the second, nineteenth-century marble tomb was the gift of Kaiser Wilhelm. If it weren't for the spectacular Ottoman tilework, the room would look positively puritanical (fig. 68).

Of all Muslim leaders, the chivalrous Saladin was the one most idolized by the Western world. But not everyone in the Muslim world shares the feeling of veneration. The medieval chronicler Ibn al-Athir summarized the case against Saladin:

Salah al-Din never evinced real firmness in his decisions. He would lay siege to a city, but if the defenders resisted for some time, he would give up and abandon the siege. Now, a monarch must never act in this way, even if destiny smiles upon him. It is often preferable to fail while remaining firm than to succeed while subsequently squandering the fruits of one's success. Nothing illustrates the truth of this observation better than the behavior of Salah al-Din at Tyre. It is his fault alone that the Muslims suffered a setback before the walls of the city.[10]

It turns out Saladin was *too* clement, not ruthless enough. Though he mopped up fifty Crusader positions, he fatally left the Mediterranean port city of Tyre in Crusader hands. According to a five-year peace treaty signed in 1192 shortly before his death, he allowed the Franj to retain the coastal territory between Tyre and Jaffa, and it was from this territory that they periodically sallied forth to harass the Muslims. It was not until 1291, almost a century after Saladin's death, that the Crusader presence was finally expelled from Arab lands.

Saladin's British biographers Malcolm Cameron Lyons and D. E. P. Jackson sum up Saladin's record and analyze his appeal dispassionately:

He was a good, but not a great, strategist and tactician, an open-handed but not far-sighted administrator and a man with his share of faults, mixed motives and weaknesses. His reputation, however, in history and legend, is based on his identification with conventional emotion. He appears to have held instinctively to the middle ground. The conventional mind was matched by virtues that were no less attractive for being themselves conventional. He was not concerned to question the relevance of his ideals or even apparently, to check how far he was guilty of distorting them. They were part of the heritage of Islam, to be accepted emotionally, not intellectually, and with such an attitude he could be presumed to ignore contradictions. The attractiveness of such a position must depend largely on the fundamental sincerity, however intellectually muddled this may be, of its holder. This is a test that Saladin must be allowed to have passed.[11]

Saladin's shortcomings were set into relief by contrast with the brutal but more efficient Baybers, who followed him some seventy years later. Baybers personified zaama from the beginning of his career, as a member of the Mamluk army, which in 1252 assassinated Turan-Shah, the last of the Ayyubid sultans, and seized power for themselves. Baybers personally finished off the dying sultan with his saber.

The Arabic word "mamluk" means "owned," and while the Mamluks have often been referred to as slaves, they were not really that. Mamluks, men who were nominally the possessions of important citizens in the Muslim empire, served in the army of the sultan. They were given an excellent military education and could achieve high office, some of them even attaining the title of Emir. By the mid-thirteenth century this elite military force had long chafed at the ineffectiveness of the later Ayyubids and their weak, conciliatory attitude toward the Franj, who since the demise of Saladin had once again gained in number and strength from their coastal strongholds at Acre, Tyre, and Antioch. The new and much more terrifying threat of the Mongols, advancing from the east, proved that current leadership was not equal to coping with the enemies who pressed in on the empire from every side. A harder, far more intransigent attitude was called for if the Muslim empire was to survive.

Baybers wasted no time. He quickly ousted Louis IX's ill-conceived Seventh Crusade from Egypt, a feat the wavering Turan-Shah had been incapable of accomplishing. A far more dangerous menace were the armies of Hulagu, Genghis Khan's grandson, who had conquered Persia and now lusted after the rest of the Muslim East. Hulagu's armies overran Damascus and

Aleppo in 1260 and were heading for Egypt when Baybers met them at Ain Jalut in Palestine, defeating the Mongols and putting an end to their further expansion. Ain Jalut is acknowledged as being one of the world's decisive battles, a historical turning point.

In 1265 he went after the great Crusader city of Antioch, which had been in the hands of the Franj a full 170 years, successfully resisting all Muslim attacks. It took Baybers and his army only four days to bring Antioch to its knees, and his style as a conqueror was very, very different from what Saladin's had been: at this moment in history, zaama decisively trumped noblesse oblige. Baybers closed the city gates that none might escape and had all the citizens who were unfortunate enough to be out-of-doors systematically slaughtered. Those who escaped this initial purge by hiding were sold into slavery. It was said that every soldier in Baybers's army got at least one new slave from among the wretched Antiochenes.

The victorious Baybers sent a gloating letter to Antioch's Prince Bohemond VI, who was lucky enough to have been absent at Tripoli when the Mamluk armies ravaged his city. "Be glad," he crowed, "that you have not seen your knights lying prostrate under the hooves of horses, your palaces plundered, your ladies sold in the quarters of the city, fetching a mere dinar apiece—a dinar taken, moreover, from your own horde!"[12] Antioch would never recover from this disaster; it was then that the great city with its historic importance as one of the centers of Christianity turned into the depressed backwater it remains today, in its modern guise as Antakya in Turkey.

Baybers continued his rampage, wiping out all the pockets of resistance Saladin and his heirs had been unable to vanquish. The mighty Krak des Chevaliers fell in 1271; the Isma'ili Assassins, broken by the Mongols, were finished off. Saladin may have become a hero in Western lore—especially through Sir Walter Scott's blockbuster bestseller *The Talisman*. (A high camp Hollywood movie was made of this in the 1950s with Rex Harrison, of all people, in the role of the great sultan.) But in Damascus's al-Nawfara café, as formerly in countless Middle Eastern cafés, it is the legends of Baybers that the hakawati recites.

Hafiz al-Asad was a leader in the mold of Baybers, a ruler who would rather be feared than loved. But he wanted to be loved, too, and much of the creative energy that went into his propaganda was turned to the purpose of eliciting a filial affection from his subjects. Traveling in Syria today, it is difficult to get anyone to openly criticize either Hafiz or Bashar, though a few will do so quietly. How much of this enthusiasm for the Asads is genuine, how much a product of fear and paranoia? On our side of the mirror the answer seems easy: obviously everyone secretly loathes and fears this undemocratically elected regime and the tyrants at its head. But on my travels I was persuaded that, while there is plenty of cynicism about the Asads and their work, there is also quite a bit of real enthusiasm and support. Populace and leader are in agreement on several key issues: resistance to Israel (and it should be remembered that resistance to Israel does not necessarily translate as anti-Americanism or anti-Semitism); solidarity with the Palestinians; the enhancement of Syria's importance as an independent regional power. While the economy is still far from healthy (partly for interior reasons and partly due to American sanctions), Hafiz al-Asad brought it into the twentieth century, in the process smashing its dreadful, feudal agricultural system. For this, he was accorded considerable gratitude by his people.

The traditional Syrian *musha'*, a system of collective farming that had distributed land on a relatively egalitarian basis for generations, broke down in the late Ottoman era. The 1858 Ottoman land code inflicted the same sort of extreme inequities that the enclosure movement had done in eighteenth-century England, with the wealthiest families (including the sultan himself) owning most of the land and the peasantry reduced to the status of serfs. They lived in misery and want, scratching a bare living from the land with primitive, inadequate tools. Landlords had the entire control of their lives and livelihoods, tax collectors and moneylenders oppressed them cruelly. Hanna Mina, one of the few Syrian novelists to be published in English, has left a tragic picture of those times in his autobiographical novel *Fragments of Memory*. In the 1960s the new Ba'ath Party launched an extensive program of land reform and nationalizations which broke up the feudal system for good.

Most of all, perhaps, the Syrians are appreciative of the stability the Asads have given the country—a boon that can be overlooked in a place like the United States, where there hasn't been a revolution or civil war in a century and a half. In the sixty years before Asad seized power, Syria had gone through a world war, the Ottoman collapse, the French Mandate, another world war, unsuccessful and unequal union with Nasser's Egypt (1958–61), and a demoralizing series of military dictators, coups and counter-coups, not to mention the Arab-Israeli wars of 1948 and 1967. Asad's respectable showing in the 1973 war put an end to the military free-fall the country seemed to be suffering and restored some confidence and even national pride. His "Corrective Movement" may have been anti-democratic, but it brought peace and a measure of economic stability. The Syrians have not underestimated the value of these things. As Hafiz al-Asad's biographer Patrick Seale reckons it:

> Arab regimes such as his, so often derided as oriental despotisms, in fact required a measure of popular consent, and the importance of public opinion could be gauged by the strenuous efforts made to mobilize it. . . . Asad did not wholly stifle political activity but confined it to in-groups such as the higher echelons of the party, the army commanders, and the security chiefs, all ultimately dependent on himself. Those outside these privileged circles soon learned they could go about their business without undue fear or constraint so long as they accepted that politics was not their domain.[13]

Hafiz al-Asad's intent was simply to establish a dynasty. This seems an outrage on our side of the mirror, but it is in the natural order of things in Syria, where one dynasty has followed another for millennia. His plan has proved quite successful so far. Whether the dynasty succeeds, whether it fails and the nation musters the political will to oust it, or whether it is overthrown by another dynasty or perhaps another country remains to be seen.

Afterword

Back on my own side of the mirror, I feel not only enriched and enlightened by my journeys—which after all is what one hopes to get from travel—but in some way essentially changed, as though my very personality has subtly shifted. Perhaps this is simply due to an enhanced depth of vision.

Mark Twain's *The Innocents Abroad* described a group of naive, bumptious Americans touring the Holy Land, including Syria, a century and a half ago. The book is still amusing and remarkably pertinent. Our country has assumed a far more active role on the world stage since Twain's time. He could hardly have foreseen our current position as the earth's sole superpower, with an unsurpassed capacity to effect both good and evil across the globe. Yet we have retained the provincial, inward-looking viewpoint of his innocents. Twenty minutes of network TV news as I stand in the immigration line at JFK airport is a swift reminder of our parochialism: news is only news if it affects *us*.

Our history is not only chronologically thin, it is also culturally so, despite our boast of being the world's melting pot. A dip into Syria's four-thousand-year recorded history has been a salutary reminder of this shortcoming, more so even than my trips across

Europe over the years. My improved depth of vision makes it painfully clear that history is a messy business, and that attempts to contain historical forces within rigid intellectual categories are doomed. The clash of civilizations; the end of history; the dictatorship of the proletariat; free-market ideology; Wahhabi purism—all these formulas fall apart in the context of history's long, involute muddle.

Twain observed, "Travel is fatal to prejudice, bigotry, and narrow-mindedness." These three evils are no less pervasive today than they were in Twain's time. Their proposed remedy, in this age of affordable jet travel, is readily available. What is keeping us all?

Select Bibliography

Ansary, Tamim. *Destiny Disrupted: A History of the World through Islamic Eyes*. New York: Public Affairs, 2009.

Arberry, A. J. *Aspects of Islamic Civilization as Depicted in the Original Texts*. Ann Arbor: University of Michigan Press, 1967.

Armstrong, Karen. *Holy War: The Crusades and Their Impact on Today's World*. London: Macmillan, 1988; New York: Anchor Books, 2001.

———. *Islam: A Short History*. New York: Random House, Modern Library, 2002.

Baghdad Burning Blog. http://riverbend.blogspot.com/.

Ball, Warwick. *Syria: A Historical and Architectural Guide*. New York: Interlink Books, 1998.

> A good compact guide, less dense than Ross Burns's *Monuments of Syria*.

Baron, Alexander. *Queen of the East*. New York: Ives Washburn, 1956.

Bell, Gertrude Lowthian. *Amurath to Amurath*. New York: E. P. Dutton and Co., 1911.

———. *The Desert and the Sown*. London: W. Heinemann, 1907.

———. *Letters of Gertrude Bell*. Edited by Lady Bell, D.B.E. New York: Boni and Liveright, 1928.

> *Amurath to Amurath* made a fascinating contrast with my own experiences in Syria, as it describes the country as it was exactly a century ago. Some things have changed so much—others not at all.

Benjamin, Sandra, ed. *The World of Benjamin of Tudela: A Medieval Mediterranean Travelogue*. Madison, NJ: Fairleigh Dickinson University Press, 1993.

Binst, Olivier, ed. *The Levant: History and Archaeology in the Eastern Mediterranean.* Cologne: Könemann, 1999.

Boase, T. S. R. *Castles and Churches of the Crusading Kingdom.* Oxford: Oxford University Press, 1967.

Brodie, Fawn. *The Devil Drives: A Life of Sir Richard Burton.* New York: W. W. Norton & Co., 1967.

Brown, Peter. *The World of Late Antiquity, A.D. 150–750.* London: Thames and Hudson, 1971.

Burns, Ross. *Damascus: A History.* New York: Routledge, 2005; paperback edition 2007.

———. *Monuments of Syria: An Historical Guide.* London and New York: I. B. Tauris, 1992; revised edition 2009.

Thorough and exhaustive, Burns's *Monuments of Syria* is the one indispensable book for any traveler with an interest in the country's history and archaeology. It is the fruit of the author's decades of experience in Syria, first as a diplomat and then as a traveler and historian. *Damascus: A History* is also a useful book, though its format is not as handy as that of *Monuments.*

Burton, Isabel. *The Romance of Isabel Lady Burton: The Story of Her Life. Told in Part by Herself and in Part by W. H. Wilkins.* New York: Dodd Mead & Co., 1916.

Byron, Robert. *The Road to Oxiana.* London: Macmillan, 1937; New York: Oxford University Press, 1982.

Carter, Terry, Lara Dunston, and Amelia Thomas: *Syria & Lebanon.* Oakland: Lonely Planet, 1999.

Almost every tourist we saw in Syria had a copy of the Lonely Planet guide. It is better for logistics—trains, banks, hotels—than for cultural history.

Dalrymple, William. *From the Holy Mountain: A Journey among the Christians of the Middle East.* New York: Henry Holt & Co., 1997.

I have not found a better book on the subject. My own encounters with Syrian Christians bore out all of Dalrymple's observations.

Darke, Diana. *Syria: The Bradt Guide.* Guildford, CT: Globe Pequot Press, 2006.

A first-rate guidebook, with more heart and more substance than the Lonely Planet guide. The author has lived in Syria for a number of years.

Faris, Nabih Amin, ed. *The Arab Heritage.* Princeton: Princeton University Press, 1944.

Fedden, Robin, and John Thomson. *Crusader Castles.* London: John Murray, 1957.

Fischel, Walter J., ed. and trans. *Ibn Khaldun and Tamerlane: Their Historic Meeting in Damascus, 1401 A.D. (803 A.H.): A Study Based on Arabic Manuscripts of Ibn Khaldun's "Autobiography."* Berkeley and Los Angeles: University of California Press, 1952.

Fletcher, Richard. *The Cross and the Crescent.* London: Allen Lane, 2003.

Fromkin, David. *A Peace to End All Peace: The Fall of the Ottoman Empire and the Creation of the Modern Middle East.* New York: Henry Holt and Co., 1989; Owl Edition 2001.

> Absolutely the best book available about the carving-up of the Ottoman Empire after the First World War. Fromkin answers countless questions about why the modern Middle East is the way it is.

Genet, Jean. *The Declared Enemy: Texts and Interviews by Jean Genet.* Stanford: Stanford University Press, 2004.

Gibbon, Edward. *Decline and Fall of the Roman Empire.* 6 vols. New York: Alfred A. Knopf, Everyman's Library, 1993.

Glubb, Sir John. *A Short History of the Arab Peoples.* New York: Dorset Press, 1969.

Grabar, Oleg, Renata Holod, James Knustad, and William Trousdale. *City in the Desert: Qasr al-Hayr East.* Cambridge: Harvard Middle Eastern Monograph Series, 1978.

Halasa, Malu, and Rana Salam. *The Secret Life of Syrian Lingerie: Intimacy and Design.* San Francisco: Chronicle Books, 2008.

Hamilton, Robert. *Walid and His Friends: An Umayyad Tragedy.* New York: Oxford University Press, 1988.

Hillenbrand, Robert. *Islamic Art and Architecture.* London: Thames and Hudson, 1999.

Historia Augusta. Translated by David Magie. Loeb Classical Library nos. 139, 140. Cambridge: Harvard University Press, 1924.

Hitti, Philip K. *History of Syria.* New York: Macmillan, 1951.

———. *History of the Arabs.* London: Macmillan, 1937.

Hopkins, Clark. *The Discovery of Dura-Europos.* New Haven: Yale University Press, 1979.

> Charming; and thrilling for those with an enthusiasm for archaeology.

Huxley, Julian. *From an Antique Land: Ancient and Modern in the Middle East.* London: Max Parrish, 1954.

Ibn Jubayr. *The Travels of Ibn Jubayr.* Translated by R. J. C. Broadhurst. London: Jonathan Cape, 1952.

Irwin, Robert, ed. *Night and Horses and the Desert: An Anthology of Classical Arabic Literature.* Woodstock, NY: Overlook Press, 2000.

> A superb anthology.

Johnson, Paul. *A History of Christianity.* New York: Atheneum, 1976.

Jones, Terry, and Alan Ereira. *Crusades.* London: Penguin Books/BBC Books, 1994, 1996.

Kennedy, Hugh. *Crusader Castles.* Cambridge: Cambridge University Press, 1994.

Kinross, Lord. *The Ottoman Centuries: The Rise and Fall of the Turkish Empire.* New York: Morrow Quill Paperbacks, 1977.

Klengel, Horst. *The Art of Ancient Syria.* Translated from the German by Joan Becker. South Brunswick and New York: A. S. Barnes and Co., London: Thomas Yoseloff Ltd., 1972.

Lawrence, T. E. *The Letters of T. E. Lawrence.* Edited by David Garnett. London: Jonathan Cape, 1938.

———. *Seven Pillars of Wisdom.* London: Jonathan Cape, 1935.

Lesch, David W. *The New Lion of Damascus: Bashar al-Asad and Modern Syria.* New Haven: Yale University Press, 2005.

The only English-language biography of Bashar al-Asad, so far as I can ascertain.

Lovell, Mary S. *Rebel Heart: The Scandalous Life of Jane Digby.* New York: W. W. Norton & Co., 1995.

Lucian of Samosata. *The Syrian Goddess.* Translated by Herbert A. Strong and John Garstang. Forgotten Books, 2007.

Lyons, Malcolm Cameron, and D. E. P. Jackson. *Saladin: The Politics of the Holy War.* Cambridge: Cambridge University Press, 1982; Canto Edition 1997.

Maalouf, Amin. *The Crusades through Arab Eyes.* Translated from the Arabic by Jon Rothschild. New York: Schocken Books, 1984.

An invaluable antidote to what Westerners, at least older Westerners, were always taught about the "heroic" Crusades.

Macaulay, Rose. *Pleasure of Ruins.* London: Weidenfeld & Nicolson, 1953; New York: Barnes & Noble, 1996.

Mackintosh-Smith, Tim. *Travels with a Tangerine: From Morocco to Turkey in the Footsteps of Islam's Greatest Traveler.* New York: Random House, 2001.

Macmillan, Margaret. *Paris 1919: Six Months That Changed the World.* New York: Random House, 2001.

Marcus, Abraham. *The Middle East on the Eve of Modernity: Aleppo in the Eighteenth Century.* New York: Columbia University Press, 1989.

Margueron, Jean-Claude. *Guide de Mari.* Paris: Clio, 1999.

Meyer, Karl E., and Shareen Blair Brysac. *Kingmakers: The Invention of the Modern Middle East.* New York and London: W. W. Norton and Co., 2008.

Mina, Hanna. *Fragments of Memory: A Story of a Syrian Family.* Translated from the Arabic by Olive Kenny and Lorna Kenny. Austin: Center for Middle Eastern Studies at the University of Texas, 1993.

Mommsen, Theodor. *The Provinces of the Roman Empire: From Caesar to Diocletian*. Translated from the German by William P. Dickson, D.D., LL.D. Vol. 2, 1885. New York: Barnes & Noble, 1996.

O'Leary, De Lacy. *Colloquial Arabic*. London: Routledge & Kegan Paul Ltd., 1926; reprinted 1965.

Procopius. *Buildings*. Translated from the Greek by H. B. Dewing and Glanville Downey. Loeb Classical Library no. 343. Cambridge: Harvard University Press, 1940.

Regan, Geoffrey. *Lionhearts: Richard I, Saladin, and the Era of the Third Crusade*. New York: Walker and Co., 1999.

Rice, David Talbot. *Art of the Byzantine Era*. London: Thames and Hudson, 1963.

Rice, Edward. *Captain Sir Richard Francis Burton: The Secret Agent Who Made the Pilgrimage to Mecca, Discovered the* Kama Sutra, *and Brought the* Arabian Nights *to the West*. New York: HarperCollins, 1990; Harper Perennial Edition, 1991.

Rosenblum, Mort. *Mission to Civilize: The French Way*. San Francisco and New York: Harcourt Brace Jovanovich, 1986.

Rostovtzeff, Michael. *Caravan Cities*. Translated from the Russian by D. and T. Talbot Rice. Oxford: Oxford University Press, 1932; New York: AMS Press, 1971.

Roux, Georges. *Ancient Iraq*. London: George Allen and Unwin, 1964; Penguin, 1992.

Runciman, Steven. *A History of the Crusades*. 3 vols. Cambridge: Cambridge University Press, 1951; paperback, 1996.

> The definitive history of the Crusades, at least in English. A treasure-trove of information, but it should not be the *first* book you read on the subject, for there is simply too much information to take in. A better choice for the novice would be Karen Armstrong's *Holy War*.

Russell, Bertrand. *The History of Western Philosophy*. New York: Simon & Schuster, 1945.

Said, Edward. *Covering Islam: How the Media and the Experts Determine How We See the Rest of the World*. New York: Pantheon, 1981.

Salti, Rasha, ed. *Insights into Syrian Cinema: Essays and Conversations with Contemporary Filmmakers*. New York: Rattapallax Press, 2006.

Seale, Patrick. *Asad of Syria: The Struggle for the Middle East*. London: I. B. Tauris & Co., 1988.

> An excellent, intelligent biography of Asad the Elder from a long-time journalist and scholar of the region.

Shaheen, Jack G. *Reel Bad Arabs: How Hollywood Vilifies a People*. Northampton, MA: Olive Branch Press, 2001; revised 2009.

Stanhope, Lady Hester. *Travels of Lady Hester Stanhope: Forming the Completion of her Memoirs. Narrated by her Physician.* 3 vols. London: Henry Colburn, 1846.

Stark, Freya. *Letters from Syria.* London: John Murray, 1942.

Stewart, Desmond. *T. E. Lawrence.* London: Hamish Hamilton, 1977; Picador Books, 1979.

Stoneman, Richard. *Palmyra and Its Empire: Zenobia's Revolt against Rome.* Ann Arbor: University of Michigan Press, 1994.

Syria Comment Blog. http://joshualandis.com.blog/.

Thackston, W. M., trans. *Jumi'u't-Tawarikh (Compendium of Chronicles): A History of the Mongols.* Sources of Oriental Languages and Literatures 45 (1998–9).

Theodoret of Cyrrhus. *A History of the Monks of Syria.* Translated by R. M. Price. Kalamazoo: Cistercian Publications, 1985.

> Simply mind-blowing.

Tibawi, A. L. *A Modern History of Syria, Including Lebanon and Palestine.* London: Macmillan, 1969.

Tuetey, Charles Greville, ed. and trans. *Classical Arabic Poetry.* London: Taylor & Francis, 1985.

Twain, Mark. *The Innocents Abroad.* New York and Oxford: Oxford University Press, 1996.

Al-Ush, M. Abu-l-Faraj, Adnan Joundi, and Bachir Zouhdi. *A Concise Guide to the National Museum of Damascus.* Translated from the Arabic by Muhammad Khalifa. Damascus: Publication of the General Directorate of Antiquities and Museums, 1999.

de Volney, C. F. C. *The Ruins, or Meditation on the Revolutions of Empires.* Boston: Josiah P. Mendum, 1869.

Waddell, Helen. *The Desert Fathers.* London: Constable & Co., 1936; Ann Arbor: University of Michigan Press, 1957.

Wallach, Janet. *Desert Queen: The Extraordinary Life of Gertrude Bell: Adventurer, Adviser to Kings, Ally of Lawrence of Arabia.* New York: Doubleday, 1996; Anchor Books, 1999.

Wedeen, Lisa. *Ambiguities of Domination: Politics, Rhetoric, and Symbols in Contemporary Syria.* Chicago: University of Chicago Press, 1999.

Weiss, Harvey, ed. *Ebla to Damascus: Art and Architecture of Ancient Syria.* Washington: Smithsonian Institution Traveling Exhibition Service, 1985.

Woolley, C. Leonard. *Dead Towns and Living Men: Being Pages from an Antiquary's Notebook.* Oxford: Oxford University Press, 1920.

Zenner, Walter P. *A Global Community: The Jews from Aleppo, Syria.* Detroit: Wayne State University Press, 2000.

Notes

I. The Destination

1. Amnesty International Memorandum, "The Dangers of Speaking Out in Syria," 28 January 2008.
2. Ibn Jubayr, *The Travels of Ibn Jubayr,* translated by R. J. C. Broadhurst (London: Jonathan Cape, 1952), 299.
3. Ibn Jubayr, 271.
4. Translated from the Arabic by Shareah Taleghani. *Words without Borders,* June 2005, http://wordswithoutborders. org/article/barada.
5. *Tishreen,* May 23, 1991, as quoted in Eyal Zisser, *Asad's Legacy: Syria in Transition* (New York: New York University Press, 2001), 129.
6. Quoted by Margaret Macmillan, *Paris 1919: Six Months That Changed the World* (New York: Random House, 2001), 381.
7. Ibid., 386.
8. *Covenant of the League of Nations,* Article 22: Creation of Mandates, June 28, 1919.
9. Janet Wallach, *Desert Queen: The Extraordinary Life of Gertrude Bell: Adventurer, Adviser to Kings, Ally of Lawrence of Arabia* (New York: Doubleday, 1996; Anchor Books 1999), 150–51.

II. Time

1. C. Leonard Woolley, *Dead Towns and Living Men: Being Pages from an Antiquary's Notebook* (Oxford: Oxford University Press, 1920), 239–40.
2. Mark Twain, *The Innocents Abroad* (New York and Oxford: Oxford University Press, 1996), 462.
3. Ibn Jubayr, 277.

4. Robert Byron, *The Road to Oxiana* (London: Macmillan, 1937; New York: Oxford University Press, 1982), 39.
5. T. E. Lawrence, *The Letters of T. E. Lawrence*, ed. David Garnett (London: Jonathan Cape, 1938), 69.
6. Muhanned al-Mallah, quoted in "Retail Therapy," *Syria Today* no. 50, June 2009, 52.
7. Ross Burns, *Damascus: A History* (New York: Routledge, 2005; paperback edition 2007), 244.
8. Twain, 457–58.
9. Ibid., 462.
10. Charles Greville Tuetey, ed. and trans., *Classical Arabic Poetry* (London: Taylor & Francis, 1985), 175–76.
11. De Lacy O'Leary, *Colloquial Arabic* (London: Routledge & Kegan Paul Ltd., 1926; reprinted 1965), 8.
12. Lady Hester Stanhope, *Travels of Lady Hester Stanhope: Forming the Completion of her Memoirs. Narrated by her Physician.* 3 vols. (London: Henry Colburn, 1846), 3:88.
13. Mary S. Lovell, *Rebel Heart: The Scandalous Life of Jane Digby* (New York: W. W. Norton and Co., 1995), 169.
14. William Dalrymple, *From the Holy Mountain: A Journey among the Christians of the Middle East* (New York: Henry Holt & Co., 1997), 168.

III. Ruins

1. Count C. F. C. de Volney, *The Ruins, or Meditation on the Revolutions of Empires* (Boston: Josiah P. Mendum, 1869), 13–14.
2. *Scriptores Historiae Augustae*, translated by David Magie (Cambridge: Loeb Classical Library, Harvard University Press, 1932), 3:259–61.
3. Alexander Baron, *Queen of the East* (New York: Ives Washburn, 1956), 80.
4. Stanhope, 2:35.
5. Ibid., 2:255–56.
6. Gertrude Lowthian Bell, *Amurath to Amurath* (New York: E. P. Dutton and Co., 1911), 71.
7. Jean-Claude Margueron, *Guide de Mari* (Paris: Clio, 1999), 24.
8. Clark Hopkins, *The Discovery of Dura-Europos* (New Haven: Yale University Press, 1979), 3.
9. Ibid., 91.
10. Ibid., 121–22.
11. Ibid., 133.
12. Ibid., 203.
13. Procopius, *Buildings*, translated by H. B. Dewing and Glanville Downey (Cambridge: Harvard University Press, Loeb Classical Library 343, vol. 7, 1940), 151.

14. Warwick Ball, *Syria: A Historical and Architectural Guide* (New York: Interlink Books, 1998), 169.
15. Procopius, 157.
16. Stanhope, 2:265.

IV. Faith

1. Dalrymple, 150.
2. *Internet Medieval Source Book*, Fordham University.
3. Lord Kinross, *The Ottoman Centuries: The Rise and Fall of the Turkish Empire* (New York: Morrow Quill Paperbacks, 1977), 474.
4. Ibid., 475–76.
5. Quoted in Lovell, 246.
6. Sandra Benjamin, ed., *The World of Benjamin of Tudela: A Medieval Mediterranean Travelogue* (Madison, NJ: Fairleigh Dickinson University Press, 1995), 210–11.
7. Walter P. Zenner, *A Global Community: The Jews from Aleppo, Syria* (Detroit: Wayne State University Press, 2000), 54.
8. Quoted in Patrick Seale, *Asad of Syria: The Struggle for the Middle East* (Berkeley: University of California Press, 1989; revised 1995), 174.
9. Robert Irwin, ed., *Night and Horses and the Desert: An Anthology of Classical Arabic Literature* (Woodstock, NY: Overlook Press, 2000), 319.
10. Robert Hamilton, *Walid and His Friends: An Umayyad Tragedy* (New York: Oxford University Press, 1988), 122.
11. Georges Roux, *Ancient Iraq* (London: George Allen and Unwin, 1964; Penguin, 1992), 213.
12. Ross Burns, *Monuments of Syria: An Historical Guide* (London and New York: I. B. Tauris, 1992; Revised Edition 2009), 295.
13. Ibid., 4.
14. Theodor Mommsen, *The Provinces of the Roman Empire: From Caesar to Diocletian*, translated by William P. Dickson (New York: Barnes & Noble, 1996, originally published 1885), 2:134.
15. Lucian of Samosata, *The Syrian Goddess*, translated by Herbert A. Strong and John Garstang (Forgotten Books, 2007), 36.
16. Ibid., 43–44.
17. Ibid., 44–45.
18. Ibid., 52–53.
19. Ibid., 54.
20. Edward Gibbon, *Decline and Fall of the Roman Empire* (New York: Alfred A. Knopf, Everyman's Library, 1993), 1:142–43.
21. *Historia Augusta*, 2:111–13.
22. Gibbon, 1:164.
23. Bertrand Russell, *The History of Western Philosophy* (New York: Simon & Schuster, 1945), 284.

24. Lucian, 27.
25. Philip K. Hitti, *History of Syria* (New York: Macmillan, 1951), 363.
26. Lawrence, *Letters*, 78.
27. Gibbon, 4:14.
28. Ibid., 20–21.
29. Paul Johnson, *A History of Christianity* (New York: Atheneum, 1976), 94.
30. Theodoret of Cyrrhus, *A History of the Monks of Syria*, translated by R. M. Price (Kalamazoo: Cistercian Publications, 1985), 114.
31. Ibid., 122.
32. Gibbon, 4:22.
33. Ibid.
34. Theodoret, 171.
35. Quoted in Helen Waddell, *The Desert Fathers* (London: Constable & Co., 1936; Ann Arbor: The University of Michigan Press, 1957), 5.
36. Theodoret, 165.
37. Amin Maalouf, *The Crusades through Arab Eyes*, translated by Jon Rothschild (New York: Schocken Books, 1984), 143–44.
38. Bell, *Amurath to Amurath*, 14.

V. Fighting

1. Hugh Kennedy, *Crusader Castles* (Cambridge: Cambridge University Press, 1994), 98.
2. T. S. R. Boase, *Castles and Churches of the Crusading Kingdom* (Oxford: Oxford University Press, 1967), 52.
3. Steven Runciman, *A History of the Crusades* (Cambridge: Cambridge University Press, 1951; paperback 1996), 3:272.
4. Lawrence, *Letters*, 78.
5. Robin Fedden and John Thomson, *Crusader Castles* (London: John Murray, 1957), quoted in Kennedy, 85.
6. Ibn Jubayr, 260.
7. W. M. Thackston, trans., *Jumi'u't-Tawarikh (Compendium of Chronicles): A History of the Mongols* (Sources of Oriental Languages and Literatures 45, 1998–99).
8. Terry Jones and Alan Ereira, *Crusades* (London: Penguin Books/BBC Books, 1994, 1996), 117.
9. Quoted in Maalouf, 185.
10. Quoted in Maalouf, 193–94.
11. Walter J. Fischel, ed. and trans., *Ibn Khaldun and Tamerlane: Their Historic Meeting in Damascus, 1401 A.D. (803 A.H.): A Study Based on Arabic Manuscripts of Ibn Khaldun's "Autobiography"* (Berkeley and Los Angeles: University of California Press, 1952), 38–39.
12. Quoted in Maalouf, 39.

13. T. E. Lawrence, *Seven Pillars of Wisdom* (London: Jonathan Cape, 1935), 646–47.
14. Ibid., 660.
15. Desmond Stewart, *T. E. Lawrence* (London: Hamish Hamilton, 1977; Picador Books 1979), 210–11.
16. Jean Genet, *The Declared Enemy: Texts and Interviews by Jean Genet* (Stanford: Stanford University Press, 2004), 147.
17. The Baghdad Burning Blog, comment posted Sept. 6, 2007, http://riverbendblog.blogspot.com/
18. Ibid., comment posted October 22, 2007.

VI. Leaders

1. Lisa Wedeen, *Ambiguities of Domination: Politics, Rhetoric, and Symbols in Contemporary Syria* (Chicago: University of Chicago Press, 1999), 60.
2. Quoted in David W. Lesch, *The New Lion of Damascus: Bashar al-Asad and Modern Syria* (New Haven: Yale University Press, 2005), 45.
3. *Emerging Syria 2005* (London: Oxford Business Group, 2005), 14.
4. Quoted in Lesch, 200.
5. Quoted in Peter Beaumont, "No Longer the Pariah President," *The Guardian*, November 16, 2008.
6. Interview with Ian Black, "Syria's Strongman Ready to Woo Obama With Both Fists Unclenched," *The Guardian*, February 17, 2009.
7. Quoted in Lesch, 95.
8. Beaumont.
9. Quoted in A. L. Tibawi, *A Modern History of Syria, Including Lebanon and Palestine* (London: Macmillan, 1969), 191.
10. Quoted in Maalouf, 203.
11. Malcolm Cameron Lyons and D. E. P. Jackson, *Saladin: The Politics of the Holy War* (Cambridge: Cambridge University Press, 1982; Canto Edition 1997), 373–74.
12. Quoted in Maalouf, 250.
13. Seale, *Asad of Syria*, 178–79.

Credits